ROBESPIERRE

Or the tyranny of the Majority

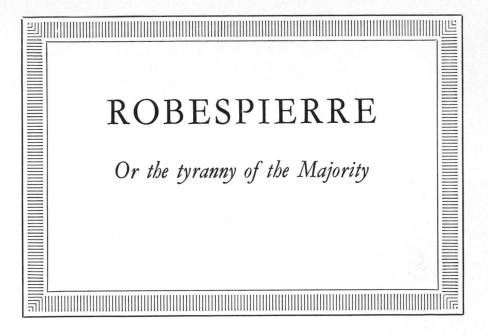

ROBESPIERRE

Or the tyranny of the Majority

JEAN MATRAT

TRANSLATED BY ALAN KENDALL

WITH FELIX BRENNER

CHARLES SCRIBNER'S SONS
NEW YORK

Printed in Great Britain
Library of Congress Catalog Card Number 74–16891
ISBN 0–684–14055–1

[[TABLE OF CONTENTS]]

[[LIST OF ILLUSTRATIONS]]

· 7 ·

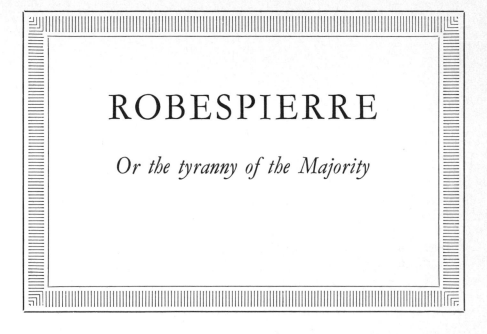

ROBESPIERRE

Or the tyranny of the Majority

· I ·

A HARD-WORKING

PUPIL

THE DEROBESPIERRES WERE A VERY OLD AND WORTHY ARRAS family. For the most part they were legal people, attorneys, royal notaries, barristers; but some of them were simple farmers, who at the end of the seventeenth century lived in the little towns and villages around Arras—Lens, Vaudricourt, Carvin, Hélin-Liétard and Epinoy. Some of their ancestors, with a pretension to nobility which seemed justified, had used the "*de*" in front of their name. In a document dated 1328 there is a mention of Bloquelle de Robespierre, an archer in the Duke of Burgundy's army. In the next century we find Gilles de Robespierre, a prior; then Jean, who served in the royal cavalry; and Baudouin, who held ecclesiastical estates at Cambrai and Hesdin granted by Pope Eugenius IV. Round about 1550 at Lens a Robert Derobespierre was a dealer in candles and torches and in "bread and wine for use in the mass". One of his descendants was successively keeper of the judicial decrees, and notary and attorney at La Tour de Harnes. Another reached the rank of lieutenant of the baliff's court at Epinoy. He had two sons. Yves, the elder one, gave the family a coat-of-arms of "*or à bande de sable chargé d'un demy vol argenté*". The younger son, Maximilien, was a barrister who in 1720 went to live in the provincial capital, Arras, where he had his name entered at the bar of the Council of the Province of Artois.

He was a respected barrister and an influential member of the local lodge of freemasons. Some ten or so years after his arrival Maximilien married the daughter of an Arras merchant, Marie Poiteau, and they had five children. A boy and a girl died young. The only surviving son, François, grew up; he showed that he had an odd, undisciplined mind, which caused his parents a certain amount of anxiety. At this time religion offered a convenient resort in such cases, so the boy was put as a novice into the Premonstratarian Abbey of Dommartin, in Ponthieu, in the hopes that his teachers would succeed "through a severe and just education, in containing his dangerous tendencies". But at the age of seventeen, when it came to making his vows, François withdrew, telling the abbot "that he felt that he had no inclination for the religious state". The convent authorities returned him to the outside world, but hot-heads are not necessarily unintelligent, and François then studied at Douai University. A few years later he successfully completed his law studies, became a barrister and joined his father's practice.

All the same, neither age nor the respectability of his profession had subdued François. His behaviour was the talk of the town. In 1757, the year in which Damiens attacked Louis XV with a knife to remind him of his duty, Francois had an affair with Jacqueline Carrault, the daughter of a brewer from the suburbs. He was twenty-six. When the girl realized that she was pregnant, he decided to marry her. Of course to his family such a marriage was a disgrace, and to show their disapproval, not one of them was present at the wedding ceremony.

As so often happens, however, the birth of a child four months later, on 6th May 1758, reconciled everyone. The elder Robespierre agreed to hold his grandson at the christening in the Church of the Madeleine, and gave him his own names of Maximilien Barthélemy Isidore. From the rather clumsy signature in the register, all we know about the godmother is that she was called Marie-Antoinette.

François Derobespierre seemed to calm down under the gentle influence of his wife. He showed himself to be a faithful husband and a good father, retaining only one of his old quirks of behaviour, which was a need to move around. François and Jacqueline changed houses frequently. François's barrister's practice was going fairly well, with about thirty briefs a year, and according to the Oratorian Gaillard, "he held an honourable position among his colleagues of the Superior Council of Arras".

More births followed that of Maximilien, but they were too close together for the delicate health of the young wife, and they exhausted her. First came two girls, Charlotte in 1760 and Henriette in 1761, then a large boy, Augustin Bon, in 1763. The fifth child, born in July 1764, died after a few days. A doctor was urgently summoned from Paris, but he was unable to save Jacqueline.

The death of his wife "striking François like a thunderbolt to the heart", left him listless. "Entirely ruled by the grief which consumed him," said his daughter Charlotte much later, "he began his odd behaviour again." He refused to sign the death certificate and did not attend the funeral. He abandoned his law practice, began to drink, and then in order to overcome his boredom started to travel. From time to time he returned to Arras to provide himself with money, by borrowing from one of his sisters and subsequently by claiming his share of the family

Maximilien Barthélemy Isidore Derobespierre was born 6th May 1758 in this house

inheritance. In 1770, when the inheritance question was broached, François was in Germany, but supplied confirmation of the fact that he had received his portion. The next year he made a short visit to Arras, during the course of which he apparently pleaded one or two cases before setting off again, this time for good. No one knew where. According to vague rumours, François died in Munich in 1777.

The family shared the four orphans. The two aunts—François's sisters—Eulalie and Henriette—took care of the little girls. Grandfather Carrault took the boys into his house.

Maximilien was a little over six when his mother died, and eight when his father went away, and he was deeply influenced by the sudden break up of the home in which he had experienced happiness. As his sister, Charlotte, later explained: "Whenever we spoke about our mother in our private conversations I heard his voice falter and saw his eyes fill with tears. A complete change came over him. Previously he had been like all boys, scatter-brained, wild and carefree. But when he realized that he was, as it were, head of the family by virtue of the fact that he was the oldest, he became sober, serious, and hard working. He spoke to us with a kind of gravity which we respected. When he took part in our games it was so as to direct them. He loved us tenderly, and he lavished care and caresses on us."

Because of his delicate health Maximilien amused himself as would a serious child. People said that his mother had taught him to make lace. He found a great deal of pleasure in making model chapels, and collected pictures, which he liked his sisters to admire. In the garden his grandparents had a dovecot made, and Maximilien reared a few pigeons. Little Charlotte and Henriette begged him to give them a pigeon, but for a long time he refused, fearing that they would neglect it. Finally he gave in, but he soon regretted it—the scatter-brains forgot to bring the cage in one night, there was a storm, and the bird died. "When he heard about the death, Maximilien's tears flowed and he overwhelmed us with reproaches."

He had his first schooling as a dayboy at the Collège d'Arras, where he spent three years and learnt the rudiments of Latin. Charlotte's memoirs tell us that he was a good pupil "astonishing his masters by his consistent progress, and they unanimously praised his keenness and application". For the rest of his life Robespierre was to work with dedication and perseverance. One of his classmates in Arras, Le Blond, attributed Maximilien's scholastic success to "determined work" but also emphasized the "inflexibility" of his nature.

Such a promising pupil was considered to be worthy of a better education than that provided by a provincial school. A friend of the family, Canon Aymé, applied on Maximilien's behalf, through the intermediary of the bishop, for him to be awarded one of the four scholarships from the Abbey of Saint Vaast to the Collège Louis-le-Grand in Paris. In October 1769, when he was eleven years old, Maximilien left Arras for Paris. As Charlotte described the departure: "Many tears flowed on both sides. In spite of his sensitivity he had a certain determination of character and consoled us as best he could, though weeping with us. He made presents to my sister and myself of all the things that had been his playthings, but he did not want to give us his beloved pigeons, in case they might suffer the same fate as the one we had allowed to perish. Instead he entrusted them to someone who would not neglect them!"

The old College of Clermont which had been renamed Collège Louis-le-Grand in 1681 (after a visit from Louis XIV) was the most respected university in France. Until 1764 the professors had been Jesuit priests, after which they were replaced by secular priests and Oratorians. When Maximilien arrived in 1769 the principal was the Abbé Gardin du Mesnil, who was succeeded a few months later by Abbé Poignard, a learned doctor of theology, but not much of a disciplinarian. Discipline ceased to be fashionable in the years before the Revolution. The move towards liberalism was even more pronounced when Abbé Bérardier was appointed head of the college in 1778. He was a likeable scholar, seeking above all popularity with his pupils. During his tenure religious practices such as confession and monthly communion ceased to be obligatory.

A calm, hard-working pupil is naturally well thought of by his teachers; Maximilien's teachers regarded him highly, in particular his Latin master, Abbé Hérivaux. "He found a kind of Roman aspect to his character. He would praise and cajole Maximilien endlessly because of this precious similarity."

The boy devoted himself to earnest, regular work. "Although at first he had to struggle against competitors who were more formidable than those in Arras, he managed to do this with such determination that in less than two years he succeeded in shining among his equals," said Abbé Proyart. Maximilien was not one of those

Since its foundation in 1563 by the Jesuits as Clermont College, the Collège Louis-le-Grand was pre-eminent in France for the brilliance of its teachers and of its students

boys with a great deal of intelligence who are capable of flashes of brilliance but who generally let themselves sink into idleness. Charlotte tells us in a rather vague way that she "had heard people say that he always carried off the first prizes". Inspection of the college honours list somewhat rectifies this conception of Robespierre's being always at the top of his class. In fact, there is not one first prize attributed to him, and the honours for him seem to have run from second to sixth prize. Apparently he redoubled his efforts in rhetoric, since the results he had obtained at first did not satisfy him. "Having had only mediocre success in composition at the university, he had no hesitation in starting this course over again; and as he had expected, application guaranteed for him, this second year, the reward that genius had refused him the first time." The rewards were in fact somewhat modest: a fourth in Latin translation.

His scholarship of 500 *livres* covered the cost of board, tuition and upkeep, with the privilege—which his love of solitude must have made him greatly appreciate—of not having to sleep in the dormitory but in a private room. He was so fastidious in his appearance, not to say foppish, that he spent his pocket money at the barber's having his hair curled. Charlotte said that the people were liars "who said that in his childhood Maximilien wanted for things". Moreover, he seemed to know how to ask for what he wanted. In a letter to Abbé Proyart, the college bursar, he says that he would like to pay his respects to the Bishop of Arras while he is in Paris, and could he be given a new suit "and several other things" without which, he maintained, he could not get along.

"My brother," wrote Charlotte, "during all the time that he was at the Collège Louis-le-Grand, had not one argument with his fellow pupils. His disposition was so gentle and calm." Even so, no more than at Arras did he show himself inclined to share their games. "He liked to be alone in order to think, and he spent many hours meditating." One of his fellow students later wrote: "He was melancholy, and I do not remember ever having seen him laugh." Apparently any sort of injustice done to someone made him angry. "He made himself the protector of the little ones against the older ones, spoke on their behalf and even fought in their defence when his eloquence was unsuccessful." If need be, Maximilien had no hesitation in denouncing students even in front of the masters.

A boy who criticizes his fellows is rarely popular, and a majority of Maximilien's seem to have felt that he had a "detestable character". All the same, over the years he did manage to form several friendships. At Louis-le-Grand there was a small group of students who were eventually to play their part in the Revolution: Stanislas Fréron, Suleau, Duport-Dutertre and Lebrun-Tondu. Some friends remain unidentified, such as Dubois, who later wrote to Maximilien to remind him of their student days. His favourite was Camille Desmoulins, three years younger than himself—a strange boy, swarthy, enthusiastic and suffering from a slight stammer. He was quite the opposite of Maximilien, for whom he had limitless admiration.

[[·]]

There is no doubt that it was his teachers, almost all of them full of the "new ideas", who made a revolutionary out of Robespierre. Abbé Bérardier found nothing wrong in allowing the boys to be taught by d'Alembert, one of the authors of the *Encyclopédie*, and a notorious atheist. In their turn the Abbés Porion and Dubois were to become deputies to the States-General; the Abbé Dumanchel was to represent Le Gard in the Legislative Assembly; and the Abbé Audrein was to sit in the Convention, where he voted for the death of the king, "without appeal or delay".

With such masters the teaching of Latin, then the basis of study, had become a sort of catechism of democracy. They taught their pupils to admire the civic virtues of Brutus and the Gracchi rather than the merits of the saints. "The republicans," according to Camille Desmoulins, "were for the most part young people who, nourished by reading Cicero in the colleges, conceived a passion for freedom there. We were brought up in the schools of Rome and Athens, and in the pride of the Republic, only to live in the abjection of the monarchy and under the reign of a Claudius and a Vitellius. It was foolish to imagine that we could be inspired by the fathers of the fatherland and the Capitol, without feeling horror at the man-eaters of Versailles, and that we could admire the past without condemning the present."

Two writers in particular, Voltaire and Rousseau, vied for the title of mentor of the young. Maximilien was not attracted to the sarcastic mind of Voltaire, but was seduced by the champion of the oppressed, Jean-Jacques Rousseau. Reading his works taught him to "reflect" on the great principles of the social order. Nature had made man good and happy. Society had corrupted him. One sentence in particular from the *Social Contract* had engraved itself upon Robespierre's memory. "The State, in regard to its members, is master of all their goods. The sovereign —that is to say the people—may legitimately take away the goods of everyone, as was done at Sparta in the time of Lycurgus."

The atmosphere at the college was no less favourable to religious innovations. Since they had no deep religious beliefs themselves, the masters could scarcely inculcate them in others. Under their influence the majority of the pupils lost their faith. Desmoulins wanted Catholicism replaced by "a happy religion, the friend of pleasure and women, a religion in which dancing, theatre and celebrations would be part of the worship". Robespierre, as he himself admitted, stopped being a good practising Catholic, but he retained a deep religious feeling. *La Profession de foi du vicaire savoyard* ("The Faith of a Vicar from Savoy") became a new gospel for him and was more suited than atheism to his sensitive and serious nature. And because he loved justice, he felt the need to believe in a Supreme Being, and in the immortality of the soul. Only in this way could the good be rewarded and the wicked punished.

Hoping for a liberal reign, the people greeted Louis XVI and Marie-Antoinette joyfully

[[·]]

In July 1775, a great honour fell to Maximilien. The new King Louis XVI (four years older than he), was to make his solemn entry into Paris after the Coronation at Rheims. Among other ceremonies, the chief citizens were to welcome the queen en route at St Geneviève; and in front of the entrance to Louis-le-Grand in the rue Saint-Jacques, the university officials were to greet the king.

Whenever an important person visited the college there was a tradition that one of the pupils would make a speech of welcome; in those days it was in Latin. As a sort of reward the teachers naturally chose the most deserving. It was a matter for pride to be chosen to speak to such a good king, beloved by all his people. Abbé Hérivaux had been appointed to write the speech.

Rain unfortunately spoilt the ceremony. So as not to get their clothes wet, the royal couple did not get out of the carriage, but listened through the open door to the youth kneeling on the pavement according to etiquette, "singing their praises and forecasting their reign of happiness". A few words of thanks seemed to be called for but Louis, always timid and embarrassed in public, remained silent and contented himself with giving Robespierre a "look of goodness".

[[·]]

Three years later both Rousseau and Voltaire died (when Maximilien was just twenty years old). Since 1770, apart from the last weeks of his life, which he spent at Ermenonville, Jean-Jacques had lived in Paris in the rue Plâtrière. It was a place of pilgrimage for many Parisians, who tried to get a glimpse of him. Maximilien had this good fortune, even though it seems unlikely that he was ever actually "received" by Rousseau. In a dedication addressed to the memory of the author of *Emile*, Robespierre says: "I saw him in his last days, and this memory is for me the source of proud joy. I looked at his august features, I saw the imprint of the black disappointments to which the injustices of men had condemned him."

The following year, when humanities were finished, Maximilien began his legal studies: a perfectly natural choice of career for the son and grandson of barristers. His scholarship was extended, the college kept his room for him, and he seems to have had few worries about money or lodging. The details of this period in Robespierre's life are unclear, but according to Brissot, he worked for a time as a second clerk with the attorney Nolleau. During this period he may have met President Dupaty, a magistrate much admired for having resisted "despotism" in the previous reign. At least he wrote asking him "to let him know the time when he might have the honour of talking to him". We do not know what reply he received.

Only three facts are certain. In June 1780 Robespierre received his *baccalauréat* in law, and his degree in May 1781; two months later in August 1781 Maximilien Robespierre was listed in the register of barristers of the Parliament of Paris.

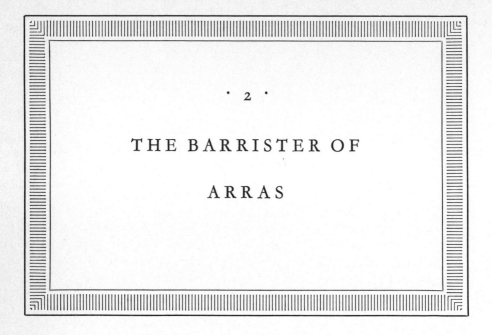

· 2 ·

THE BARRISTER OF

ARRAS

I T WAS ONLY NATURAL THAT A YOUNG MAN FROM THE PROVINCES, armed with his diplomas, should want to practise in the capital, but Robespierre lacked the necessary backing and family connections to make a name for himself at the bar. When after three months he did not have a single client in Paris, Maximilien decided to return to Arras rather than vegetate in Paris.

It is quite probable that his teachers advised him to make this move. The college had awarded him a leaving prize of 600 *livres*. This was the highest amount that a graduate from Louis-le-Grand had ever received, and was a testimony of Robespierre's good conduct over a period of twelve years and of his academic achievements. Moreover, he was able to have his scholarship transferred to his younger brother, Augustin Bon.

Robespierre knew that he already had a flattering reputation in Arras, and this was a guarantee of success. During his years in Paris, his aunts had boasted about his scholastic and university success. He had kept on excellent terms with the Oratorians of the college and had never missed a visit to them during the vacations. One of them, Canon Devie, was for a while one of his masters at Louis-le-Grand, and he never ran out of praise for Robespierre. The citizens of Arras were proud of Maximilien and ready to welcome him as a young prodigy. His appearance and immaculate dress helped to confirm the adulation established by Maximilien's aunts. Back in Arras he rather quickly reintroduced the *de* into his name, which both his father and grandfather had dropped. In those years it was smart to appear to be noble. It was about the same time that a young barrister in Paris was calling himself Monsieur d'Anton. But this concern for things aristocratic did not prevent Robespierre—no more than it prevented anyone else, and the nobility above all— from being keen on ideas about freedom and equality. No more than any of his contemporaries did he foresee the possibility of a revolution, much less the setting up of a republic. The good young king ruling from Versailles could be depended upon to carry out the necessary reforms.

Naturally, in common with many of the young people of his age, Robespierre wanted to play a part in the transformation of France towards a more just society. Following the example of his intellectual master, Jean-Jacques Rousseau—"the divine man"—he would become a writer, and a moulder of public opinion. In the meantime, he had to plead cases in order to live. He did not dream of making his fortune. Rousseau had taught Robespierre that the virtuous man ought to despise money, and in fact he did not feel a need for it. As he explained to Charlotte, he had a lofty idea of the role of a barrister. In the same way that he had protected the weak at Louis-le-Grand, he defended the poor, the most ill-provided for. It was of little concern to him that noble causes brought in hardly any money.

At twenty-three Robespierre was thin, even slight, rather short—five feet three inches—and held himself well. He walked quickly, and was sometimes the victim of nervous tics. His face was as wide as it was long, with prominent chin and cheekbones. His chestnut hair was carefully powdered in the fashion of the time, and brushed back. His skin was pale, with a greenish cast "like that of a sick man, or a man worn out with meditation and vigils". His face was slightly marked with smallpox. His brow bulged, his eyes were grey-green, his nostrils were large, his mouth large and his lips thin. He was very short-sighted, and wore spectacles which he often pushed up on to his brow.

His style of dressing was irreproachable, even elegant. He usually wore a brown or olive-green jacket with a waistcoat of a light colour, black trousers, white stockings, silver-buckled shoes and lace cuffs.

While Robespierre had been in Paris there had been some changes in the family. His paternal grandparents had died, as well as his sister Henriette, probably of tuberculosis. His aunts had married late in life; Eulalie to a former lawyer, who had become a dealer, and Henriette to a doctor called Durut. There was an atmosphere of coldness between him and Maximilien. This resulted from Durut's claiming the 700 *livres* of the Carrault inheritance which Henriette had lent to François Derobespierre.

Robespierre now had about 2,600 *livres*, a modest sum, but enough all the same to live for a few months until he acquired some clients. He rented a little house in the rue du Saumon, and his sister Charlotte went to live with him as housekeeper. There had always been great affection between the two, which separations and mutual disappointment only strengthened. She expressed the highest admiration for her older brother possibly without really understanding him all that well.

Following in the steps of his father and grandfather, Maximilien was admitted as barrister to the Superior Council of Artois on 8th November 1781. His sponsor was Maître Liborel, a likeable man who was always helpful to his young colleagues.

Liborel enjoyed a great reputation at the bar in Arras. He took Maximilien under his wing, and got him his first brief in February 1782. It was a boring business about a marriage contract, which he probably did not feel very keen on dealing with himself. In fact, it was impossible to have won the case, since it had been dealt with by a previous judgement. The next day the young barrister took his revenge by winning another. True, he did not make much of a showing, and the judgement was given in his favour in default of his opponent. But this is quite often how it turns out for beginners.

All the same, Robespierre's name was well enough known in Arras for curiosity to be aroused. A colleague who had come to listen to the case later wrote to a friend in Paris mentioning in particular Maximilien's skill in building up his argument, his choice of expressions and the clarity of his speech. During the first year he pleaded about fifteen cases, which was an encouraging beginning. According to Charlotte, Maximilien took on only those cases he considered just and often advised his clients to settle out of court. In a letter to Abbé Touques, Robespierre explains that he has no chance of winning the Abbé's case and that he ought therefore to give it up. Alissan de Chazel said: "One must agree that love of money was never the motive for his actions. On the contrary he was highly indifferent to it. For several years he gave free consultations and did not want to take money from his clients, even when he won their cases for them." This testimony came from a man who did not like Robespierre. There is no doubt that court judges held him in high esteem. During his first year of practice, Monsieur de Madre, the Vice-President of the Council of Artois, appointed him as secretary. The title was a purely honorary one, carrying neither salary nor special duties.

As another mark of esteem, only four months after his enrolment at the bar, the Bishop of Arras, Monsignor Conzié, Maximilien's former protector, appointed him "man of fief promoted to the seat of the episcopal chamber for judging all cases, civil as well as criminal". The jurisdiction of this ecclesiastical tribunal extended over a part of the city of Arras, the borough of Vitry and several neighbouring villages. It was a highly coveted post, usually given to a jurist who had shown his capabilities, after ten or twelve years in the profession. There must have been a great many worthy candidates and the bishop must have thought very highly of Robespierre to have chosen him.

There is a story told about his duties as a judge (in the Episcopal Court). Once he had to pass the death sentence upon a murderer. Such an idea was against all that he believed in. Charlotte tells us that he spent two days without sleep or food, and even thought of resigning, so as not to have to sign the order for execution. He paced up and down the apartment saying: "Of course he's a wicked man who deserves to die. But to kill a man; to put a man to death!"

One of the cases he pleaded in 1782 was the defence of a certain Alexander, disinherited by his Protestant father because he had converted to Catholicism. It is rather surprising to find in Robespierre's speech a condemnation of Protestantism. At the end of the eighteenth century "advanced" people thought that Protestantism was more philosophical than Catholicism. "This religion can only attract idle, censurious men, the eternal enemies of the truth that has been generally accepted. The apparent severity and the actual licence that it permits those who believe in it may successfully appeal to those of a sombre and austere character, but they are the very opponents of restraint, whose proud and overbearing mentality refuses to submit to the dogma and practice of the Roman religion."

On several occasions the Oratorians of the Collège d'Arras, his former teachers, asked Robespierre to make the annual speech at the prize-giving ceremony. One of the ideas he developed in his speeches was in praise of King Henri IV, the "reforming" king, whom some had seen reborn in the person of Louis XVI. Henri IV was much in fashion in liberal circles, such as the salon of Madame de Lévis (the wife of the Marshal and Governor of Arras) where Robespierre met his colleagues from the Episcopal Court—men like Maître Manduict de Martin, provost of the Council of Artois, and Maître Demazières, assessor to the Abbey of St Vaast. All these people talked a great deal about the need for political reform, and in the salons of the aristocracy, more than anywhere else, the "new ideas" were discussed and the Revolution began to take shape.

Parisians assembled at the statue of Henri IV acknowledging him as the king's preceptor

[[·]]

Quite early on Robespierre fell out with his first patron. We do not know why. But on two occasions after their estrangement Robespierre pleaded successfully against Maître Liborel, which the latter took rather badly. Soon their relationship became strained. By way of compensation, Robespierre became the colleague and friend of Maître Buissart, and this friendship was to last. Buissart was regarded by many people as the foremost figure at the bar in Arras. He was very learned, a member of the Academy of Arras, a brilliant barrister, and in addition keenly interested in scientific matters.

Through him Maximilien became involved in a case which was quite famous at the time, and was talked about even in Paris—the case of the lightning-conductor. Monsieur de Vissery, a former barrister of St Ouen, had had this invention—new at the time—put on the roof of his house. The local people became excited when they saw this metal post erected because it seemed to threaten the sky in a sacrilegious kind of way. Some of them wanted to blow up the house, and a delegation went to fetch the bailiff, who ordered the owner to take down his "engine". Monsieur de Vissery tried to explain to the bailiff about the latest theories of electricity, lightning and the power of points. He had to give in.

But at the same time he brought an appeal against the bailiff's order to the Council of Artois, and appointed Maître Buissart to plead his case. The case, which was considered to be on the side of progress, provoked a lot of sympathy in Arras. Maître Buissart consulted several famous scholars—Condorcet, Abbé Bertholon, and even a certain "Doctor" Marat—who provided him with the necessary scientific arguments. When he had collected enough information, he prepared a memorandum.

It was common practice at this time for a senior barrister who had prepared the dossier of a case not to plead in court himself but to give the job to a young colleague. In this way the young man had a chance of making himself known. Buissart chose his friend Maximilien, whom he wished to help.

The case began on 14th May 1783, and Robespierre made two speeches which were amplifications of Buissart's text. He was talking about things of which he was totally ignorant, since he had had no scientific education at all, but then no more than the magistrate who had to give judgement. That did not matter very much, however, because what he said had the backing of famous scholars. He began: "The arts and the sciences are the most noble gifts from Heaven to humanity." He recalled the persecution of Galileo, Harvey and Descartes, and gave a detailed summary of the history of lightning-conductors from Dalibard's experiment in 1752 to the most recent discoveries of Benjamin Franklin, giving examples of the use of the apparatus in France and abroad. "A man," he declared, "has appeared in our time, who has dared to arm men against fire from heaven. He has said to lightning: 'You shall go no further.'" In conclusion Robespierre cited the example of the king, who had had an electric bar put in the physics laboratory at the

Château de la Muette "a royal house honoured by the presence of our monarch. If there were any doubts about the effects of these devices, the scientists involved would never have experimented on such a dear and such a sacred head. This example cannot be ignored. I bear witness to the feelings of the whole of France for a prince who is its delight and its glory." Such arguments could not fail to convince the tribunal, who were in any case already favourably disposed. By an order of 31st May 1783, Maître de Vissery was authorized to have the lightning-conductor put back on the roof of his house—which he lost no time in doing.

Following a custom then quite common, Maître Buissart published his memorandum of the case. It was presented as a "treatise on physics" and published in *Le Mercure de France*, with a critical note, probably written by Maître Buissart himself, in full praise. His young assistant was not forgotten. "Monsieur de Robespierre, a barrister of rare merit, deployed in this matter—which was the cause of science and the arts—an eloquence and wisdom which give the highest indication of his knowledge."

It was an honour to have his name mentioned in a newspaper read by all the best minds in France, and Maximilien appreciated the fact. It was an opportune moment for him to make his name even more well known. Through one of his Oratorian friends, Father Devienne, he asked Monsieur de Vissery to pay the cost of having the two speeches printed. At first the former barrister hesitated, but then agreed. He was rich and, most important, happy with the result of the case. This young man had contributed to that success and deserved a reward. Once more *Le Mercure* mentioned: "These two speeches do the greatest honour to Maître de Robespierre, who is hardly out of his adolescence."

He gave away copies to his friends and colleagues, knowing that they would be interesting for all who read them. Several women and young ladies found themselves among the happy recipients. He wrote to one of them in the letter which accompanied the gift: "I thought that a paper dedicated to the defence of the oppressed could not be a homage unworthy of you." He also sent copies of the speeches to many famous scholars, among them Franklin: "I hope, sir, that you will consent to receive this work with kindness, the object of which was to get my fellow citizens to accept one of your inventions. Happy as I am to have been useful to my country in persuading her chief magistrates to welcome this important discovery, I would be more happy still if I might add to this advantage the honour of obtaining the approval of a man whose least worth is that of being the most brilliant scholar in the universe."

[[·]]

Robespierre became reconciled with his aunts and went to live for a few months with the Duruts, then once again rented a house for Charlotte and himself in the rue des Jésuites. A young barrister who was beginning to establish a reputation owed it to himself to have his own establishment. He soon left this address for the rue du Collège, and then for the rue des Rapporteurs. There were several more changes of address during the next few years. The only characteristic that Maximilien seemed to have inherited from his father was his taste for changing his address. But as far as the rest was concerned, he made a complete contrast with his father.

Charlotte, in her memoirs, gives us a detailed account of one of Maximilien's days, most of which were very similar, for there were few men as regular as he was in his habits. He was generally up by six or seven, and worked until eight. Then he began his toilet, which was a rather long operation, and one to which he paid the most meticulous attention. A barber would come to dress and powder his hair. After this he took his frugal breakfast of a little bread and a bowl of milk. At ten o'clock he would go to the law courts. When he returned home for dinner he would have a light meal, consisting mainly of fruit. His wine was always diluted with water, and he would finish with a cup of coffee. More substantial dishes tended to give him indigestion. When it came to choosing the menu he was completely indifferent. Charlotte, who was a good housekeeper lamented his indifference: "Many times I asked him what he would like to eat at dinner, and he would reply that he had no idea."

After dinner he would work in his study until seven or eight, and the rest of the evening would be devoted to family gatherings. Charlotte tells us that he was "naturally bright in society", capable on occasions of "laughing until the tears came". All the same, his mind seemed to be for the most part elsewhere. "My aunts and I would reproach him for being distant and preoccupied in our company. In fact, when we played cards, or when we talked about unimportant things, he would go off into a corner of the apartment, bury himself in an armchair and give himself up to his thoughts as if he were alone." Charlotte gives an example of one of his curious distractions. "Once we had spent the evening together at the house of a friend and were returning home at a rather late hour when all of a sudden my brother, forgetting that he was accompanying me, walked twice as fast, left me behind, arrived alone at the house and shut himself up in his study. I got back a few minutes after him. I found the incident so funny that, seeing he was getting ahead at such a brisk pace, I let him go on without making him realize that I was with him. I went into his study, and found him already in his dressing gown, working very hard. He asked me with a rather surprised look where I had come from so late at night, and I answered that I had come home alone so late because he had left me behind. Then he remembered what had happened, and we both began to laugh at such a funny adventure."

A serious young barrister with a promising future was considered a fine match in the little town. One may easily imagine the machinations engaged in by the aunts and Charlotte to marry Robespierre off. He was not against their plans, quite the opposite. "The friendship of my brother towards women captivated their affection, and some of them, I think, even had more than ordinary feelings for him."

Charlotte Robespierre was fiercely proud of her brother and possessive towards him. Despite the equanimity of her memoirs, it is quite likely that Robespierre found her a disturbing influence in his Paris household. Nevertheless he was a loyal and fulsome correspondent throughout his career, for family and political reasons

"One amongst others," says Charlotte, "was Mademoiselle Dehorties [the daughter of Aunt Eulalia's husband by a previous marriage], who loved him and was loved by him." There was talk of marriage on several occasions, and very likely Maximilien would have married her if his civic conscience had not called him away from the gentle pleasures of private life and thrown him into public life. "The news of her marriage, some years later, to one of his colleagues," Charlotte maintained, "deeply affected him."

One of Robespierre's "near" fiancées was Mademoiselle Dehay, to whom he addressed a letter about canaries. She had made a present of a cage of these birds to Charlotte, and Maximilien thanked her. "We expected that, having been reared by you, they would be the most gentle and most sociable of canaries. Imagine our surprise when, going to their cage, we saw them rush against the bars with an impetuosity that made us fear for their lives. Surely such a face as yours should easily have made your canaries familiar with others. Or is it that, after having seen yours, they could not bear any others? Explain, please, this phenomenon to us." As a token of gratitude he sent Mademoiselle Dehay three printed copies of his latest speech.

[[·]]

Robespierre was esteemed by his colleagues, was a protégé and friend of Maître Buissart and his wife, and made close friendships with three other young barristers, Lenglet, Leducq and Charamand. They introduced him to a sort of literary club called the Rosati—"Young people united in a taste for verse, roses [from which the group took its name] and wine." In the group there were other barristers; some priests; a chevalier of St Louis, Carré; a painter, Berseigne, the vicar of St Aubert, Herbert; a surgeon, Gignet; a musician, Pierre Cot, and two other friends of Robespierre, Dubois de Fosseux and Foacier de Ruzé. Meetings were held on the banks of the Scarpe "in a garden full of flowers and shade, very rural, under an arbour of privet and acacia, reflected in the purest of streams", and they sang, drank and danced. The thought of Robespierre engaged in such frivolous pastimes is rather hard to imagine. Nevertheless, no one was surprised then to see him indulging. "One cannot help oneself from feeling that he was made to take his place among the Rosati," wrote Dubois de Fosseux, "when one sees him mingle with the young ladies of the region and enliven their dances with his presence."

The admission of a new member was accompanied by certain rituals, to which he submitted with good grace. He sniffed three times the rose presented to him, before pinning it to his jacket, and drank the obligatory glass of *vin rosé*. He replied to the poem of welcome with some couplets he had written for the occasion:

> *I see the thorn on the rose*
> *In the bouquets you offer me.*
> *The rose is your compliment,*
> *The thorn is the duty to reply.*

Two other members worthy of mention. Lazare Carnot, the future architect of victory, then captain of the engineers in the garrison at Arras, and Joseph Fouché. The latter, a lay brother of the Oratory—in other words he wore the habit without having taken priest's orders—taught physics at the little seminary. He was already known to be fervently adept at accepting any new idea. Maximilien sympathized with him, and invited him home to dinner several times. He was delighted to see his new friend courting Charlotte, and then proposing to her.

Joseph Fouché, to whom Charlotte was long engaged, resembled Talleyrand in two ways: both had been priests of a sort, and both had a talent near to genius for political survival

[[·]]

All the same, the Rosati was only a pleasant diversion. In Arras, as in most provincial cities, there was an academy where the local intelligentsia met to discuss serious matters, read and listen to essays on literature, law or science. There were thirty members. Maximilien, succeeding a canon of the cathedral, and sponsored by Maître Buissart and Dubois de Fosseux, became a member in 1783.

Robespierre's ambition to be a writer was stronger than his interest in being a barrister. The printed speeches were merely a beginning. In 1784 the Academy of Metz held a competition, and Robespierre decided to take part in it. The subject of the competition was "What is the origin of the opinion that the shame of a crime attaches to the criminal's family as well as to himself? Is this opinion more detrimental than useful? In the event of deciding in the affirmative, how would one guard against the consequent inconvenience?" Robespierre's entry was awarded second place, and won a prize of 400 *livres*. The writer Lacretelle was first. "This work is well written throughout," said the report, "although it contains little warmth. The ideas are set out clearly and simply, the argument is concise, the means of expression good. Occasionally one would have liked more development."

At the end of the eighteenth century, Robespierre naturally took up the defence of the unfortunate family, as did the other competitors. No one with any pretensions to enlightenment would have dreamed of supporting the opposite view. He argued that the feeling that makes us attach the dishonour that goes with a crime to the family of the criminal depends on the nature of the government. In this way the disgrace is less great in a democracy than in a despotism, because justice is dispensed there more fairly. Moreover, in a democratic state the dignity of the individual is raised to the point where it cannot be affected by the reputation of another. The blot may be wiped out by an act of personal courage. Man will have learned to put the good of his country above personal feelings. There is one sentence which shows the future Robespierre who devised the Laws of Prairial (the ninth month of the Republican calendar, from 20th May to 18th June): "Each citizen has a share in the sovereign power and may not, as a consequence, acquit his best friend if the safety of the State requires him not to do so." As a whole, Robespierre's defence is very moderate in tone, particularly the conclusion: "There is no need for us to change the whole system of our legislation; it is dangerous to look for *the remedy for a specific ill in a general revolution*." In fact, Robespierre stood for detailed reforms, qualified as "more supple means, more pliant and perhaps more certain"—an attitude which was quite in keeping with popular opinion in the years leading up to 1789. He envisaged abolishing the confiscation of a criminal's property, as an encouragement to the king to help the families of criminals and, in a rather unexpected proposal, extending to all classes of society the privilege of decapitation, instead of being hanged, since "it is a punishment to which we attach a certain amount of honour".

Robespierre used the prize money to have his entry printed and published as a brochure of sixty pages. Some passages were modified and others developed more fully. In particular, he inserted a paragraph in praise of virtue: "Morals are more powerful than laws, so it is incumbent upon us to uphold them, to improve them, so as to bring about the reign of virtue on the earth, which produces happiness as the sun produces light." He ended with an appeal "to the good king who could gain honour by suppressing this barbaric custom. This pressing proposal will not be presented in vain to the young and wise monarch who occupies the throne. We have as a guarantee for it his sacred passion for the happiness of the people, which is part of his august character."

The following year, Robespierre, encouraged by his success, entered a competition organized by the Academy of Amiens. For the fourth year in succession the subject chosen was a eulogy on Gresset (since the Academy had not found a work worthy of the prize up till then). What was there to say about Gresset, the author of *Vert-Vert*? He was such a mediocre writer, and certainly more to be commended for his attitudes than his writing. Robespierre lavishly praised his character, his love of religion, and his virtues, which had merited his being ennobled by Louis XVI. But what a curious idea to have drawn parallels with Voltaire! "Voltaire has more spirit, more finesse, more correctness, but in Gresset there is more harmony, more abundance, more naturalness, more talent. Voltaire's attributes seem more brilliant, more selective, more lively, brighter, while Gresset's are simple, spontaneous, gay and touching. The first amuses, surprises, enchants my mind. The second brings to my heart a gentler delight." Another passage which is surprising is a tribute to the Jesuits: "this famous society which offers such a gentle retreat to men who are devoted to the charms of study and literature".

In spite of his efforts Robespierre did not win the competition, nor did any of the other competitors. As before, he had his work published, and distributed copies to friends and acquaintances. Lacretelle thanked him for his copy in a letter full of compliments; and the closest of his friends, Dubois de Fosseux, sent a letter in verse:

> Fly into my arms with confidence,
> Support of the unfortunate, avenger of the innocent.
> You live for virtue, for gentle friendship,
> And you may command half of my heart.

In June 1786 his colleagues of the Academy in Arras elected Robespierre director, and in this capacity he presided over meetings, delivered official speeches and welcomed new members. There was a lady among them, Mademoiselle de Kéralio, who was a prolific writer of novels. On one occasion he spoke in her honour about the role of women in literature and the arts, with the usual gallant sentiments.

In common with other academies, the Academy of Arras held competitions. Robespierre was appointed one of three judges responsible for reading the manuscripts. During all the time that he held this office, no prizes were awarded.

Possibly this severity was a sort of revenge for his own disappointments. Here, for example, is the opinion he gave on one of the works submitted: "This entry has neither plan nor development. There is nothing new in it, nothing useful. It is badly written and badly presented. Its only merit is that it is short."

Several of his poems from these years have survived, and in them there is evidence of a certain amount of poetic skill, an attempt to be full of feeling and gallant, as was the fashion at the time. Many of Robespierre's madrigals are also in existence. There was a young English girl called Ophelia Mondlen who is supposed to have inspired one of them:

> Believe me, Ophelia so young and fair,
> Whatever the world and thy glass avow,
> Be happy to be pretty and never mind how,
> Guard with care thy modest air,
> Ever aware that the strength of thy charm
> Is always something to fear,
> And if only thus thee appear,
> Thy friends' hearts to thee shall warm.

He wrote a song for a certain Mademoiselle Henriette, and more songs on the marriage of a friend, Mademoiselle Demoncheaux. There are several graceful ballads: *I saw just now the lovely Flora*, and *I loved her so much when she was faithful*. On another occasion, changing the style, he wrote a hymn in the heroical-comic style *To the glory of cream tarts*. But the most unexpected of all his writings is without doubt the poem in Alexandrines on the handkerchief—*The Art of spitting and blowing one's nose*:

> No, no, never would a Roman of courage inflexible,
> Submit his bold, free and majestic nose
> To the caresses of soft cotton as he blows.

[[·]]

Shortly after the case of the lightning-conductor, Robespierre was invited by some cousins who were farmers to visit Carvin. A long letter to his friend Maître Buissart, describing the trip in great detail, is worthy of being quoted almost in its entirety because of the insight it gives into his character. The opening is strongly reminiscent of Racine:

> It was five o'clock in the morning when we set out. The chariot which was conveying us left the gates of the town at precisely the same moment that the chariot of the sun was flinging itself onto the bosom of the ocean. It was decorated with a cloth of dazzling whiteness, part of which floated freely, abandoned to the breath of the zephyrs.

Unfortunately at the gates there was an incident which spoilt his pleasure:

In this way we passed in triumph in front of the sentry-box. You may well imagine that I did not fail to look on that side. I wanted to see whether the worthies of the farm would belie their ancient reputation for civility. I myself, filled with noble emulation, dared to aspire to the glory of outdoing them in politeness, if that were possible. I leaned over the side of the coach and, taking off a new hat that covered my head, I greeted them with an almost gracious smile. I counted on a fair response. Would you believe it? The workers, static as boundary stones stood at the door of their cabin, looked at me fixedly without returning my greeting. I have always had a vast amount of personal dignity. This sign of contempt cut me to the quick, and made me unbearable for the rest of the day.

He was still thinking about the incident when, towards evening, they reached Carvin:

The inhabitants of this village gave us a welcome which amply recompensed us for the indifference of the workers at the Méoulens gate. Citizens of all classes vied with one another in their keenness to see us. The cobbler, just as he was about to nail a sole to a shoe, put down his hammer and came to have a look at us. The barber, leaving a half-trimmed beard, ran in front of us, his razor in his hand. The housewife, to satisfy her curiosity, ran the risk of having her tarts burn. . . . I saw three good women break off a very animated discussion to come to the window. Finally we savoured during this journey—which was, alas, all too short—the situation, flattering for one's dignity, of seeing a good many people looking at us.

"How pleasant it is to travel," I was thinking to myself. It is quite true that a prophet is not without honour except in his own country. At the city gates they despise you, but six leagues further on you are a personality worthy of public curiosity. I was occupied with these wise reflections when we arrived at the house which was the object of our journey. I will not attempt to paint for you the transports of tenderness which then burst out in our greetings. The sight would have moved you to tears. I know of only one scene of this sort which is comparable, and that is when Aeneas, after the fall of Troy, landed in Epirus with his fleet and found there Helenus and Andromache.

The kind welcome of his cousins cheered him up:

Since we arrived, all our time has been spent in delights. Since last Saturday I have been eating tarts to spite desire. Fate has decreed that my bed be placed in a room that is a depository for pastries, and thus exposes me to the temptation to eat them all night. But I reflected that it was a fine thing to master one's desires, and I slept in the midst of all these seductive objects.

I give thanks to thee who, with subtle mast'ry,
Was the first to tame the lowly pastry
And gave to mortals this delicious dish.
But did they recognize this precious benefice?

France, in common with all Europe, was primarily an agricultural country. Roads were poor and toll booths stood before the villages and towns. Principal cities were surrounded by defensive walls

He jokingly suggested that a temple should be built to the inventor of the tart:

> I would even say, between you and me, that I have a plan for it, which I intend to put before the States of Artois. I bet that it will be powerfully supported by the clergy.

His cousins had invited the local celebrities to a dinner given in his honour: ". . . three lieutenants," he stressed with evident satisfaction, "and the son of a bailiff; the entire magistrature of the neighbouring villages was gathered round our table." He ended addressing Buissart's wife: "I am getting ready to return to Arras soon. I hope, when I see you, that I will experience a more genuine pleasure than the one I have written to you about. However attractive a lieutenant may be, believe me, madame, he cannot enter into competition with you." In a letter to the husband he was able to allow himself to include, jokingly, gallant things about one woman: "Her face, even when champagne had turned it a gentle pink, did not offer the charm that nature has given to your wife's, and the company of all the bailiffs in the universe would not be able to compensate me for your kind conversation."

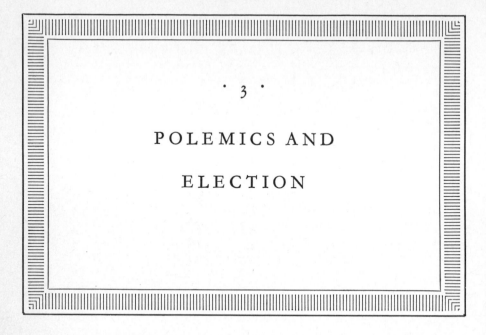

· 3 ·

POLEMICS AND

ELECTION

SHORTLY AFTER HIS RETURN, A MAN CALLED FRANÇOIS DETEUF, a master ropemaker in a little town near Carvin, asked Robespierre to undertake his defence. The treasurer of the Benedictine abbey of Anchin, Dom Brognard, accused Deteuf of having stolen 300 *livres* from the abbey's strongbox. Deteuf was poor and defenceless, which was just the sort of case that Robespierre liked to handle. But before the case came up before the tribunal, Dom Brognard was himself arrested at the request of his superiors. They had just discovered that the dishonest and pleasure-loving monk had misappropriated a large part of the abbey revenues for his own entertainment. The charges against Deteuf therefore lapsed *ipso facto*.

Nevertheless, as a conscientious lawyer, Robespierre reckoned that his client had a right to compensation for the wrong to which he had been subjected. He claimed damages in his client's name of 30,000 *livres*. This was no doubt an excessive amount, but there was a considerable problem. Who was to be responsible for paying the damages? Dom Brognard, who was now in prison, was penniless. Robespierre maintained that the abbey ought to pay, since it was responsible for the conduct of its members. In his dossier he argued that the thieving monk's superiors had turned a blind eye to his actions, not only out of moral weakness, but out of a sort of moral complicity which made them the truly guilty party. They had entrusted the administration of the monastic finances to him, yet they must have known that with the money he was organizing orgies in the monastery. "Let all of us who glorify ourselves with the title of citizen demand that laws be passed for all, that every injustice be made good, whatever the rank and condition of the person who committed the injustice. No, never, under any pretext whatsoever, let us watch the oppressor defy the cries of the weak, oppressed man. May magistrates never afford society this spectacle, meant to encourage crime and instil the innocent with fear.''

The tone of this argument was new, smacking more of the political pamphlet than of a judicial document. Moreover, Robespierre did not wait, as was customary, for the end of the trial to have his text printed and distributed. In a way he was making an appeal to public opinion over the heads of the judges. The Benedictines considered that they had been libelled and made an official complaint. They retained Maître Liborel to look after their interests. Liborel's relations with Robespierre had been very strained ever since they had separated. It seemed a good opportunity to teach a lesson to the pretentious despicable young man. By publishing his text before judgement was given, he maintained that Robespierre had been guilty of a serious breach of practice. Consequently, he demanded that: "A severe reprimand be inflicted on the lawyer for having made use of an infamous libel."

The quarrel was the talk of Arras, where people took sides for or against Robespierre. All those who professed to hold advanced ideas were for him—the majority of the lawyers, the Oratorians and the bishop himself, Monsignor de Conzié, who had had several contretemps with the abbey. Opposed to Robespierre were the judges, who were aroused by his attack on the magistrature, led by the President of the Council of Artois, Briois de Beaumetz, and all the conservative elements of the town. In fact, the abbey of Anchin stood for the traditionalists of the Church, in opposition to the Oratorians, who constituted the progressive wing. But the abbey did not have a very good reputation in the district, and the prior realized that public debate might do them even more harm. Wishing to stop the matter from going any further, he had a sum of 6,000 *livres* offered to François Deteuf in return for which he would withdraw his case. Not only did Deteuf accept this windfall—it was a huge sum for a poor master ropemaker—but he publicly repudiated his lawyer and the dossier. He said that he had never intended to "cause any harm to the regularity that prevailed in the said monastery, no more than he intended to damage the esteem it had acquired for itself by the moral purity of those who were members of the monastery."

It was a humiliating experience for Robespierre, in spite of the 1,100 *livres* given him by Deteuf by way of a fee. He had taken on the case not for the money, but because he had seen in it a cause that deserved to be won. As for the public reprimand, what a humiliation for his personal dignity! He saw in it a "plot against him on the part of the judges and prosecutors". All he wanted to do now was to take his revenge.

Another case soon provided him with the opportunity. Defending a certain Dame Penge, he launched himself into an indictment of the organization of justice.

*Despite the fact that France was the richest country in Europe, she was faced with bank-
ruptcy. Neither the clergy nor the nobility paid taxes. Both extracted their tithes and rights
of enforced labour from the peasants and working classes making still more onerous their
heavy burden of taxation*

"I see this mob of unfortunates being smashed by a thousand similar cases—of a
type one cannot divine—against the blood stained reefs that are the dangers in our
criminal jurisprudence, and I feel the need to supply the strength of justice and
humanity to the assistance of those who have been robbed by the imperfections of
the law."

The judges considered that they had been insulted yet again, and reacted. In a
decree of 30th January 1787, the Council of Artois ordered "that all the injurious
terms undermining the authority of the law, put about in the printed memorandum
signed Robespierre, lawyer, will be suppressed, and the present decree will be
printed and posted in the towns of Arras and Béthune, and everyplace deemed
necessary".

War had now been declared between the magistrature of Arras and Robespierre.
He replied to their decree with a eulogy on President Dupaty. We know how much
he admired the conscientious magistrate, who died the following year. The persecutions he had suffered and the coarse jokes made about him seemed to
Robespierre to come from a common source. "Dupaty, the philanthropist and

criminal expert, denounced to the nation the outrages of our criminal legislation, which seems made for a barbarian race, not a civilized people."

He took up the ideas of Rousseau on the inequality of wealth, and in it pilloried the source of the ills of society:

> You who charge dearly for the help dragged out of you by necessity, through importunity; you who cry out constantly against the mass of unfortunate people who bore you blind, come and learn to blush for your lack of sensitivity. Do you know why there are so many needy people?
>
> It is because you hold all the wealth in your greedy hands. Why is this father, why are these children, exposed to all weather, with no roof to cover them, suffering the horrors of hunger?
>
> It is because you live in sumptuous houses, where your gold commands all the arts to serve your soft way of life, and occupy your idleness. It is because your luxurious existence devours in one day the substance of a thousand men.

This singled Robespierre out as the strongest champion of reformist opinion. The poorer people began to speak his name with admiration, but at the same time his pronouncements brought about a break with some of his former friends, among them Dubois de Fosseux and Foacier de Ruzé. He stopped going to the Rosati meetings. Because attorneys had turned against him they stopped providing him with clients. In any case, despite an encouraging start, one could hardly say that he had succeeded as a barrister. In 1787, his best year after five years of practice, Robespierre pleaded twenty-two cases, which was one of the lowest figures. In 1788 he had only sixteen. He did not have enough money, which held such little attraction for him, to survive this drop in income without problems. Nor had his literary aspirations been fulfilled.

It seems that in the course of the first few months of 1788, discouraged, and attributing his disappointment to persecution, he considered leaving Arras, which was a miserable city, incapable of understanding him, to try and establish a new career in Paris. It was at that point the rumour began to spread that there was soon to be a meeting of the States-General.

[[·]]

In 1788 France was a prosperous country, with more than half the wealth of the rest of Europe. Life there was better than in any other country, as all the accounts of foreign travellers testify. This did not prevent numerous subjects from being discontented, however.

Each section of the population had its individual grievances, often contradicting each other. The middle class were rich, shrewd and cultured, and found it hard to swallow the fact that they did not have the influence in the State to which they felt themselves entitled. They demanded greater participation in government, and the end of privileges. In a rather clumsy way, exactly the opposite had been achieved. Since 1781 access to ranks above that of sub-lieutenant in the Army were closed to the middle class.

Above all, the people wanted a decrease in the taxes which they alone paid—in particular, feudal taxes, which were a survival from the past and could no longer be justified. The people attributed their problems to the king's agents who, they thought, constituted an obstacle to his desire to do good. They had to rid him of these impediments, therefore, to enable him to be a better ruler.

Both the middle class and the aristocracy, on the other hand, feared the abuse of absolute power. They wanted to "organize the monarchy", in other words, to force a constitution on the king. The parliaments were particularly active in their opposition. Throughout the eighteenth century they had contested the authority of the central government, thereby gaining a reputation as champions of public freedom and reform. All the same, they wrecked the most necessary reform, that of taxes, because it threatened their privileges.

What people wanted most was to make a clean sweep of the past. The Comte de Ségur was to say: "Everything ancient seemed to us cumbersome and ridiculous."

People expected the king to carry out reforms. Despite the fact that the government and the régime were keenly criticized, Louis XVI was held in greater affection by his subjects than any monarch before him. The previous reign had ended in contempt and disgust, but anything and everything might be hoped of the young king who had come to the throne in 1774. He was known to be hard-working, conscientious, full of good intentions and concerned for the happiness of the people. In fact, he had all the virtues, except those essential for a king. He was particularly afflicted by an inability to make a decision and stick to it. His brother, the Comte de Provence, compared his character to greased ivory balls which a person could never hold together. The first fourteen years of his reign had been no more than a long attempt at improvements never brought to fulfilment. Mallet du Pan wrote: "From one day to another they change systems and ideas about policy at Versailles. The sun never rises there three days running on the same opinion." The perspicacious Louis XV had prophesied that his successor would "spoil everything". In the meantime Louis XVI was the darling of the people and the object of the aristocracy's sarcasm, to whom his middle-class virtues seemed ridiculous. Alluding to his favourite hobby, they nicknamed him the locksmith.

As far as the government was concerned the problem was not one of reform, but of how to cope with the deficit in the treasury—125,000,000 *livres*—caused in part by the American war and in part by the pensions paid to a few great aristocratic families. A policy of economy and collecting taxes from everyone would easily have provided the remedy. Successive ministers, Necker, Calonne and Brienne, tried in vain to extract this fiscal reform from Parliament, then from an Assembly of Notables. An appeal to the nation then seemed the only solution. Brienne decided to summon the States-General by a decree of 8th July 1788. A subsequent decree of 8th August fixed the date of 1st May of the next year for the meeting.

Meanwhile Necker succeeded Brienne, who was persuaded to resign. Public opinion was for the return of the Genevan banker, since people saw in him a man of providence, the only one capable of avoiding bankruptcy. Yet Louis XVI did not like him. "They have made me recall Necker, I did not want him, and they will not be long in regretting what they have done." This way of acting on the advice of others in opposition to his personal opinion was characteristic of the king.

[[·]]

France had not seen a meeting of the States-General since 1614, and the news that it had been summoned aroused immense hope. There was no doubt that it would bring back the golden age. The king was thanked for his initiative in consulting his subjects. Thanks to him the nation would soon have a constitution, a marvellous institution, from which one might confidently expect the solution of all problems.

The extravagant fashions of the upper classes were in marked contrast to the dress of the lower orders

The legend in this engraving reads in part: '. . . our august monarch who joyfully follows in the footsteps of that great king Henri IV . . . has chosen as his mentor Necker, himself a second Sully . . . who has placed his own fortune at the disposition of his master . . .'

Everyone had precise ideas about it. Mallet du Pan said that any Frenchman who had the least bit of education thought himself capable of drawing up a Constitution, and had his own plan. Without delay every association, circle and group in France began to discuss the Constitution. In Arras the President of the Council of Artois, Briois de Beaumetz the younger (who had just succeeded his father in the office), held weekly meetings in his house of the foremost barristers to study improvements to be made to the common laws of the province. Robespierre was not invited. It was Beaumetz's way of showing his disapproval of the attacks on the magistrature. Since the meetings were private, he certainly had the right to invite whom he pleased. But Robespierre, already extremely hurt by the public reprimands, took his exclusion as an affront.

He protested in a new pamphlet which was published anonymously, but whose author was easily identifiable: "A letter from a lawyer of the Council of Artois to a friend who is a lawyer of the Parliament of Douai."

The general idea developed in it was that the older lawyers, monopolizing all the cases, did not leave any for their young colleagues. Whether this was right or wrong, the accusation had been made by each successive generation; but after five years of practice, Robespierre could no longer consider himself as a beginner. He attributed the drop in the number of his cases to the prosecutors' ill-will towards him "from whom one has to beg. Woe to those who make no effort to please them, or who fail in the attempt! Whatever talent nature has endowed them with, whatever taste they have for work, they can be sure to vegetate for ever." In an ironical tone which, with Robespierre, was an indication of wounded pride, he explained why they refused him the "honour of being summoned to the number of the chosen of Monsieur de Beaumetz. In the selection that has been made, each one has chosen his friends and kept the black ball for those who have not the good fortune to please."

Maître Liborel took it upon himself to reply. There is nothing more bitter than a quarrel between old friends. He laid into Robespierre well and truly. "Woe, thrice woe to you if you do not feel the nobility of the profession to which you claim to belong. Sordid interest and base greed reign in the depths of your heart, and rampant jealousy leads you to try to bring down to your level enlightened men and impartial jurists, who owe the confidence the public has in them to nothing more than their talents and their enlightenment." The war of the pamphlets, which began in this way between Beaumetz and his friends on one side and Robespierre on the other, was destined to last for a long time.

[[·]]

The second half of 1788 saw the appearance of hundreds of brochures and memoranda, from authors known and unknown, on the reform of the State and society. Volney's *The Sentinel of the People* appeared at Rennes; Thouret's *Advice to good Normans* appeared at Rouen; Mirabeau's *Appeal to the Provençal Nation*; Camille Desmoulins's *Philosophy of the French People* and Abbé Sieyès's *What is the Third Estate?*

As soon as the summoning of the States-General was proclaimed, Robespierre conceived the idea of seeking election. It was only natural that he should take up his pen to set out his manifesto. But unlike other authors, who purported to speak to the whole of France, he thought it better for his readers to deal with local matters, thus providing them with issues of more immediate interest.

The ills of Artois, according to him, were above all the consequences of the composition of the provincial Estates. It therefore followed that the remedy lay in a reform of the electoral system. He explained that the Estates were not representative since they were "constituted of a league of a few citizens who had seized power which belongs only to the people". Thus the First Estate (the clergy) was made up of bishops and regular abbés who held their seats by virtue of their rank, and not by election. "By what right have they excluded the curés, the class that is without contradiction the most numerous; the most useful of this body; the most valuable because of the close relationship which binds it to the needs and interests of the people?" The priests read these words and approved of them. Robespierre then went on to consider the composition of the Second Estate (the nobility) and found it no more representative. All the lesser aristocracy of Artois, with its liberal views, was in fact kept out of the Estates in favour of a few old families, therefore the lesser aristocracy also welcomed Robespierre's views. And so Robespierre's reputation spread among various sections of society. As for the deputies of the Third Estate, he rightly stressed that they represented neither the townspeople nor the country folk. "And whilst the enemies of the people are bold enough to play around with humanity, I lack the courage needed to demand its rights. I would stand in cowardly silence before them, at the very moment when, for so many centuries, the voice of truth could make itself heard with force."

He denounced the waste of public money by quoting detailed facts which everyone knew. There was the story of a person employed at the town hall who was dismissed for corruption, and then subsequently reinstated through his protectors. Robespierre protested strongly against forced labour among the farmers of Hainaut, which was one of the most unpopular institutions of the time. In the country areas where the peasant vote could be decisive, Robespierre was talked of favourably. "The ending of all the evils which overwhelm us depends on the virtue, courage and feelings of those to whom we will entrust the redoubtable honour of defending our interests in the national assembly."

He presented himself to the electors in these terms:

"My heart is true and my resolution strong. I have never borne the yoke of baseness and corruption. If there is anything with which I am to be reproached it is that I have never been able to disguise my way of thinking, that I have never said 'Yes' when my conscience cried out 'No', that I have never courted the potentates in my country."

This electoral manifesto ended with an invocation to Louis XVI: "Let us listen to the august and moving voice of our king, who offers us happiness and freedom."

[[·]]

From then on any occasion was opportune for him to make political speeches. He pleaded on behalf of a man called Dupont who had deserted, was condemned to death for failure to appear in court, and then locked away as a madman in a hospital at Armentières, which was run by a religious order. Robespierre soon ignored his client and devoted his attention to a denunciation of *lettres de cachet*, the sealed letters which contained secret orders from the king. He said that judges were "oppressors of the laws" and that a person was an "enemy of the fatherland" who "placing his convictions under the protection of arbitrary power, dares to restrict the authority of the law to oppress citizens without impunity". As for the monks of Armentières, he described them as "the dregs of the people, motivated by vile and cruel instincts, who live in opulence on the remains of their victims". There was also, as a sort of peroration, the call to the king: "Sire, from that great height on which the grandeur of your amazing destiny places you, deign to cast a glance

Mons. de Jumilhac mon Intention
étant que le nommé Hugonet
soit conduit en mon Chateau de La Bastille, je
vous ecris cette Lettre pour vous dire que vous
ayez à l'y recevoir lorsqu'il y sera amené, et à l'y
garder et retenir jusqu'à nouvel ordre de ma part.
La presente n'étant a autre fin je prie Dieu qu'il
vous ait Mons. de Jumilhac en sa sainte garde.
Ecrit à Versailles le treize Janvier 1765.

Louis

In this lettre de cachet *Louis XV ordered the governor of the Bastille to allow the courtier
mentioned to be admitted to the château and confined there until further notice*

of commiseration on the entire human race. You see before you this enormous
family of brothers, which the Father of the universe assembled to raise themselves
by their joint efforts to that perfection of which their nature was capable. They are
cast down through the abuse of arbitrary power and by the crimes of tyranny, to
the last degree of corruption, abasement and misery."

When Robespierre had his memorandum on Dupont printed, he added an appeal
to Necker. "I will not mention you by name, because the whole of France and the
whole of Europe will easily be able to identify you. Your great mind and character
ensure both the mission and the means of putting into motion the most interesting
of revolutions. You are a great hearted citizen, do not despair of the French, and
on a stormy sea abandon the rudder of this superb vessel loaded with the destiny
of a great empire, which you must bring to port."

Several more pamphlets followed, which he had distributed by the hundred. He
spoke, he denounced, he presented himself as the victim. "I am risking, sacrificing,
my life for the defence of the people. Let us join forces with each other at this

critical time to overthrow the terrible conspiracy. Oh citizens, the fatherland is in danger, enemies at home, more fearsome than foreign armies, secretly plot its ruin. Rush to its help, and let us rally all its defenders to the cry of Honour, Reason and Humanity."

Nowadays elections require large financial means. It was not so at this time. Robespierre was not inconvenienced by his lack of money. What little he had was enough for printing his memoranda and pamphlets. He found money among those close to him, and a few dedicated friends acted unsparingly as his publicity agents. Most important were Maître Buissart and his wife, who were useful because of their close connections with the upper middle class and the liberal nobility. Through them Charles and Alexandre de Lameth supported Robespierre, as did his cousins in Carvin who had influence over the peasants in their area. Augustin, Robespierre's younger brother, who greatly admired him, "went from village to village canvassing votes". Through Uncle Durut, Robespierre was able to influence not only the Oratorians, who were already well disposed towards him, but also their spiritual charges. Finally, by a happy chance, Charlotte had just made friends with Madame Marchand, who owned a newspaper. She threw herself with zest into the battle, in Robespierre's favour. It was in this way that the possibilities of election were fairly hopeful, as far as the young candidate was concerned. Naturally there was no lack of opponents who were determined to prevent Robespierre's election. Among them were several of his former friends. Chief of these was Monsieur de Beaumetz, regarded as the leader of the conservative faction. He was to be the deputy representing the nobility. Others included the Benedictines; the magistrates he had offended, and some of the barristers. On the other hand, his memorandum on the Estates had won for him genuine popularity with the common people.

[[·]]

Voting began on 23rd March (1789). The system varied from province to province, had several stages, and was complicated, but it was more or less universal. In Arras each corporation had to name delegates to the electoral assembly, which was in turn responsible for choosing the deputies. Those who, in common with Robespierre, did not belong to any corporation, met in the Church of the Oratorians. From the very beginning of the meeting there was a problem as to who was to be chairman, and this raised a sharp but minor altercation. The Mayor of Arras, d'Aix de Rémy, maintained that it was his prerogative. There were immediate protests. A barrister named Delorgue proposed that a commission of five people be appointed. This motion was hotly supported by Robespierre, who urged the people present to: "Use their sovereign rights to be governed by those whom they had freely chosen and to refuse to be ruled by those whom a despotism had designated to fulfil this function." A commission was appointed, and the members immediately began to count the votes of those electors present.

The reform party had just won an important victory which was mainly due, as everyone acknowledged, to Robespierre's intervention. The mayor and the aldermen had been booed and whistled at; and they had withdrawn their names, declaring that they would appear no more at the Assembly "in view of the disrespect that had been shown to them", and so were eliminated. In public meetings, more than anywhere else, those who are absent are always in the wrong. In much

Throughout France ballots to nominate deputies to the first convocation of the States General in 114 years were distributed on the 27th December 1788. The system of nomination and selection for ultimate election was very complicated and was not completed until five months later

the same way Maître Demazières, a deputy of the Third Estate to the Estates of Artois, who proposed himself as a candidate, was declared ineligible by the barrister Ansart, a colleague of Robespierre's, and was described as "this prop of despotism". In any case, whether rightly or wrongly accused, Demazières only got a very small number of votes.

Robespierre headed the list of the twelve elected delegates, along with his friends Buissart and Delorgue. A few days later the first general meeting of the representatives of the corporations took place at the town hall. The business was to draw up a list of complaints. Among the guild of cobblers, the most pitiful of all, there was not one member who could write. On the recommendation of one of their members called Languillette, they asked Robespierre to undertake this task for them. The choice shows how much the poorer people trusted him. The chief complaints of the cobblers were competition from the shoemakers, a recent increase in the price of leather and too many inspections by municipal agents who claimed that they were checking the quality of workmanship. Robespierre added his own ideas to these professional problems. Through his pen, the cobblers protested "against the inhuman processes which could only degrade a people already despised, whereas the first concern of those who govern is to elevate, as far as it is possible for them, by their very nature, to inspire in others the courage and the virtues which are the springs of social happiness."

The next session was to be devoted to condensing all the individual lists of grievances into one report, which turned out to be much more difficult than expected because of the numerous contradictory complaints. It took five days to complete. The conflict between Robespierre and his former friend Dubois de Fosseux made the debate very heated at times. And so a friendship was destroyed by politics. One of the items on the general report called for the restoration of the right of the Commons to be their own administrators. Robespierre had already elaborated this point in his "*Appel à la nation artésienne*", and made a fervid contribution to the debate. The present municipal authorities, he said, had been appointed by the ruling powers, and therefore had no legal constitutional authority "to represent the unfortunate citizens of Arras, who had been oppressed for so long". Fosseux became indignant at these words, since he was a member of the ruling body, and he protested. He accused Robespierre of inadmissible slander. Robespierre replied that "Monsieur de Fosseux's indictment can only be regarded as a new attack on the freedom of vote—more so, since it is made by a person alien to the Third Estate, and consequently without the right to express an opinion in the assembly of the Third Estate."

In their turn the 550 delegates from the towns and villages arrived. They also brought complaints which had to be incorporated with those of the city. A commission was set up which carried out this task in three days. Robespierre was a member of it, and in this way his name was brought more and more to people's attention.

In Paris, a week after the election of the States General, paper plant workers whose wages
had been frozen at 15 sols a week held a sit-in strike. When besieged by soldiers, the strikers
hurled stones and tiles at them. The Guards fired on their assailants, killing a great number

[[·]]

The great occasion of the election of deputies to the States-General arrived. It began on 20th April with a religious ceremony. The delegates of all three Estates heard mass together in the great nave of the abbey before they took the oath. Bishop Conzié and the Duc de Guines both made "patriotic" speeches which included a great deal about reform. After this, each Estate met separately. Because the clergy and the nobility had made it known that they intended to renounce some of their privileges, the Duc de Guines, who was presiding over the assembly of the Third Estate, proposed sending them a message of compliment. The majority appeared to approve, but according to the minutes "a barrister got up and protested that there was no call to thank people who had only renounced abuses", and the motion was abandoned. The barrister was Robespierre.

There were eight deputies to be elected individually by the Third Estate, a clumsy process which took five days. Three had already been elected. First was Payen, then Bassart and Fleury: two farmers and a barrister. Then Robespierre came forward. A man called Vaillant, Keeper of the Seals of the Chancellery of Arras, opposed him. The first round was inconclusive, and in the second Vaillant won.

This setback was of no importance for Robespierre, since there were four more delegates to elect. He had only to keep his candidature in. He took great pains, however, to make sure of his success. According to his opponents, he intrigued and formed cabals. However, a candidate cannot be reproached for trying to win votes. The support of two liberal deputies for the nobility—Charles and Alexander de Lameth—was extremely useful to him. They wished to play a major part in the meeting of the States and therefore wanted Robespierre to be present as a devoted second. All the same, it would seem that the decisive element in his election was the intervention of Robespierre's Carvin cousins, who persuaded the other delegates from the country to vote for him.

When the election was over, the traditional banquet brought electors and elected together. Cobbler Languillette was present, a fact which astonished some of the guests, who were not accustomed to such company. Dubois de Fosseux asked the men sitting next to him, in a mocking tone, if in the new era about to dawn, such a man would one day be able to become Mayor of Arras. Robespierre overheard this remark and responded. "Yes", he said. "Everything in France is going to change now. Before very long, poor Languillette, whom Monsieur Dubois de Fosseux so despises, will be able to mix in any company. Languillettes will become mayors, and mayors will be Languillettes."

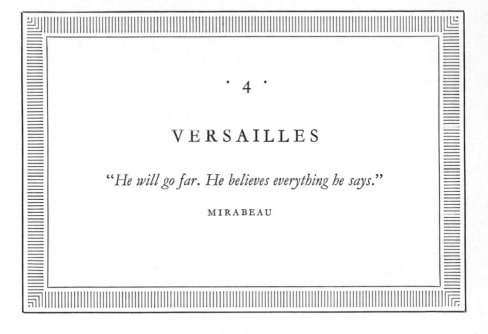

· 4 ·

VERSAILLES

"He will go far. He believes everything he says."

MIRABEAU

THE DELEGATION FROM ARTOIS LEFT ARRAS ON 1ST MAY. Robespierre's relatives and a small group of close friends, among whom was Fouché, went with him to the carriage. Madame Marchand had lent him a large trunk in which to put his things. Charlotte, like a careful châtelaine, drew up the inventory: he took with him, among other things, three pairs of black breeches "very worn"; a black velvet coat that had been dyed; six shirts in good condition; three pairs of silk stockings "one of which was almost new"; a little black cloak; a barrister's gown; a hat to carry under his arm(!), and a supply of copies of his "*Appel à la nation artésienne*".

Robespierre and his colleagues arrived at Versailles on 3rd May. The night before, the royal reception had taken place, and this was the first in a long series of blunders by the Court in dealing with the deputies of the Third Estate. The double doors of the great salon were wide open for the privileged orders, whereas they passed before the king in his bedroom. This was the old etiquette. But this was not good enough reason for men who had come to Versailles with the intention of changing the basis of the State. They were offended by this difference in the way they were treated, and let it be known "how much such distinctions were painful for that section of the people which alone of the three estates was truly national". Unfortunately no one had the goodness to take any notice of this.

If the king had only given them a cordial welcome the wound would have been healed, but Louis XVI was always timid and embarrassed in public, and could

At the States General in Versailles the nobility and the clergy were seated in rows to the left and right of the king, while the Commons were further away, facing them

scarcely find a word to say, apart from "Good day, my good man", to a Breton deputy whose traditional costume surprised him. From afar the representatives worshipped their sovereign as a god. Close to, they were disappointed. One of them, Barère, said: "His appearance was very awkward and gave everyone the impression of a badly brought up, big, fat boy."

On 4th May in front of an enthusiastic crowd, there was a procession through the streets of the "delegates of the nation". Robespierre received his share—anonymously—of the cheers for the deputies of the Third Estate. There was a ceremony in the cathedral to ask Heaven's blessing on the work of the States, but the places allotted them at the end of the nave displeased the delegates considerably. Bailly wrote: "It is by such childish pettiness that the seeds of bitterness are sown, which never fail to flourish." Nevertheless, the Bishop of Nancy's "patriotic" sermon partially removed this bad impression. He condemned the established order, the abuses of the régime, and particularly denounced the unfair distribution of the burden of taxation. "It is in the name of a good king, a just and sensitive monarch," he exclaimed, "that these villainous extortionists perform their outrages." The fact that a representative of the privileged orders held such views gave all manner of hope. When he left the pulpit the deputies broke into applause.

The next day, however, at the opening session, the Third Estate were to have their third disappointment. The States-General began with a misunderstanding.

The deputies were expecting the announcement of a programme of reform by the king. Not only did he not say a word about it, but he warned them against "the exaggerated desire for innovation". They applauded him warmly all the same, because they liked him. There was not a man among them who was not a monarchist. After the king, the Keeper of the Seals, Barentin, spoke. His speech, which was supposed "to explain the king's intentions", was delivered in so mumbled a manner that no one understood very much about the propositions. Necker's statement was therefore awaited all the more impatiently. He appeared and was greeted with cheers. But he was mistaken for a reformer. The American Ambassador, Morris, said, "he knew nothing about politics". As Minister of Finance his only concern was to balance the budget. His financial statement was very technical, and full of figures, so that the deputies had the greatest difficulty in following him. He was, moreover, tired, and had an assistant finish off the speech. The session, which had opened in hope, ended in indifference and boredom.

[[·]]

Versailles was an unknown city for most of the provincial deputies. First of all, they had to find somewhere to live. Feeling themselves lost among strangers they formed groups according to the place they came from, or to their political affiliations. The deputation of the Third Estate from Arras split into two. On one hand were the middle-class members, and on the other the peasants Payen, Fleury and Petit. Robespierre chose the company of the second group in preference to his barrister colleagues. They stayed as a group in the Hôtellerie du Renard in the rue Sainte Elisabeth, on the edge of the town. Some weeks later they rented a house in the rue de l'Étang, nearer to the conference hall.

Robespierre's first political move was to introduce himself to Necker, who made the little deputy welcome and asked him to stay to dinner. This gesture granted to a possibly future adherent, which no minister neglects to do, was especially useful in this case, since Necker was beginning to have his doubts about the intentions of the States. It would be a good thing to have a few of his own men there. All the same, the meeting ended in total failure, since each of them realized that they did not have the same aims. They never saw each other again.

So, at one fell swoop, Robespierre lost all respect for Necker. He was no less disappointed in his contacts with the big names of the Assembly—Mounier, Target and Malouet—who were greeted by the crowd with cheers. He suspected that there was nothing revolutionary about them. On 24th May he wrote to Buissart:

Monsieur Mounier will not play such a large role here as in his province, since people suspect him of having pretentions. Moreover he is far from being an eloquent man. I saw Monsieur Target arrive here preceded by a great reputation. He opened his mouth and we were prepared to listen to him with the greatest interest. He said ordinary things with a great deal of emphasis. Count Mirabeau is nothing because his moral character has robbed him of all confidence. But the most suspect and the most odious of all patriots is Monsieur Malouet. This man, armed with impudence and riddled with guile, manipulates the springs of intrigue. Generally speaking, there are few talented men in the nobility. Every day d'Eprémesnil piles up folly upon folly.

The plan of the nobles to give up some of their privileges as a sop to the Commons seemed highly suspicious. It was doubtless only "in the hope of negotiating more successfully with us at the expense of the rights of the nation, after they had made this illusion of sacrifice, which no longer depends on their will, and which ought not to be the gift of the nobility, but a constituent law that the States-General alone ought to bring in. . . . As for the clergy," he concluded, "there is no trick they do not use to seduce their priests. They have even gone as far as to insinuate that we want to strike at the Catholic religion."

[[·]]

In his evaluation, Robespierre showed himself to be shrewd. Mounier, Target and Malouet, whom people had thought would be the leading men in the States, played only a limited part. As for Mirabeau, his immorality, which lost him the confidence of his colleagues, did indeed prevent him from succeeding. Robespierre had little admiration for anyone except for Lafayette and the Duc d'Orléans. He soon had reason to revise this opinion. As far as Mirabeau was concerned, his openly revolutionary attitude made Robespierre go back on his first impression, and he made friends with him. In fact, Mirabeau was a difficult person to judge. His enormous potential had previously been revealed in disorder and adventure. He saw in the Revolution a way of reaching the top, and threw himself into it with verve. He was excluded from his Order because of his scandalous private life, and had himself elected deputy of the Third Estate at Aix-en-Provence. Unlike Robespierre, he was not a revolutionary by conviction but out of opportunism. He had given himself the role of playing up to the weak Louis XVI, as Cardinal Richelieu had to Louis XIII. He led the extremists not because he shared their ideas, but because he wanted to make himself so popular that the extremists would force him on the Court. His plan was to make the aristocracy tremble, to avenge himself for their disdain, and then to appear in the disorder as the only possible saviour. The cheers of the crowds made him believe that he could, by force of words alone, set the Revolution in motion, quicken its pace, then stop it at what he thought the proper moment. Meanwhile, to bolster his influence, he looked forward to creating a following for himself of promising young people, deputies and journalists—what we would call a brains trust today—attracted to Versailles by the meeting of the Estates. That is how Camille Desmoulins came to be his secretary for a time. During the first four weeks of the Assembly Robespierre was seen in his company quite often, enabling his enemies to label him Mirabeau's monkey. Under his direction, Robespierre drew up a list of motions to be put to the Assembly. The behaviour of his young colleague, cold and calculated, interested in neither money or women—the two things to which he was particularly devoted—astounded Mirabeau.

[[·]]

Brittany was, to all appearances, one of the most "advanced" French provinces. In fact, more than any other it had a tradition of resistance to royal administration. From the outset, the Breton deputies were accustomed to meeting at the Café Amaury to discuss beforehand the proposals to be presented to the Assembly. These deputies formed what was known as the Club Breton. The leaders were Le Chapelier and Lanjuinais. Soon representatives from other provinces, who shared their views, joined them when they saw the advantages of the organization. This was at a time when political parties did not exist. Duport, Sieyès, Abbé Grégoire, Mirabeau himself, and Robespierre went along. The latter wrote: "Forty deputies, with whom we have joined forces, most of them talented men, and full of spirit and energy."

The first issue to be decided by the States was the question of voting. Traditionally after each debate it had been by the Estate as a whole, but now there was strong feeling that it should be by each individual. In order to gain popularity, Necker agreed that the Third Estate should have a representation equal in number to that of the clergy and nobility combined. If voting by Estate were to be maintained, the concession was nonsensical. The representation of the Third Estate might just as well have been ten times greater, without giving it any advantage. Individual voting, on the other hand, with the support of the liberal nobles and a section of the clergy made up of curés, would have assured them a majority.

In a rather clumsy fashion, the government left it to the States to decide for themselves how they would vote. They were unable to agree. The debate went on without coming to any conclusion, and was in danger of bringing things to a standstill. The 24th May came and the business of checking the credentials of the delegates had not even begun. Faced with the reforming mood of the Third Estate, the Court wanted to retain the practice of voting by Estate, so as to defeat them, but knew full well that it would be very difficult to make them accept the idea. At all costs they had to break the deadlock. Rabaut Saint-Etienne, a deputy of the Third Estate, proposed that commissioners be appointed to consult with representatives from the clergy and nobility. Le Chapelier opposed the motion, which he described as useless and dangerous. At such a meeting, he maintained, the Third Estate was in danger of being in the minority. What he suggested was a solemn appeal to the other two Estates to join with them. Several speakers followed Rabaut, in favour of his motion. Robespierre was strongly against it. He was afraid that a meeting would provide an opportunity for the clergy and nobility to undermine the resolution of the Third Estate. Le Chapelier's motion, on the other hand, seemed to him "energetic and vigorous", and had his wholehearted approval. Nevertheless, he saw that the majority would not follow him, so he proposed a third plan. All that was needed was to send to the clergy "a brotherly invitation to join the national body and to add their efforts to those of the Commons [the new name which the Third Estate gave itself] to persuade the nobles to follow their example". The clergy were in fact the most likely of the two privileged orders to join with the Third Estate. It was therefore a good tactic to speak to them first of all. When they had agreed to join forces, the nobles would not be able to remain in isolation for very long. Mirabeau realized the advantages to be gained from Robespierre's idea, and quickly gave his support. But since the discussion up to that point had been restricted to the other two motions, the commissioners refused to allow a vote to be taken on it. "Many people," Robespierre said, "told me that they were grateful to me for the path that I had opened up, and assured me that they had no doubt that it would have been adopted, if it had been proposed first."

Robespierre made a second contribution on 28th May, but the question of voting was still not decided. That day the Archbishop of Aix came to the Commons, carrying a piece of black bread. He exhorted the deputies not to waste any more time in useless discussion, but to send a delegation as soon as possible to discuss with the representatives of the clergy and the nobility and decide what were the best ways of improving the lot of the people. His speech appeared to agree with the ideas of the reformers, and was greeted with applause from everyone except Robespierre. He suspected that there was some hidden motive behind the archbishop's humanitarian sentiments: to get the Third Estate to accept the idea of voting by Estate under false pretences. Mirabeau's secretary, Étienne Dumont, tells how he replied to the archbishop: "Go and tell your colleagues not to hold up our discussions with spurious delays. They are ministers of a sublime religion, founded on the scorn of wealth. Let them copy their divine master and give up their displays of luxury which offend the people in their dire need. The ancient canon law states that one may sell sacred vessels to relieve the poor, but there is no need for such a desperate remedy. Dismiss your proud servants, sell your magnificent coaches, your sumptuous furniture, and the luxuries which are an offence to Christian humility. Give the unfortunate the immense fortune you hold in the name of charity."

Dumont reports that a flattering murmur greeted these words. Everyone asked who was the young man? They stood up the better to see him. The deputy Raybaz, who was standing next to Dumont, remarked that such a speaker would not be lost in the crowd for very long.

On 10th June the king replied rather vaguely to a message from the Third Estate, which did not satisfy the delegation. "It was," said Robespierre, "the work of his perfidious advisers, who ceaselessly plot the end of the National Assembly." He still had complete confidence in Louis XVI's goodwill. As far as the government was concerned, however, his distrust constantly increased. Not much is known about Robespierre's speeches in the Assembly at this time. He is generally credited with a speech made on 12th June addressed to the king, in which he protested against the use of flattering titles by a popular assembly.

His first two or three appearances in the Assembly had been well received. Even so, some time was to pass before his colleagues listened to him with interest. There were some well-known speakers in the Assembly, and all attention was turned on them. When an unknown such as Robespierre got up to speak, many deputies would leave or turn to other matters. Robespierre had two disadvantages; a weak voice and a certain amount of nervousness. One day he admitted to Dumont that he always shook with fear when he began to speak. In the Salle des Menus-Plaisirs, which was unsuitable for public meetings, the acoustics were very bad, and moreover everyone talked at once. "More than five hundred people," said Mirabeau, "thrown into a room without knowing each other, all free, all equal, none having the right to command, none feeling himself obliged to obey, and all wishing—in the French manner—to be heard rather than to listen." There were no rules of order at all. The chairman, elected for a fortnight, lacked the authority to enforce silence. France had to serve its apprenticeship in parliamentarianism. Meanwhile, in order to be heard, one had either to have a powerful voice or a name which aroused curiosity. Robespierre's pride was terribly wounded to think that anyone could fail to pay attention to what he had to say, and this disconcerted him. The report in Duplain's *Courrier* says: "Monsieur de Robespierre took the floor, but the Assembly having shown a certain amount of impatience, the honourable member withdrew, like Jeremiah, with tears in his eyes." But he was determined, and was not long in learning to face up to it. Between the end of May and the end of the year he was to make twenty-five speeches. Mirabeau made 122. One day Robespierre said "I am not at all put off by those who interrupt me. I even propose telling other truths that will excite more than murmurs."

Before making a name for himself in the Assembly, he was brought out of anonymity, as far as the public was concerned, by the newspapers. There had been a considerable increase in the number of journals since the opening of the States. Their chief purpose was to report the debates. At first they published long extracts from speeches which were certain to be of interest to their readers. They gave only short résumés of speeches made by unknown deputies, most of the time without even giving their names. This is what happened in the case of Robespierre's first speeches. All the same, quite quickly the more radical papers mentioned him, and he knew some of the editors personally—for example Mademoiselle de Keralio from the *Mercure national*. She was a former colleague from the Academy of of Arras, and was now Madame Robert. Then there was Gorsas's *Courrier de Versailles à Paris*; *Le Moniteur*; Beaulieu's *Les Nouvelles*, and *La Sentinelle du peuple*, which mentioned his name with praise. Several newspapers were owned by colleagues, such as Mirabeau's *Courrier de province*; and when they were on good terms, Mirabeau always mentioned Robespierre's speeches. There was also *Le Point du jour*, which belonged to Barère, who had become friendly with Robespierre because of their similar beliefs. Moreover, he had met again his old school friend Camille Desmoulins, who was becoming one of the most widely read of journalists, since he was the most witty and amusing of them all. Camille was always enthusiastic, and made admiring comments about "his dear Robespierre", while Barère spoke about "his fine dialectic, his clarity of speech, the purity of his intentions and his patriotic fervour". He singled him out as one of the new talents who had just appeared "in such a brilliant way alongside Barnave, Le Chapelier and Pétion".

[[·]]

Robespierre does not seem to have played a special part in the events which led up to 14th July. On 17th June, at the suggestion of Sieyès, the Third Estate declared itself the National Assembly. Two days later some members from the clergy came and joined them. A fusion of the three Estates was announced, and the establishment of individual voting. The Court could not agree. Advised by those close to him, and in particular by Marie-Antoinette, Louis XVI wanted forcibly to impose a division of the three Estates, and voting by Estate. On 20th June the deputies arrived to find the doors closed—for alterations, according to the notices posted there. After a moment's hesitation they met in the Jeu de Paume—a tennis court—and there, under the chairmanship of Bailly perched on a table, they swore never to leave before they had given France a constitution. Robespierre took the oath, along with all his colleagues but one, and was the forty-fifth person to sign the document.

On 23rd June, in the royal session, Louis XVI spoke as an absolute monarch, arrogantly shattering the decrees passed by the Commons on the preceding days, and ordering them to divide up into Estates. Thinking that he would frighten the deputies, he threatened dissolution. "If, by an unimaginable calamity, you should abandon me in such a worthy undertaking, alone I should see to the good of my people. I alone would deem myself their true representative."

The king's weakness—and the strength of the deputies—lay in the financial situation. After having tried all other methods, he had summoned the Estates in an attempt to get money through new taxes. Were he to dismiss them, he would be back where he started but in an even worse situation, since in the meanwhile the deficit had increased. The deputies, knowing this, did not obey. Customarily

(OPPOSITE, ABOVE) *In the Great Conference Room, and in the presence of the king, the Commons declared themselves the National Assembly. Members of the other two estates were invited to join them.* (OPPOSITE, BELOW) *Barred from the Conference Room, delegates re-assembled in the Jeu de Paumes. They took an oath to be inseparable, and wheresoever they met they were the National Assembly, and that should a member fall ill he was to be carried in*

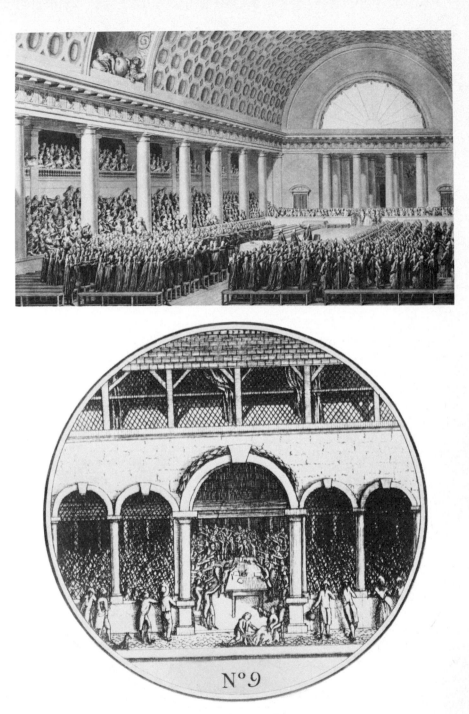

Louis XVI gave in when resisted. When Dreux-Brézé came to report to him two hours later, all he could say was: "So they want to stay; well let them stay." After this he ordered the nobility to join forces with the clergy and the Third Estate. At this spectacle of alternate resistance and capitulation, Mirabeau was inspired to remark: "This is how kings are led to the scaffold."

Louis XVI never knew how to stand by a decision once he had taken it. A week after giving in, he returned to a policy of resistance, bringing Swiss and German troops into the area round about Paris under the pretext of keeping order. The Assembly saw this as the prelude to its dissolution. On 9th July, at the instigation of Mirabeau, the delegates voted to ask the king to disband them. This initiative increased Robespierre's estimation of him, and Robespierre wrote to Arras: "You doubtless know of an address presented to the king by the National Assembly, prepared by the Comte de Mirabeau, who has behaved fairly well for some time now. It is a truly sublime work, and full of majesty, truth and energy." If only he had known that a few weeks earlier Mirabeau, thinking that the time had come to make a truce with the Court, had sought an interview with Necker to offer his services. Necker showed him the door, and he left in a fury, bent on revenge. Be that as it may, because of his support Robespierre was a member of the delegation which delivered the address to the king, who took it very badly.

"Only men of evil intent," said the king, "would mislead my people over the precautionary measures I am taking."

In the planned *coup d'état* not only were the Estates to be dissolved, but there was to be a change of government. Necker was to be dismissed and a Ministry of Combat was to be set up under Breteuil. It would be difficult to commit a graver blunder. Breteuil was famous for his brutality, and his name alone was provocation enough. As for Necker, sincerely devoted to both Louis XVI and the good of the State, he enjoyed unequalled popularity with the people. "It was," wrote Rivarol, "at that time as stupid and dangerous to the Court of France to get rid of Monsieur Necker as it would be to the Court of Naples to have the flask of St Januarius' blood thrown into the sea."

Three days later the people of Paris took the Bastille. In the face of this "revolution" the king capitulated. Breteuil was dismissed, and the king recalled Necker, disbanded the foreign troops and the new municipality of Paris was recognized. The taking and the destruction of the old fortress, the epitome of despotism, could only have Robespierre's approval. On the left, only a journalist named Marat did not share the general enthusiasm, reproaching people for rejoicing in the fall of a building which held its enemies. Usually only nobles were imprisoned there, in fact. On 17th July the king resigned himself to going to Paris, so that in some way his presence would legalize the events of the past few days. Robespierre was one of the two hundred deputies chosen to be in the procession. In reply to the harangue to which he was subjected at the Hôtel de Ville, Louis XVI pronounced these surprising words: "Gentlemen, I am very satisfied. . . ." Then

The citizens of Paris, assisted by members of the Guards, stormed the Bastille on the 14th July 1789. De Launay, the governor of the prison, was seized by a Grenadier and a clockmaker

he said: "You may always count on my love." In fact, there were few sovereigns who loved the people so much. Unfortunately it was no longer a question of love, but of accepting the Revolution. The king could not do so with sincerity. It was altogether at odds with his education and his ideas. The reception in Paris, in spite of the cheers, was not destined to reconcile him to the Revolution. Jefferson, who witnessed the occasion, wrote in his memoirs: "Thus finished an honourable apology such as no king has ever made, and no people ever received."

Robespierre, writing to his friend Buissart, naturally had other, quite different, sentiments:

It is impossible to imagine such a dignified, such a sublime sight, even less the feeling it aroused in those capable of emotion. Just imagine a king whose name, the day before, an entire capital and an entire nation had held in awe, making his

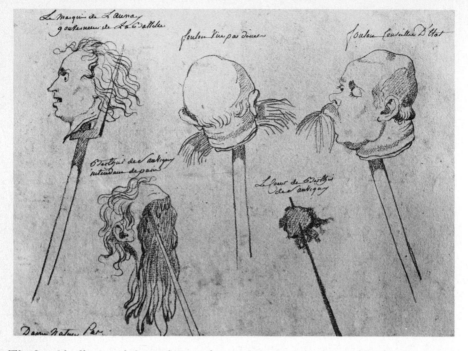

The first bloodletting of the revolution culminated in a parade of severed heads; de Launay's on a trident, councillor Foulon's, the mouth stuffed with straw, on a pole, Berthier de Sauvigny's faceless head on one pike, and the heart which had been ripped from his body on another

way for some two leagues before an army of citizens drawn up three deep along the whole of the route, amongst whom he might recognize his soldiers, hearing the people everywhere shouting: "Long live the nation. Long live liberty." These shouts reached his ears for the first time.

He went to see the Bastille, which was already in the process of being demolished:

On the day of the king's journey I was taken there by a detachment of the good townspeople's militia which had captured it, for after we had left the Hôtel de Ville, the armed citizens enjoyed escorting deputies whom they met, and wherever we marched we were cheered by the people. How pleasant a place the Bastille is now that it is in the hands of the people. Its cells are empty, and a multitude of men are working ceaselessly to demolish this hateful monument of tyranny. I could scarcely tear myself away from this spot whose aspect gives feelings of pleasure and ideas of freedom to all citizens.

The storming of the Bastille was the signal for all those who had prepared the *coup d'état* to flee. The next day the Comte d'Artois, the king's second brother, the princes of Condé, Conti, Lambesc, Maréchal de Broglie, Barentin, Breteuil, and the

Polignacs, set off to leave France. Louis XVI could perfectly well say at the moment of danger: "I have been abandoned by all."

On the whole, the event produced mixed feelings in the National Assembly. The revolt in Paris, the deputies fully realized, had saved them from dissolution. They therefore approved of it. But at the same time they were dismayed at the violence which broke out almost everywhere. In Paris itself the execution of de Launay, Governor of the Bastille and of Flesselles, provost of the merchants, was followed by those of the former minister Foulon and his son-in-law, Berthier. There were riots at Chartres, Troyes, Saint-Denis and Caen. In the countryside the peasants began to attack the châteaux, burn parchments and patents of nobility on which feudal rights were inscribed. On 20th July, one of the members of the liberal nobility, Lally-Tollendal, proposed a proclamation which conveyed the anxiety of his colleagues. He wanted to give municipalities the right to use armed force to suppress riots. This brought protests from several deputies of the Breton Club, especially Buzot and Robespierre. They proposed that the concern of the majority of the members that an end be put to the disorders must be contrasted with their apprehension of a reaction on the part of the aristocrats. If counter-revolutionaries were armed, they would use force to crush the Revolution. Robespierre protested that Lally-Tollendal's proposal would extinguish the love of freedom, and would mean handing the nation over to despots. "They talk about riots, but this riot, sirs, is freedom. There have been a few heads cut off, no doubt, but guilty heads. One cannot classify as rebels men who rise up to defend a sacred cause. And who is to say that new attempts against the Assembly will not be made? And if citizens are classified as rebels for arming themselves in the interest of our safety, who will repel these new attempts?"

A few days later there was a debate in the Assembly on the secret nature of correspondence. This had been sparked off by the seizure of several letters from Castelnau, the king's ambassador in Geneva, to the Comte d'Artois. There was no doubt about their political nature. Perusal of them would doubtless uncover a counter-revolutionary plot. The violation of the privacy of the post, a normal practice of despotic governments, could only be repugnant to the liberal men who formed the majority of the National Assembly. Yet again, Robespierre disagreed. Of course he did not deny the principle that normally the secrecy of letter writing is sacred. But when national liberty is endangered, the case is altered. The State, as Rousseau taught, was above the individual. "When the entire nation is in danger, when people plot against its freedom, when respectable citizens are proscribed, a thing which is a crime at other times becomes a praiseworthy action. Lenience towards conspirators is treason against the people."

It was therefore decided to press for their punishment. The Assembly began a discussion on 31st July on the case of Besenval. For having attempted—so inefficiently, moreover—to oppose the riot of 14th July, the former commander of the army was accused of *lèse-nation*. Can an officer do other than obey his orders?

Vainqueur de la Bastille

This aspect of the question did not seem relevant to Robespierre. For him, Besenval represented, as did Launay, "a guilty head". He ought to be punished. He therefore demanded for him the application "in all their force, of the principles to which men who were suspect to the nation ought to submit, to exemplary judgements. The people must be assured that its enemies will not escape the vengeance of the law." For the same reason, a few days later, he demanded the arrest of the Marquis de Salle, who had had gunpowder removed from the Arsenal to prevent the people from seizing it. Robespierre protested against his acquittal because "the people could only regard it with suspicion". When people talked about violence Robespierre replied that the best way of preventing it was not by police measures, but by punishing suspects. "Do you want to calm the people? Speak to them in the language of justice and reason. Let them be certain that their enemies will not escape the vengeance of the law, and feelings of justice will follow those of hate."

Another speech by Robespierre a few days later brought the warm applause of the public. The Assembly was discussing the events at Mariembourg, where a number of townspeople had carried out a kind of revolution of their own, and thrown out the municipal authorities, whom they replaced with others. Afterwards four of the ringleaders were arrested. Most people saw in these incidents an example of the violence which threatened France, and which they wanted to halt. For Robespierre, right was on the side of the rioters, otherwise—he said quite logically —one might as well condemn the taking of the Bastille, which had also been followed in Paris by the creation of a new municipality. In his eyes the arrest constituted an attempt on national freedom. "It is inconceivable that anyone has dared to threaten people who have only availed themselves of the right that all towns have, of choosing their own municipal officers."

[[·]]

The Revolution pursued its course. Its first two summits had been 20th June and 14th July. The third was going to be the night of 4th August. At the suggestion of a liberal nobleman, the Vicomte de Noailles, the National Assembly abolished, in a wave of enthusiasm, "amidst tears, embraces and applause . . . the hateful remains of the feudal system". So disappeared forced labour, the sale of offices, hunting rights, ecclesiastical tithes, the compulsory use of the lord's mill and seigniorial jurisdiction. Provinces and towns renounced their immunities and individual rights. In the face of this sweeping change, Mirabeau declared: "How typical of the French! They spend a whole month discussing syallbles, and in one night they overturn the whole order of the monarchy."

(OPPOSITE) *Engravings of the idealized 'Brave Victors of the Bastille' were splattered with slogans proclaiming* Peace to the cottages *and* War to the Château, Death to the Tyrants, *spearheaded by the date, 14th July 1789*

The Declaration of the Rights of Man was everywhere, in painted panels or engraved placques

A Declaration of the Rights of Man, a preface to the Constitution, was to serve as a basis for the new order. This declaration proclaimed freedom; propriety; the safety of the individual; resistance to oppression; the sovereignty of the nation; the participation of all citizens in the drawing up of laws; and the admission of all to situations and honours, with no other distinction than that of their virtues and their talents. Some of the clauses provoked lively discussion, for example those on the freedom of the press, conscience and opinion, which came up for consideration on 23rd August. Robespierre, supported by Barère, was against the establishment of any censorship. "There ought to be no compromise in the matter. The freedom of the press ought to be established without any reservation. Free men cannot set out their rights in equivocal terms. Freedom of the press is the corollary of freedom of speech. In a free state each citizen is a guardian of freedom, who must shout at the smallest rumour, and at the least sight of any danger which threatens it."

Three days later the Assembly considered the question of taxes. Some deputies asked whether the freedom to believe what one liked and to say what one liked, ought not to be accompanied by the freedom to pay what one liked. The argument had the appearance of logic about it. Robespierre refuted it by an argument drawn from the *Social Contract*, his political Bible—the will of the individual was to be submitted to the general will. The free citizen is a member of the free nation, that which is a free act of the body corporate may therefore become an act which is binding on the constituent parts. "As soon as the legislative power is put into the hands of the nation, so also is the right to establish taxes; and unless the nation can force each citizen to pay, this right would cease to exist."

The debates on the Constitution itself began on 28th August. Mounier, the secretary, read the first of its clauses in a dreadful uproar. The usual noise of the sessions, which was greater than usual on that day, prevented anyone from hearing a single word. Some deputies, among whom was Robespierre, were furious at this method of drawing up laws, in disorder. For some time he had intended proposing the creation of rules of procedure so that people could be heard in silence. He went up to the rostrum and asked that "before deliberating, one adopt a method which satisfies the conscience, I mean the establishment of a possible form of discussion. That each one might be able, without fear of murmurs, to offer to the Assembly the tribute of his thoughts." One would scarcely have thought it possible, but hardly had he made this very reasonable suggestion than protests were made on all sides, as if he had said something completely ridiculous. Obviously most of the deputies considered the right to carry on their own conversations as essential, even when one of their colleagues was speaking on the rostrum. We read in Gorsas's journal: "He was called to order, but he was moved to carry on by the zeal which animated him. He was interrupted again, and at last, seeing that it was still not permitted to hold sound opinions, and that one could give offence by expressing them, he left the rostrum. The president was unable to avoid remonstrating with the Assembly that this conduct was not fair. Monsieur de Robespierre was invited to take the rostrum once more. He did so. However, whatever excellent things he might have had to say, the discourteous opposition he had experienced had sapped his energy." The time had not yet come when Robespierre would be able to face up to a hostile Assembly. It was useless Mirabeau coming to his assistance by backing his proposal—the wisdom of which he appreciated. No decision was taken. The affairs of France continued to be discussed in disorder.

Agreement was rapidly reached on the organization of the legislative power, by 849 votes to 89. Differences arose when the question of the royal veto was discussed. It was a matter of deciding whether the king would be granted the right to oppose the application of a law voted by the legislative body. There were three schools of thought. On the extreme left of the Assembly was a little group of about thirty deputies, among whom were Barnave, the de Lameths, Duport, Buzot, Pétion and Robespierre, who were against any kind of veto. In their eyes the will of the people, as expressed by its representatives, was sacred. No obstacle should be put in its way. The right wing was made up of most of the nobility and bishops, with a number of deputies from the Third Estate such as Mounier and Malouet. They were alarmed by the progress of the Revolution and wanted the king to have an absolute veto, for without it, they maintained, he would be a sovereign in name only. The majority, of the centre and left, leaned towards a temporary veto, which would leave the king a role and constitute a safeguard against over-hasty decisions, while in the end allowing the clearly expressed will of the nation to carry the day. Mirabeau was the spokesman for this group. He said that he would prefer to live in Constantinople than in France, if they turned down the idea of a veto. He realized that absolute rule, with no check, on the part of a deliberating assembly, might also be tyrannical. But he particularly wanted the veto for reasons of his personal ambition. He thought that he was the only real statesman in France and counted on being called to be a minister soon. His eloquence convinced the Assembly, and they voted for the temporary veto by 574 votes to 325.

As far as Robespierre was concerned, Mirabeau's position constituted a betrayal, and he was furious. All Robespierre's initial distrust, kindled by Mirabeau's unscrupulousness, returned. Instinctively he felt that Mirabeau had sold himself to the Court. From that moment he began to watch his every movement, ready to denounce him. Robespierre had prepared a speech against the veto with especial care, since the question seemed an all-important one to him. Not to be able to deliver it was a disappointment. One hundred or more speakers had put their names down. To hear all they had to say would have taken months. The Assembly preferred to end debates. Several deputies thus thwarted in their right to speak decided to have them printed. Robespierre was one. For the moment he doubtless deplored this setback, but the advantages were not long in making themselves apparent. For one thing, printing gave wider diffusion to his proposals. As he had done with his pleas previously, he decided to send copies to influential citizens, and especially to patriotic clubs, which had been formed almost everywhere. He was aware that the Assembly was hardly disposed to accept the measures he proposed. It was better to speak to the entire French nation.

His speech against the veto was read and talked about everywhere, and firmly established him as an intransigent patriot. It brought him numerous letters and commendations, a sure sign that his arguments had made their point. In fact, they did not lack logic or solidity. Those who were for the veto had conjured up its practical advantages. He replied in terms of principles. A civil servant had no right to prevent a law being put into operation. What was the king, if not the chief civil servant?

> Whoever says that a man may oppose the law, says that the will of an individual is above the will of all. He says that the nation is nothing and that a single man is all. If he adds that this right belongs to the man who wields the executive power, he says that the man chosen by the nation to have its wishes carried out has the right to constrain and limit the wishes of the nation. He has created an inconceivable monster in terms of morals and politics, and this monster is nothing more than the royal veto. What a terrible thing it would be if the first article of this constitution, which is awaited with so much interest by the whole of Europe, and which seems that it must be the epitome of the events of this century, were to be a declaration of the superiority of kings over the nation, and the outlawing of the sacred and inalienable rights of peoples.

The royal veto was discussed in many pamphlets. Those who were for it concluded that the will of the people was such that the king might have a veto. Robespierre disagreed, for the sanction of the law was utterly explicit in its denial of the right to oppose it. Moreover a representative of the people was not so much the representative of those who elected him, as a person responsible to the whole country. He had to sacrifice their wishes when they threatened the general interest. "You are the representatives of the nation, and not simply bearers of votes."

He also dismissed the idea, put forward by some people, of a plebiscite on the veto. Such a step, he maintained, would strip the Assembly of its sovereignty. "The people can only exercise its power through its deputies." Robespierre did not believe in direct democracy, which was in any case only practical in very small states. Rousseau had pointed out why this was so. "The people may indeed always want what is good, but sometimes they do not see in what direction it lies." It followed from this that the temporary veto ought to be rejected, as being as bad as the absolute veto. Each time a law was vetoed by the king, it effectively constituted a sort of call to the people, transmitting the legislative power of the General Assembly of the representatives of the nation to individual primary assemblies of the different provinces. Robespierre put the dilemma before the deputies: "Either you put legislative power in the hands of each local assembly or else you entrust it to the National Assembly. In the first instance this is superfluous, in the second, instead of exhausting it and enslaving it, you ought to leave it with all its strength and all the authority it needs in order to defend freedom, of which it is the guardian against the ever formidable enterprises of the executive power."

He naturally recognized the existence of the danger of possible abuses by the legislative body. At the same time, he pointed out the remedy which lay in the choice of deputies "for their virtues and their talents", and above all for a short term which was not renewable: "Appoint your representatives for a very short term, after which they should retire into the mass of citizens, to whose impartial judgement they submit."

[[·]]

There were no organized parties at the time. All the same, the Assembly was divided into four principal homogeneous groups. On the right were the out-and-out monarchists, whom their opponents called the blacks, embracing the former privileged class of nobles and bishops, who were against any reform. Mirabeau's brother, called Mirabeau-Tonneau (barrel) because of his girth and his gluttony, was one of this group. Aware of their powerlessness, and full of sarcasm and contempt, they interrupted the sessions with their jokes and their laughter. Soon most of them stopped going. The second group were those monarchists, liberal nobles and affluent commoners, who had begun the Revolution and were now afraid of its disorders and wanted to stop it. Their best speakers were a military man from the south, Cazalès, and Abbé Maury, a fighting clergyman built like an athlete. The old stars of the Third Estate—Malouet, Bergasse and Mounier, belonged to this group. The majority consisted of constitutionalists who, along with Mirabeau, sought a balance between the powers of the king and those of the Assembly. These were Lafayette, Thouret, Target, Le Chapelier, Sieyès, Camus and Bailly. On their left was a small splinter group, under the direction of three talented men, Barnave, Alexandre de Lameth and Duport. They were known as the Triumvirate, or *triumgueusat* (trio of beggars) by Mirabeau, as he angrily called them when they directed their attacks at him. Finally, on the extreme left was a group of isolated members who were previously unknown, but were beginning to make their presence felt: Abbé Grégoire, Pétion, Buzot, Dubois-Crancé, Prieur de la Marne and Robespierre. Whenever they came to the rostrum, they were greeted by applause from the public in the galleries.

The plan of the moderates to halt the progress of the Revolution, but without going back at all, required the collaboration of Louis XVI. But this took no account of his entourage. Malouet said: "Unfortunately the king and queen were surrounded by a buzzing of counsels, virulent in intent but without any sort of restraint, and lacking ability in their execution. It was sufficient to exasperate the patriots and drive them to extremes. It was not sufficient to intimidate them. The contempt with which the Court talked of the 'popular party' persuaded the princes that they had only to pull the wool over their eyes to get rid of them, but when the time came they did not even know how to bluff them."

On their advice the king returned to a policy of resistance. To start with, he refused to ratify the decrees abolishing feudality. Mirabeau and Barnave explained on the rostrum that the decrees were an integral part of the Revolution and therefore did not have to be submitted for royal approval. The veto could not be applied to them. Robespierre gave them his support.

In Paris, which was badly supplied with fresh provisions, all sorts of rumours were flying about, as on the eve of 14th July. The bookseller Haray wrote: "They were saying that money and cash were totally lacking, to the point where, at the end of the month, all payments of income, which were already in a sorry state, would come to a complete stop." On top of this it was learned that troops were building up around the capital. The regiments thus summoned were—it was said— "To help the departure of the king for Metz, from where he would return to his kingdom at the head of an army of confederates and would in this way attempt to enslave it by right of conquest."

The private banquet in the opera house at Versailles on 2nd October was the spark which set the powder alight. Duport denounced it as "an orgy, at which wisdom takes fright and misery murmurs". There had been shouts of "Long live the King! Long live the Queen!" from some young gentlemen and some slogans against the National Assembly. The popular journalists pounced on the incident. Camille Desmoulins said that Marat made as much noise about it as the trumpets on the Day of Judgement: "People of Paris, it's time to open your eyes. Shake yourselves out of your torpor. Wake up! Once more, wake up!"

His call was heard. On 5th October some five or six thousand women set off for Versailles with the intention of bringing the royal family back to Paris, in the

Enraged by food shortages and high prices, the women of Paris, armed with knives, pikes, sabres, whatever weapons they could grab, marched on Versailles shouting slogans and singing

belief that their presence in the capital would put an end to rumours of a counter-revolution. They invaded the Assembly, where scenes of incredible disorder took place. Their spokesman was Maillard, one of the victors of the Bastille and an usher at the Châtelet, a tall thin man with a lugubrious appearance. He harangued the deputies: "The aristocrats want to make us die of starvation. This very day a miller has received a note for 200 *livres* inviting him not to grind, and promising to send him the same sum every week." When asked to give proof of his accusation, he could remember neither the names of those who had been denounced nor the names of those who had made the denunciation. Robespierre supported him. *Le Moniteur* wrote: "The deputy from Artois spoke and said that the stranger introduced into the solemn assembly was very right, and that he thought that it had been so that morning, and that Monsieur l'Abbé Grégoire could give details." But Abbé Grégoire preferred to remain silent.

(OPPOSITE) *On the very next day the women were followed by their men and together they stormed the palace, slaughtering some of the Guards and were stopped at the very doors of Marie-Antoinette's apartments*

·5·

THE ASSEMBLY IN PARIS

"In our reform of abuses we are not going to rely on the zeal of those whose concern is in preserving them."

ROBESPIERRE

THE NEXT DAY THE MEN AND WOMEN OF PARIS RETURNED IN triumph from Versailles bringing with them "the baker, his wife and the baker's boy", as they referred to the king, the queen and the dauphin. Disregarding the truth, the official version of the incident declared that the king had come of his own free will. The General Council of the Commune reported to the provinces that "the open and freely expressed love of His Majesty had procured for his capital the happiness of taking him to its heart". Marat, for once letting himself be swept along by the general euphoria, wrote: "It is a festival for the Parisians to have their king in their midst at last." Many thought that this return was finally going to put an end to the Revolution, a fact which the republican Madame Roland rather regretted: "I think that the great political shock that has just disturbed Paris and called the king within its walls will be the last."

In fact, initially Louis XVI won back some of his former popularity, which had been seriously affected since the opening of the States. A crowd gathered in front of the Tuileries and clamoured to see him, and cheered him when he appeared at the window. His cheerful appearance pleased the people. The queen, who had been so severely criticized during the last few months, now received demonstrations of sympathy. Full of illusions, she wrote to her confidant, Mercy-Argenteau, the former Austrian Ambassador: "I am well, so keep calm. Forgetting where we are, and how we came to be here, we ought to be happy with the expressions of the people. I hope, if bread is not short, that many things will sort themselves out."

Unfortunately bread was to continue to be in short supply. The production of it did not depend on the presence of the king in Paris.

[[·]]

About ten days later the Assembly also decided to transfer to Paris. There were practical reasons why they should be near the king, despite the fear of several deputies that they would no longer be able to debate freely because of the pressure of the Parisian mob. Robespierre, on the other hand, saw an advantage in this. With the eyes of the people upon them the representatives would not dare betray them.

The Assembly chose to meet in the Manège, originally a riding-school near the Tuileries. It was a long narrow building, and hardly suitable as a debating chamber. Most of the deputies took lodgings in near-by houses, in a district which then consisted of dark, narrow little streets. Robespierre had the advantage of knowing Paris. He settled on the rue Saintonge in the Marais, which was more pleasant. The owner of the building was Humbert, one of his old school friends at Louis-le-Grand, who held advanced opinions. The number of the house is not known, but the apartment was on the third floor. There were two rooms. For a time Robespierre shared it—possibly for reasons of economy—with a man called Pierre Villiers "a young man with whom he was friendly", Charlotte tells us, "and whom he liked very much". From time to time he acted as Robespierre's secretary, copying out his speeches. "Their household was that of two bachelors, who are hardly ever at home and who eat in restaurants."

In his memoirs, Villiers depicts Robespierre as "being very badly off, and totally without ideas of making money. I turned down offers and gifts of money that asked for nothing in return, not even an expression of thanks. If I allowed myself to insist from time to time, he took me to task." An English authoress who was quite well known at the time, Miss Freeman Shepherd, one day sent him a cheque, asking him to use it for the good of the people. But he sent it back, to the dismay of the lady, who reproached him for lacking civility.

If he had had a mind to do so, like the majority of his colleagues, he could easily have had a more pleasant life—in fact, quite a luxurious one—on his salary of eighteen *livres* a day, which the deputies of the Assembly had voted for themselves. As for the mistress which Villiers claimed Robespierre had—"a young woman of twenty-five years who idolized him, and to whom he generally had his door shut"—it is difficult to accept her existence. From the moment when Robespierre busied himself with affairs of State, he believed that he had to give up all distractions. In rare moments of leisure he allowed himself the pleasures of feeding the sparrows in the Tuileries or going to the theatre from time to time. "He liked declamatory tragedies which dealt with the tyranny of people or judges, or in which one heard the voices of crime and virtue."

Some of Robespierre's eighteen *livres* were sent to his sister in Arras. Since he had left, she and Augustin had been through some difficult moments.

Charlotte wrote to him: "Would you like to send me what you promised me, my dear brother? We are still very needy." Augustin, who was not being very successful as a barrister, also wrote to him: "We are short of everything. Remember, I beg you, our unhappy little household." He wanted Maximilien to use his influence as a deputy to find him a job in Paris, but the big brother turned a deaf ear to all his suggestions.

[[·]]

The Manège had a feature that Robespierre greatly appreciated, namely a large gallery for the public. He regretted the fact that it could not hold more people. His ideal meeting-place for the Assembly was: "A huge and majestic building, open to twelve thousand spectators. Under the eyes of so many witnesses, neither corruption, intrigue nor perfidy would dare show themselves. Only the general will would be consulted. The voice of the nation and of public interest alone would be heard."

The majority of his colleagues did not share his opinion. With apprehension they saw the role played by the public in the gallery as becoming daily more active, interrupting the debates with applause or booing. The day would come when a deputy would need courage to brave them, as when Mirabeau-Tonneau, sword in hand, bandied insults with the crowd. Because it was impossible to make themselves heard, 120 of the moderate deputies stopped taking part in the proceedings. Among them were Lally-Tollendal and Mounier, who had drawn up the Tennis Court Oath. With their departure the middle class, which was satisfied with the results they had achieved—the end of feudalism and the restriction of royal power—ceased to be represented; and thus the field was left open to extremists. Soon most of the moderate deputies were to emigrate.

Some deputies, on the other hand, decided to turn the gallery's approval to their advantage. The chief speakers soon had their paid cliques. Robespierre had no need for such devices. In a few weeks he became the idol of the Parisan public. His colleagues now listened to him with respect. No one dared to interrupt a person applauded by the people. Rather than to the Assembly it was to the gallery, and through it to the country as a whole, that he spoke: "Always looking beyond the narrow confines of the sanctuary of legislation, when I spoke to the body of representatives, my aim was above all to be heard by the nation and by humanity. I wanted to arouse unceasingly in the hearts of citizens the feeling of the dignity of man."

He was to have the opportunity of an even more splendid platform than that of the Manège. As soon as a suitable meeting-place was found, the Breton Club started to meet again, after a break of some weeks caused by the transfer of the

When the Assembly moved to Paris the members of the Breton Club took over the refectory of St Jacob, a Dominican order, as a meeting-place. Originally they called themselves the Friends of the Constitution, but later were known as Jacobins, after the monastery

Assembly to Paris. They began meeting in the refectory of a Dominican monastery in the rue Saint-Jacques. At the same time the club became known as the Friends of the Constitution. To their opponents they were known as Jacobins, since that was the name of the monastery. Many of the original members, such as Le Chapelier, were soon eclipsed by more impressive people such as Mirabeau and Barnave, and eventually they stopped attending meetings. Almost four hundred deputies joined the club. It was decided to admit writers, who were involved in work devoted to the cause of the public welfare. The first to be admitted in this category was the philosopher Condorcet, then the Prussian, Baron Cloots. When simple, private individuals were also granted this facility, a larger meeting-place was needed to cope with the numbers, and first the library and finally the chapel of the monastery were taken over. At last the club had its public gallery just like the Assembly.

At this time Robespierre was not yet a well known or influential member of the club. Mirabeau, Barnave, Duport, the de Lameths, Sieyès, Lafayette and others were all more famous than he. But Robespierre had found the atmosphere that suited him. The size of the chapel meant that he could easily make himself heard without having to raise his voice, whereas Mirabeau had to tone his down.

Robespierre almost dictated his speeches. A journalist wrote: "In view of the fact that the eloquent Robespierre frequently stops to lick his lips, one has the time to write." By diligent attendance at all meetings, and the admission of members who were not deputies, it took only a few months for him to take a preponderant role in the club. In January 1790 the royalist newspaper *Les Actes des Apôtres* ("The Acts of the Apostles") named him as one of the leaders of the club. Provincial clubs became affiliated in ever-increasing numbers with the one in Paris. They were sent accounts of the meetings, and in this way France came to know the name of Robespierre as one of the most assiduous defenders of the people.

[[·]]

On 20th October Robespierre made his first speech in the National Assembly since its move to Paris. The matter under debate was an instruction from the Bishop of Tréguier which was hostile to the principles of the Revolution, which he described as phantasmagorical. Robespierre demanded an immediate discussion. In opposition to the President, the Comte de Clermont-Tonnerre, who insisted that the agenda be adhered to, he maintained that in the bishop's writings 'reigned the spirit of revolt, and the most dangerous fanaticism. Can we put off examination of the Tréguier affair when the fire of civil war has been lit in the diocese?" He inserted a note of alarm: "I must express my anxiety frankly. The safety of the State is in danger. One of the most atrocious conspiracies has been formed. The fatherland is still threatened; the enemies of the public good have probably still not stopped their odious plotting, and we are immersing ourselves in a state of false security." The Assembly was impressed by the gloomy considerations and decided to refer the case to the Châtelet tribunal on a charge of "*lèse-nation*".

Robespierre had good reason to be anxious. It was becoming more and more difficult to feed Paris, and bread in particular was short. There were riots. During one of them, on 21st October, a baker called François was killed. In his shop were found little white loaves of bread which were, it was said, intended for the members of the Assembly. It was this detail that aroused Robespierre's suspicions. This was simply a counter-revolutionary manoeuvre with the perfidious aim of discrediting the Assembly, and creating a situation to justify the imposition of martial law. It was completely normal that the people should riot because they were hungry, and he would never dream of blaming them; but the story could have been put about by counter-revolutionaries who were preventing supplies from getting through, inciting the people to riot, and in this way trying to compromise the Revolution in the eyes of ordinary people by frightening them.

In the afternoon several deputies proposed that municipalities should be given the right to proclaim martial law, and this strengthened Robespierre's feelings. Buzot was the first to speak against the motion. He said that there was no need whatsoever for martial law to re-establish order, and that they should set up a court to judge the enemies of the people: "It is not enough to frighten the people, they must be calmed down." Robespierre followed him on the rostrum. He said that in going back to the cause of the riots they would find a plot. The shortage of bread was the work of speculators, who had bought flour wholesale in the hope of making a profit by retailing it; and now the enemies of the Revolution were exploiting the situation in the hope of driving the Assembly to use force to create bad feeling between itself and the people. "If we do not wake up, it will be the end of freedom. They have just asked you for soldiers and bread. Why? To drive the people back at this time when it is in the interests of the powerful to find a way to put an end to the present revolution. Those who want to quicken the pace of revolution have foreseen that they could turn it against you. They have foreseen that popular sentiment would be the best way of demanding laws which could be used to oppress the people and freedom. When the people are dying of hunger they mob together. We must therefore go back to the cause of the riots to pacify them. They are asking for soldiers. Does not this mean simply that the people are in revolt. They are asking for bread. We do not have any. Shall we destroy them? One person asks for martial law, but who will carry it out? Will it be the citizen soldiers? Must their hands be stained with the blood of their brothers whose ills they share? No!"

The remedy lay in assuring the people that those who plotted against them would not escape punishment. In a general way Buzot had said the same thing. Robespierre put forward two proposals. First of all, he asked the municipality of Paris to hand over to the Assembly "all the pieces of evidence it has relating to this host of conspiracies against the people, which follow each other unceasingly". Once the plotters were identified and arrested, they had only to be judged by the civic courts, since the career judges were all aristocrats who would not fail to acquit them. "We must appoint a truly national tribunal, we must not leave it to the king's prosecutor at the Châtelet to carry out the function of prosecutor-general to the nation. Only representatives from within the nation may judge this sort of crime." This new tribunal, only concerned with "plots and conspiracies against the people and freedom", would be made up from members of the Assembly. Then the people, certain of the punishment of its enemies, would feel reassured and would calm down.

The gallery applauded and the leftist newspapers approved. But the Assembly did not follow Robespierre. It voted for martial law, not for a court. A citizen wrote to the editor of *Révolutions de Paris*: "Robespierre's motion impressed me. His appeals were not heard, extravagant eloquence won the day against reason."

[[·]]

As Robespierre's fame grew throughout France, his popularity in Arras declined. The day after the election [in April 1789] *Les Affiches de l'Artois* had published an article which strongly took him to task. "This hotheaded, infuriated, headstrong little pony is as vicious as a mule, knowing neither the bit nor the riding crop, but only daring to bite from behind for fear of the whip." The campaign of denigration had continued since then, organized by the former President of the Council of Artois, Briois de Beaumetz, whose son was Robespierre's colleague in the Assembly. As the people of Arras were of a conservative nature, the attacks were successful. Hostility to Robespierre was so severe in some quarters that one of his supporters warned him that if he should return to Arras, his life would be in danger. He received similar warnings from his friends and family. They wrote to him that the alienation of his birthplace was partly his fault. The other deputies informed their electors regularly of what was going on, but he had not kept in touch with the people who had elected him, doubtless too involved in his work in the Assembly. Even so, the situation was not beyond remedy. But a memorandum would have to be written to justify his position and inform the people.

There were two reasons for Robespierre's lack of communication with his electors. In the first place, he looked upon himself as a representative of the French people in general, and not of one province in particular. Then Artois, with the painful memory of the polemics of the last few years, was a closed book for him. In his letters he referred to it in a disdainful way as "that place". Basically it mattered little to him that his popularity should diminish there. He found ample compensation in the applause of the Jacobins and the flattering correspondence with the popular clubs of several towns in the south. From Marseilles they wrote: "It is doubtless impossible to add anything to the patriotism which inspires you and to the courage that you have shown in the most difficult circumstances." Even so, he decided that Beaumetz's attacks should not be allowed to go unanswered. In a few days he wrote a message to the people of Artois.

In the introduction he warned that his message was intended only for worthy citizens, in other words, the people: "I have nothing to say to that multitude of men who, bound by the ties of personal interest and pride to the terrible abuses that we have just outlawed, seem made to hate and forever slander the friends of humanity." He had nothing but disdain for their miserable lies, "for truth and patriotism need only make their voices heard to plunge back into nothingness this whole absurd legion of factious and slanderous people". At a time "when one was still far from predicting the present revolution, he had defended the cause of the poor, and he had rushed to the aid of the oppressed innocents". He sent his respects "to the misery of the people, and not to the pride of men in position". During the campaign for election to the States-General "he had not withheld himself from any sacrifice to avenge the outrages suffered by the people and to press for their rights against all the tyrants who were oppressing them". Now, taking advantage of his absence, his enemies were trying to persuade the people, "that he had become a cowardly deserter of the public interest, a traitor, a scoundrel, a monster". But "the fury of the wicked is the greatest compliment that can be paid to the patriotism of honest people". In fact their goodwill and praise would have merely afflicted it.

"Oh good, generous people, take care, lest you be snared by the gross insinuations of these vile flatterers who surround you, and whose only aim is to plunge you back forever into the misery from which you are beginning to escape; to recover for themselves the unjust power that oppresses you. Why were you protesting so vigorously against their injustices a few months ago? Why did you look upon the National Assembly as your last hope if you are already tired of waiting for the happiness that is being prepared for you, to throw yourselves back into the arms of your former aggressors? Do not discourage all those who, in the future, might have the courage to take up your cause. The rich people and powerful men will always find enough slaves to serve their injustices. Keep at least a few defenders for yourselves."

The debate on the electoral law was to give Robespierre the chance of appearing in this very role. In October 1789 the Assembly adopted three conditions for being an elector or a candidate for election: French nationality, twenty-five years of age and a month's domicile. A fourth proposition, on the other hand, created electoral discrimination and aroused violent controversy. The Constitutional Committee proposed restricting the title of elector to citizens who paid the equivalent of three days' salary in direct taxes, for candidates the equivalent of ten days': in other words, one silver *marc*. French people were in this way to be divided into two categories: active citizens, with the right to vote—and for some of these the right to be elected; and passive citizens, who would have neither right. The committee put forward the argument that a large section of the nation who were illiterate were incapable of participating in the slightest way in the direction of public business. They should therefore be kept away from it. Some of the leftist deputies approved of the measure, but for an entirely different motive. They were afraid that the people's lack of political maturity would become, at some juncture, a weapon of the aristocrats. Their votes might endanger the work of the Revolution. In this way servants, without distinction of income, were put in the category of passive citizens. It was argued that they would vote inevitably the same way as their masters, the nobles and the rich.

But whatever reasons might be advanced, the new electoral law constituted a regressive step in relation to what had gone before, since election to the States-General had been by universal suffrage—or almost. It contradicted the Declaration of Rights, voted by the Assembly a few weeks before, setting forth the equality of all men. The Declaration said that the law was the expression of the general will and that all citizens without exception had the right—personally or through the intermediary of their representatives—to take part in its creation.

Naturally the motion provoked the anger of all those—about three million people—who were going to find themselves excluded from the electoral body because they did not pay enough taxes. Protests were heard at once among the districts of Paris where the "passives" were most numerous. It would have been a wonderful opportunity for Louis XVI to win back his popularity by opposing this unjust law. Robespierre immediately threw himself into the fight. These poor people who were being kept out were the ones he championed, the most concerned section of the nation, because they were the most virtuous. He was in a good position to show that a distinction based on taxation could not be equated with a person's capacities. Under such a system Rousseau would not have been an elector. "The aristocracy of the rich," he wrote to his friend Buissart, "is setting itself up on the ruins of the feudal aristocracy, and I do not see that the people, who ought to be the aim of any political institution, could in any way gain from this kind of arrangement."

He mounted the rostrum to deliver a passionate appeal to the deputies to abandon a division of the French into two categories, which, in his estimation was so unfair: "The cause which I defend affects the interests of the people. All citizens, whoever they be, have the right to aspire to every degree of representation. Nothing is more consistent with your Declaration of Rights, in the face of which all privileges, all distinctions and all exemptions should disappear. The Constitution establishes the fact that sovereignty resides with the people, in all individuals of the people. Each individual has therefore the right to contribute to the law under which he is governed, and with the administration of the republic which is his. Otherwise, it is not true that all men are equal in law and that all men are citizens. If there were any question of proportion, then the man with an income of 100,000 *livres* would therefore be one hundred thousand times more of a citizen."

The Assembly greeted this speech with grumbles. Those whom they had deprived of the vote were the very ones they were placing under martial law. Robespierre's proposal for universal suffrage was sent back to the Constitutional Committee, which quickly killed it. But he was not the sort of man to give up. The suppression of the silver *marc* became the *leitmotif* of his speeches, his *delenda est Carthago*. He fought for it ceaselessly until the end.

[[·]]

For a time the question of suffrage was to cause a resurgence of controversy in Arras. Among other arguments advanced in his speech, Robespierre had pointed out that in Artois only the rich paid direct taxes, and the rest of the population paid duty and indirect taxes. As a result, Artois would have only a small number of active citizens in relation to the number in other provinces.

It is always tempting to try to undermine an adversary by twisting his words. Beaumetz thought that he saw a chance to ruin Robespierre's reputation once and for all in his native region. He wrote to his father, saying that Robespierre had stated in the Assembly that Artois did not pay enough taxes. It is easy to imagine what effect such an accusation might have had on public opinion. Beaumetz advised his father to publish his letter, "to enlighten the electors on the actions of their representative", especially in the rural areas, knowing how touchy the peasants were about taxation. The old man sent the letter to the Attorney-General, Foacier de Ruzé, who had it widely circulated, with his own commentary added, to make doubly certain of its effect.

The storm was let loose. Desolation reigned among the tiny group of Robespierre's friends and relatives. Charlotte wrote to him: "I will be able to tell you sometime later how those on whom you counted most were no more than cowards." Doubtless she was referring to Madame Marchand who was annoyed at having been neglected by her former protégé since his departure, and had joined his opponents. Augustin-Bon, somewhat bewildered, wondered anxiously whether his brother had not, without realizing the fact, "committed a slight fault", and called on him urgently to defend himself. "I beg of you, let us hear your news, tell the public about your motion and the scandalous attempt to make you appear to be an enemy of the people. Your virtues and your patriotism must triumph. Our simple village people are dreadfully credulous. It is no good their knowing what you have done for them. They have forgotten everything you have done for them, and only remember their abject misery under these crushing taxes, for which they also blame you."

Maximilien realized that he had to reply. It would also be a subtle way of making the Assembly have second thoughts about the electoral law, by showing how far it was destroying political equality in Artois. Certainly other French provinces would find themselves in the same situation. "Do you want a citizen to be a rare creature among you, solely because property owners are monks and profiteers? Freedom consists in the free nomination of magistrates whom one ought to obey, and we no longer choose our magistrates. In France, when it was in slavery, we were known to have a few tatters of freedom. In a France that has been set free, we should be remarkable for our bondage."

In order to defend himself, Robespierre accompanied his letter with a kind of certificate of good conduct signed by other Artois delegates to the Assembly, testifying that he had always defended the province's interests. Seven of the fourteen deputies signed it. Six were members of the Third Estate (Vaillant had refused), and the seventh, Charles de Lambeth, whose signature carried a lot of weight, was the leading representative of the nobility of Artois.

Augustin and his friends circulated the documents. Some time later on Charlotte wrote to Robespierre: "Your letter, my dear brother, seems to be producing a good effect. Slander has been reduced to silence, but in this you have still only had a minor victory over your enemies." Another man who worked hard on Robespierre's behalf was Joseph Fouché. Having shaken off his role as an Oratorian, he had become President of the Constitutional Club of Arras, which was affiliated to the Jacobins in Paris. He foresaw the rise of his friend Maximilien, he avowed himself his fervent supporter on every issue, and went on courting Charlotte. At his suggestion the club sent a letter to Paris, assuring Robespierre of the esteem and backing of all good patriots.

[[·]]

Even so, 1789 ended for Robespierre in disillusion. He angrily witnessed the cause of the people betrayed by the very ones who had seemed the most ardent in fighting on their behalf. The provincial parliaments were the head and spirit of these renegades. In their opposition to royal power, none had contributed more to prepare the way towards Revolution. Now that it was threatening their privileges, they were ranging themselves against the Assembly. But in doing so they were launching themselves against a more determined authority than that of the king, and they would find themselves destroyed by it. For ages they had been hailed as "the fathers of the fatherland". They were fated to disappear under a hail of boos, awaiting the guillotine. A "seditious resolution" from the Parliament of Metz provoked a debate in which the right and the left opposed each other somewhat violently. Robespierre had a skirmish with Mirabeau-Tonneau, whom he reproached with "dishonouring the dignity of the Assembly by his revolting satires".

The last speech he made that year was on 23rd December about the right of actors, Jews and Protestants to vote. The speaker from the right, the battling Abbé Maury, agreed to give it to the last-mentioned, but not to the first two. He maintained that the job of an actor was as infamous as that of an executioner. What confidence could be put in people whose profession consisted of feigning feelings? As for Jews, leaving aside religion, he considered them to be "as foreign in France as Englishmen in Holland". Robespierre took up the defence of actors and the theatre—more exactly, the sort of theatre that the Revolution was going to regenerate, "for then the virtues of the actors will reform the stage, and theatres will become once more schools of high principle, good conduct and patriotism". On the subject of the Jews he said: "How can one face them—the victims of persecution in various other countries of Europe. On the contrary, these are national crimes which we ought to expiate by giving them the inalienable rights of man, of which no human power can deprive them." Mirabeau, giving an account of the debate in his *Courrier de Provence*, wrote: "Monsieur Robespierre refuted Abbé Maury in a few words, but forcibly."

In January the question of public order came up again in the Assembly. Peasant revolts had broken out in Quercy, Limousin, Périgord and Brittany, and on top of these came the events in Toulon. Admiral de Rioms, who was in command there, was against the inclusion of workmen at the arsenal in the National Guard. The Guard replied by imprisoning the admiral along with his staff. When the matter came up for discussion in the Assembly, Malouet spoke in defence of the arrested officers and demanded that they be set free at once. Robespierre protested. The admiral had wanted to arm soldiers against the defenders of the fatherland. "To adopt such a resolution would be tantamount to blaming the inhabitants of Toulon for their conduct, whereas resistance to oppression was one of the inalienable and natural rights of man." Moreover, he went on, they did not have sufficient details to judge fairly. The Assembly concurred with this opinion and decided to delay taking a decision until they had more detailed information.

Some days later the discussion was resumed. A man called Liancourt proposed a conciliatory motion, intended to satisfy both the port workmen and the arrested officers. Robespierre again spoke. He said that he had received information from his correspondents in Marseilles. There could no longer be any doubt about the guilt of the officers. As for the workmen, "they had simply availed themselves of that which the Declaration of Rights had given them, namely the right to resist oppression. When the conduct of the inhabitants of Toulon showed the spirit of legitimate resistance to oppression, nothing was more unjust, and apolitical at the same time, than to give either praise or absolution to the officers, or the least sign of criticism to the conduct of the people of Toulon. If any insurrections are just and noble, that without doubt one of them is when the people repel force and to condemn their zeal in such circumstances is to oppress them. A great deal has been said about praise due to a worthy admiral, but I ask pity, love and respect for the people. You see what has happened at Brest, where freedom was encircled by soldiers. You see what happened in Marseilles, where the most admirable friends of freedom, thrown into cells, were ready to perish in irons. When I consider all these events, I am unable to prevent myself from thinking that, reproached by their time, they were perhaps joined together by bonds that it would not be impossible to release. Above all I fear seeing a decree of the National Assembly that would discourage patriotism, and encourage the enemies of freedom."

Nevertheless, the Assembly rallied to Liancourt's compromise, saying that bearing in mind the motives that had inspired both sides, there were no grounds for condemning either party. To prevent new disorders, Le Chapelier proposed the adoption of coercive measures by strengthening martial law. Six months of Revolution had considerably modified the opinions of the former left-wing leader. Robespierre fought against the proposal as he had fought against the previous ones, in almost the same words. He said that there was no need to resort to repression to re-establish order. No revolution had ever cost so little blood and shown so little cruelty. The remedy lay in just laws and the setting up of a people's National Guard, to which all citizens might be admitted, without any distinction of means. "It was monstrous to call peasants who burnt castles brigands. Let the people be free to express their will at the elections, and leave it to the armed citizens to deal with the real 'brigands' and defend their houses." The Assembly listened to his speech attentively but, all the same, did not follow it in its conclusions. Martial law was strengthened, as Le Chapelier had requested. Nevertheless, some days later, Robespierre achieved quite a success when the Assembly decreed that proprietors would receive no compensation for their rights of *main-morte*, which had been suppressed on 4th August. After the enthusiasm of this famous night, some people had attempted to reclaim numerous abandoned privileges. Robespierre thus had to fight against a proposal to re-establish the feudal game laws. At the Jacobin Club he strongly criticized a motion put forward by Necker to annul the decree abolishing titles of nobility.

Lettres de cachet, the most hated institution of the *ancien régime*, had been abolished at the outset of the Revolution. Even so, in a somewhat paradoxical way, most of the people who had been arrested were still in prison. In many cases, it is true, the people were thieves and criminals.

The Assembly held several debates on this question. Robespierre said that he wanted all the prisoners set free: "It is better that one hundred guilty people be pardoned than one single innocent person be kept in prison." He subsequently revised this opinion, admitting that one could not set recognized criminals free, but that they were to be imprisoned for a maximum term of twenty years.

· 6 ·

MIRABEAU

"They want to be free and do not know how to be just."

SIEYÈS

OF ALL THE MEASURES VOTED UPON BY THE NATIONAL Assembly, none was to have more influence upon the future of the Revolution than the Civil Constitution of the Clergy. It was born not of a desire to reform the Church, but of financial considerations. The national deficit, which had been the reason for summoning the States-General in the first place, was growing bigger, because in the general disorder people were not paying taxes. Two loans that Necker had tried to float had failed completely. "You are debating," cried Mirabeau, "and bankruptcy, hideous bankruptcy, is at your doors." In times of financial crisis the natural course is to take money from the place where it happens to be at that moment. The assets of the clergy, which had accumulated over the centuries, formed an immense reserve of riches. In fact, the value was put at three thousand million francs. Talleyrand's proposal—put forward on 10th October 1789—to use them to pay off the National Debt, had been approved by Robespierre: "The assets of the Church belong to the people, and to seek to use them to help the people is simply to re-apply them to their original intention."

The decree that they should be put at the disposition of the nation had been voted on 2nd November. Immediately there was an initial loan to the value of four hundred million francs, committing an equal sum in paper money, issued under the name of *assignats*. This money rapidly disappeared. The very success of the operation meant that it was easy to make further sales and further issues. The result was a terrible inflation, which was ruinous for money. In those days the phenomenon was misunderstood, and the dangers of it were not appreciated. Mirabeau saw the increase of money in circulation as "a salutary dew".

Having appropriated the assets of the Church, it was perfectly logical that the State should be responsible for the maintenance of the clergy, who thus became civil servants. The debate on the Civil Constitution opened on 21st May 1790. It was to last six weeks. Robespierre wanted the Church reorganized as a department of State: "Priests, considered as members of society, are magistrates whose duty it is to carry on public worship." Useless ecclesiastical offices, such as those of cardinal and archbishop, should be abolished. Only bishops and priests should be retained, and the number of them would be in proportion to the population. Finally, in common with other officials, they should be appointed by popular election.

This ultimate proposal caused strong protest. If all citizens, whether Catholic or not, had the right to take part in the election of priests and bishops, what guarantee would there be that the person elected would not be a Protestant or even an atheist? Those who were in favour of the Civil Constitution replied that under the Concordat the king appointed the bishops, which was in itself no guarantee of a good choice—rather the contrary. Since sovereignty had passed to the people, there was no reason why they should not make use of this right. Abbé Jacquemart suggested a compromise, namely, that the priests should be elected by the people, but the priests, meeting in synod, should in turn appoint the bishops.

Robespierre was one of those against this idea. By entrusting the election of bishops to the priests he objected, their action would be tantamount to destroying equality of political rights and reconstituing the clergy as an isolated body, thereby harming the Constitution. "The opinion of the people and the wish of the people express the general interest. The voice of a body expresses the interest of a body. The specific commitment and the wishes of the clergy would always express the spirit and interest of the clergy. The clergy is not purer than the people. I come down on the side of the people." The law was passed on 12th July with a huge majority. Pasteur Rabaut Saint-Etienne said: "Priests will march in time with the State. They have only to marry now."

Another aspect of the religious question, then very much on the agenda, was in fact the marriage of priests. The enforced abolition of clerical celibacy had been advocated in several pamphlets, and by one in particular, written by a man called Billaud-Varenne, in 1787. Quite a few of the lower clergy were for it. Abbé Cournand, one of the Jacobins, had resolved the question by taking a wife. Even so, the Assembly threw out Robespierre's motion by a large majority. Even his usual supporters voted against it. Writing in *Le Patriote français*, Brissot approved of the idea but thought that it had been advanced prematurely. There was a danger, he said, that it would cause unrest among the ignorant. Augustin wrote to his brother: "Your proposal for the marriage of priests has given you the reputation of being an unbeliever amongst our great philosophers in Artois. You will lose the respect of the peasants if you renew it. People use it as a weapon against you; they talk of nothing but about your lack of religion. Perhaps you would be better off dropping it altogether."

Robespierre had hoped for Mirabeau's support, since he knew that on this topic they shared the same view. He was, however, ignorant of one detail. Mirabeau wanted to bring the matter up himself, personally, in the Assembly. At that very moment one of his "slaves" was working on a speech for him, and he expected to make a great success of it. Robespierre's initiative, coming a few days too soon, cut the ground from under him. Moreover, Robespierre's failure made it impossible to reopen the debate. Mirabeau was furious, and this event marked the end of any cordiality in their relationship.

The number of letters of congratulation that Robespierre received were a form of consolation for him. They assured him that he expressed "the secret wishes of a good number of priests". Some priests even expressed their thanks to him in verse. He was amused by this lyricism, and he told his friend Villiers "that it was certainly not true that France had stopped producing poets".

Several other speeches by Robespierre during the course of the debate on the civil constitution are worthy of mention, despite the fact they relate to minor matters. For example, he supported Beauharnais's motion to allow priests to wear civilian clothes when they were not officiating, to denote "that they were part of the body of citizens". On the other hand, he opposed their election to other offices, since plurality was, in his eyes, dangerous for democracy. Nevertheless he did allow one exception to this rule. Priests might serve on juries, since judging criminals was an act beneficial to society and was not incompatible with the office of a minister of religion.

[[·]]

On 31st March 1790 the Jacobins elected Robespierre their president for the fortnight to come. Lafayette was so put out that he left the club and founded his own 1789 club. It was to have no future. Robespierre wrote to his friend Buissart: "I only have time to renew the proof of my inviolable attachment for you. I have not time to tell you about the important events which are happening daily before our eyes. Surrounded by the efforts incessantly wrought against them by all the enemies of the people and freedom, I will always have the consolation of having defended both of them with all the zeal of which I was capable. The manifestations of good will with which all good citizens honour me is sufficient compensation for the hatred the aristocrats have concentrated on me."

The Assembly had undertaken the reform of innumerable economic, financial and judicial institutions. The reorganization of Paris was one of these, but the Assembly was motivated by political rather than administrative considerations. Since the beginning of the Revolution the capital had been governed virtually by general assemblies in certain districts. By breaking up these districts the Assembly hoped to take away their power. All the popular movements to extend the Revolution sprang from these districts, of which there were sixty. The constitutional committee proposed replacing them with forty-eight sections in which, by careful drawing of boundaries, extremist and moderate elements would be mixed. More important was the fact that the sections would not be permanent (whereas the districts had become "permanent"), and meetings would only be held on certain dates which would be fixed by law.

Robespierre was strongly opposed to this motion. He saw the permanence of the districts as the very pivot of the Revolution, by virtue of the pressure they brought to bear on the Assembly. To suppress them would be tantamount to leaving the path wide open to the counter-revolutionaries. "Who could assure us that under their active surveillance more effective methods would not be used to inhibit our work?" Somewhat surprisingly the extreme right supported him. They wanted the maintenance of permanent districts just as much as Robespierre, but for quite a different reason. The right hoped to use them one day to get their revenge. Eventually the keenness of the citizens would flag, they would then stop going to the meetings, and then the friends of the right would take over. From being hotbeds of revolution, the districts would turn into hotbeds of reaction.

Mirabeau spoke in support of the proposal. He was on the point of being accepted as secret adviser to the Court, having failed to get his ministry because of his colleagues' mistrust. He wanted to be seen to be moderate. He also wanted to settle accounts with Robespierre. As if he were afraid of giving too much importance to Robespierre by even bothering with him, he assumed a disdainful tone: "Monsieur de Robespierre has brought a degree of zeal to the rostrum that is more patriotic than considered. Above all, let us not take the elevation of principles to be the same thing as the sublime height of principles." These words set the seal on their estrangement. As for the division of Paris into sections instead of districts, the motion was passed by a large majority, to the dismay of some and the despair of others, but it was to have no influence whatsoever on the future development of the Revolution.

[[·]]

The Assembly was engaged in reforming the judicial system throughout 1790 and for part of 1791. Robespierre took an active part in the debates, and made some twenty speeches.

In common with the majority of his colleagues he agreed with the principle of the election of judges. In this way their authority would not come from the king, but from the people. In the same way public prosecutors would henceforth represent: "The national vengeance of crimes committed against the people." Whether or not they had any knowledge of the law seemed to him of secondary importance, provided that they were "patriots". In fact, he wanted jurisprudence suppressed.

But above all he came back to his idea of a national High Court to judge "political crimes". Both judges and juries in this court were to be "friends of the Revolution", elected by the people, and provided with sufficient power to crush traitors. All these features—apart from the election—were incorporated in the future Revolutionary Tribunal. Robespierre wanted the court to sit in Paris, "the city which has rendered so many services to the Revolution, and which has always been the centre of enlightenment"; but the Assembly preferred Orléans, since there was more likelihood of independence there. In all other details they accepted Robespierre's proposals.

[[·]]

Since the earliest days of the Revolution the Army had been divided. On one side were the officers who were nobles, and therefore constituted a closed caste jealous of their privileges and exasperated by the reforms. On the other side were the soldiers who sprang from the people, and were well versed in the new ideas that were circulating in the clubs. On the eve of 14th July the French Guard had re-volted against their colonel and taken part in the riot. Since then mutinies had taken place at Lille, Hesdin, Rennes, Nîmes and Perpignan. As far as most of the Assembly were concerned these constituted acts of indiscipline which had to be suppressed or else the Army would be in danger of disintegration. But Robespierre saw a political difficulty. If he equated unrest in the Army with civil rebellion, he could only support the soldiers against their officers. To put a stop to it, punish-ment should not be used, but the Army ought to be "democratized" by dismissing noble officers. He said that it was absurd during a period of revolution to leave power in the hands of their enemies, who would have no hesitation in using it against them one day. "Take care, oh lawgivers, lest you be torn in opposite directions; take care lest you adopt measures against what is right." When soldiers realise that they are commanded by officers they can trust, they will no longer revolt.

On 1st August there were quite serious troubles at Nancy. The Assembly com-missioned General Bouillé to re-establish order, and he crushed the revolt bloodily. The reprisals he took were particularly severe. Twenty ringleaders were executed and forty Swiss men from Châteauvieux were sent to the galleys. Robespierre was very disturbed when he heard the news. "They sought to disgust good soldiers. They wanted to embitter the troops and drive them to revolt. There is no need for much more to happen to prove that the ministers and the heads of the army do not merit our confidence." The majority, far from heeding his advice, passed a vote of thanks to Bouillé and the loyal soldiers. Bouillé was Lafayette's brother-in-law and "a man who detested the new institutions in France, who said himself that he was looked upon as the enemy of the republic". Robespierre was in no doubt that he had acted on orders, and from that day he saw the commander of the National Guard as the most dangerous of counter-revolutionaries.

[[·]]

The Assembly was confronted by a constitutional problem of particular importance for the future. Would the king or the Assembly have charge of diplomatic relations—in other words, the right to declare war? A recent event had made an urgent reply to the question necessary. On 14th May 1790 Monsieur de Montmorin, Minister for Foreign Affairs, sent a letter to the President of the Assembly, announcing that a difference had arisen between England and Spain over possession of Nootka Sound on the western coast of North America. There was a risk of war between the two countries. As a result the king had ordered that fourteen ships of the line be fitted out in the Atlantic and Mediterranean ports, and ordered the naval command to be ready for any eventuality, as the Bourbon family treaty stipulated.

This message caused great excitement in the Assembly, and it was decided to hold a debate the next day. Apart from the extreme right, the sympathy of most deputies was for England, a country they saw as a natural ally of the Revolution. At that time the feeling was mutual. Some deputies wondered whether the talk of war was not simply a ploy of the Court to distract the nation's attention from the reforms. Robespierre's speech voiced these fears: "If the prospect of war is not serious, then we ought to be indignant at this trap, this mockery; if it is serious, then we must tremble at the very idea of seeing all kinds of danger that threaten our still imperfect Constitution, which totters between enemies at home and storms surrounding it." In any case, the event demonstrated that the initiative for peace or war could not be left to the king. Only the nation could decide what its true interest was, in a general manner. He therefore asked the Assembly to take direction of the negotiations in a bid for peace. "For example, you must show the world that, by following principles very different from the ones that have created people's misfortunes, the French nation, happy to be free, does not want to be involved in any war; it renounces any spirit of conquest and ambition, and wants to live with all nations in the natural state of brotherhood."

This suggestion, which echoed the general feeling, was warmly applauded. Mirabeau undertook to oppose it. It was an opportunity for him to win for himself the confidence of the Court, by defending a royal prerogative. He first of all put forward a general principle. For practical reasons the responsibility for internal and external security ought to be in the hands of the king, and not the Assembly. This would be the only way in which the nation might swiftly confront the dangers it encountered. The argument was a weighty one, and obviously made an impression. If Mirabeau had taken advantage of this turnabout to demand an immediate vote, there is no doubt that he would have carried the day. He was tired, however, and in a difficult position; he had to give the Court proof of his intentions and yet make revolutionary speeches to maintain his popularity. He made a tactical mistake in proposing that the constitutional question be put off until the morrow. For the moment the Assembly should restrict itself to the minister's

LETTRES PATENTES DU ROI, sur un Décret de l'Assemblée Nationale, qui abolit la Nobleſſe héréditaire, & porte que les titres de Prince, de Duc, de Comte, Marquis & autres titres ſemblables, ne ſeront pris par qui que ce ſoit, ni donnés à perſonne.

Données à Paris, le 23 Juin 1790.

LOUIS, par la grâce de Dieu, & par la Loi conſtitutionnelle de l'État, ROI DES FRANÇOIS : A tous ceux qui ces préſentes Lettres verront ; SALUT. L'Aſſemblée Nationale a décrété, le 19 de ce mois, & Nous voulons & ordonnons ce qui ſuit :

ARTICLE PREMIER.

LA Nobleſſe héréditaire eſt pour toujours abolie ; en conſéquence, les titres de Prince, de Duc, de Comte, Marquis, Vicomte, Vidame, Baron, Chevalier, Meſſire, Ecuyer, Noble, & tous autres titres ſemblables, ne ſeront ni pris par qui que ce ſoit, ni donnés à perſonne.

I I.

AUCUN Citoyen ne pourra prendre que le vrai nom de ſa famille ; perſonne ne pourra porter, ni faire porter des livrées, ni avoir d'armoiries ; l'encens ne ſera brûlé dans les Temples que pour honorer la Divinité, & ne ſera offert à qui que ce ſoit.

I I I.

LES titres de Monſeigneur & de Meſſeigneurs ne ſeront donnés ni à aucun Corps, ni à aucun individu, ainſi que les titres d'Excellence, d'Alteſſe, d'Éminence, de Grandeur, &c. ſans que, ſous prétexte des Préſentes, aucun Citoyen puiſſe ſe permettre d'attenter aux monumens placés dans les Temples, aux chartes, titres & autres renſeignemens intéreſſant les familles ou les propriétés, [...] décorations d'aucuns lieux publics ou particuliers, & ſans que l'exécution [...]tions relatives aux livrées & aux armes placées ſur les voitures, [...]ivie ni exigée par qui que ce ſoit avant le 14 Juillet, pour les [...] à Paris, & avant trois mois pour ceux qui habitent la Province.

The National Assembly forced the king to approve and publish a letter patent decreeing the abolition of the hereditary nobility and the suppression of all titles. No one could bear any but his family name, nor clothe anyone in livery, nor display crests. Incense was to be burnt in temples solely to honour the Divinity and not to be offered for any other purpose

message. He managed to get a vote of thanks for the king "for the measures taken in favour of peace".

Even so, his success had put heart into the monarchists when the debate re-opened the next day. One of their speakers, Malouet, set out the advantages of leaving the control of diplomacy to the king. Pétion, the deputy from Chartres, opposed him. The people were beginning to associate his name with Robespierre's. The latter followed him on the rostrum. He could not, he claimed, accept the theory that the king naturally possessed the right to declare war as the representative of the nation: "He was only the servant and the delegate of the nation to carry out its wishes." The use of "servant" in connection with the person of the sovereign seemed to imply a lack of respect to some deputies, who protested. Robespierre explained himself. He had no intention whatsoever of being offensive, but only meant by it "the supreme office", and "the sublime duty" of carrying out the national will. When he had made that much clear, he went on to show how the motives for declaring war were often futile, bearing no relation whatsoever to the interests of the nation. "The king will always be tempted to declare war to increase his prerogative. The representatives of the nation will always have a direct interest in preventing war. Someone mentioned a treaty. What treaty? Is a family pact a national pact? As if quarrels of kings were the quarrels of peoples."

The applause of the Assembly was ample evidence to him that they shared his feelings. Would Mirabeau succeed in swaying them with his eloquence? For the second time he made a mistake in putting forward a compromise, in the hopes of rallying the hesitant. The king would have the right to declare war, for the representatives of the nation to approve or disapprove subsequently. As if, after the outbreak of hostilities, it would be possible for the Assembly to revoke the king's decision with a veto.

On the 22nd Mirabeau once more took the rostrum realizing that he had lost, and full of bitterness that his ambitions were ruined. He began to deliver a biting, ironical speech, the most emotional of his career. "A few days ago they wanted to carry me in triumph, and now they shout out in the streets Comte Mirabeau's great betrayal. I did not need that lesson to know that there is only a very short distance from the Capitol to the Tarpeian Rock." All the same, to conceal his defeat he supported another compromise—as impractical as his own—which the Assembly finally adopted. Following a proposal by the king, the right to declare war would belong to the legislative body, which would then have to defer to the king for his sanction.

In this way the members of the Assembly sincerely thought they had guaranteed peace. To insure that no foreign nation had any doubt about the peaceful nature of their intentions, they decided to let the whole world know, by a solemn declaration, that France would in future fight no war of conquest.

The annexation of Avignon, shortly afterwards, was to disprove their intention. Even so, they saw no contradiction in it. There was all the difference in the world, in their eyes, between conquest and annexation. The first was the result of a military campaign undertaken with this end in view; the second was the expressed wish of the inhabitants of a region to be attached to the nation of their choice. Unhappily for the foreigners, finally deprived of territory which belonged to them, the difference was not so clearly manifest. Many who had looked on the Revolution sympathetically until then began to revise their opinion, foreseeing that it could be just as aggressive, if not more so, than the monarchy.

Avignon and Venaissin had for centuries constituted a papal enclave within French territory. But its population was French at heart and showed its approval of events in France. The people wanted to take part in them and in November 1789 began to demand that they be returned to France. In June 1790 the people of Avignon rose in revolt, drove out the cardinal-legate and imprisoned his followers. The matter was brought up several times in the Assembly during the course of the year. The first time Robespierre referred to it was in a speech on 10th June. He said that he opposed the release of the prisoners until there had been an enquiry. On 18th November his speech was reported almost in its entirety in *Le Moniteur*. He subsequently had it printed, which shows how important he considered it to be. The Assembly hesitated to pronounce the annexation, for fear of falling out with the Pope, since they hoped to have his sanction for the Civil Constitution of the Clergy. Robespierre did not have the same scruples as the rest. He wanted immediate reunion with France. He argued that Avignon could not be the property of the Pope, because a man could not be the property of another man. Annexation in no way constituted a conquest. The Assembly was duty bound to reply without delay to the appeal of the people of Avignon. They had to establish a parallel between their revolt and 14th July: "In the midst of these troubles, in the midst of blood, after a violent insurrection, the people of Avignon ask to be united to France. Are we therefore to reject their plea? Would those of such a mind also expect the despots themselves to surrender to the people the free exercise of their rights, or to reveal to the people the secret of how to regain those rights without insurrection, or moreover to turn the process over to the French people and their true representatives, or do they think that they would forgive the Avignonnais for having asked them to do so?" The strategic advantage to be gained from possession of the place had not escaped him, either. He underlined that Avignon could be either "the support or the scourge of the Revolution", according to who was in control of it, "a centre of armed opposition or the rampart of France against her enemies".

[[·]]

In between these two speeches, incidents had occurred which had induced Robespierre to make other speeches. On 27th July the Assembly learnt that the Minister of Foreign Affairs, Montmorin, had authorized a detachment of Austrian troops to cross over part of French territory to get to Brabant. The matter was of little consequence and there was nothing unusual about it, but it caused great agitation. The Duc d'Aiguillon proposed a vote of censure against the minister. It was an instance where Mirabeau might render the Court service. This time he went about it with great skill. In an indignant tone he denounced from the rostrum a counter-revolutionary manifesto that had recently been published abroad, which he attributed to the Prince de Condé. In this way he turned the wrath of the Assembly against de Condé, thus forgetting Montmorin. When they heard the revolutionary words of the speaker, deputies on the left and people in the galleries thought they were listening to their old Mirabeau again and acclaimed him. The press did likewise. Mirabeau put forward a motion demanding that the prince be required to disown the manifesto by a firm undertaking within three weeks, and if he failed to do so he would be declared a traitor to the fatherland and his goods would be confiscated.

The next day Camille Desmoulins wrote ironically in his diary: "Mirabeau thought he must give the rein to the people, instead of being seen to break it by pulling too hard." It seems that Robespierre was the only one in the Assembly to realize what was going on. The aim of his speech, therefore, was to show this. If Mirabeau had been talking about patriotism, he could only have had the treacherous intent of deceiving public opinion. To everyone's great surprise Robespierre therefore opposed the motion: "I do not want to be any more indulgent towards the enemies of the fatherland than Monsieur Riquetti [since the abolition of titles, nobles had to use their family names. Mirabeau became Riquetti and Lafayette, Moutier], but I think that his proposal is inadmissible and dangerous." He accurately pointed out that no one knew for certain who had written the manifesto. In any case, there were more dangerous enemies of the Revolution. Condé was not the only one to have shown signs of opposition. "Behind Montmorin there is the Court and the ministers; behind Condé the entire counter-revolution." That was where the real danger lay. What was required was to open a debate on the means of destroying the enemies of the Revolution. "To go for Condé alone means to avert attention. Away from whom?" Here Robespierre, who had become expert in the art of producing effects, made a short pause. He saw that his colleagues were hanging on his words, and went on: "It is averting attention from those who are entrusted with the direction of the destiny of the Revolution, but who seem to be turning against it." There was not a single person who did not understand that he meant Mirabeau, and much more forcefully than if he had mentioned his name. With that little sentence he ruined all the profit that Mirabeau had hoped to extract from his speech.

In December the Assembly began a debate on the organization of the National Guard. This caused yet another violent confrontation between Mirabeau and Robespierre at the Jacobin Club. The plebeian count was now the paid counsellor of the Court. Whether it was treason or not, according to Lafayette it was at least "where his convictions lay". Mirabeau sincerely wanted to reconcile monarchy and people, and he advised the king—to no avail, as it happened—to accept all that the Revolution had accomplished so far. This would be the only way to channel it. Otherwise he saw a terrible storm brewing. "All is lost. The king and queen will die, and you will see the rabble tearing at their corpses."

The proposal under consideration was that only active citizens should be called upon to be in the National Guard. The reason put forward for this was that the soldiers had to fit themselves out at their own expense, and therefore they had to have the means to do so. In fact, it was a question of deciding who would control the armed forces, the people or the upper and middle classes. In time of revolution this would decide the outcome. The majority, who had deprived the passive citizens of the right to vote, could obviously not envisage giving them arms. This inspired Dandré to remark: "How often passive citizens have stirred up trouble."

But Robespierre was not put out by such disturbances. Quite the opposite. He said: "As if a revolution must be accomplished without disturbance!" He saw no danger in them, but the necessary leaven to make the Revolution go on. He was the champion of the political rights of passive citizens, and it was therefore normal that he should take up, in this instance also, the defence of their interests. However, the Assembly voted before he had the time to speak.

The matter seemed so important to him that he had no hesitation in twisting his principle that a decree passed by the Assembly was not to be attacked. On the evening of 5th December he made an implacable criticism of it at the Jacobin Club. "The right to be armed in defence of freedom and the well-being of the community is just as sacred as that of national and individual defence." Robespierre's speeches at this time were cold, controlled dialectic. On this occasion he allowed himself a flight of eloquence. "Stop slandering the people by always representing them as unworthy of enjoying their rights, as if they were wicked, barbarous and corrupt. You are the corrupt ones, and the people are good, patient and generous."

Mirabeau was in the chair. He was not dissatisfied to hear criticism of a decree inspired by Lafayette, but what followed pleased him much less. "You are cruel and clever sophists, but it is useless for you to claim, by little charlatan tricks and Court intrigues, to guide a revolution of which you are unworthy. You will be dragged along like weak insects in its irresistible train. Your successes will be as fleeting as dreams, and your shame as immortal as truth."

Mirabeau obviously realized that it was himself that Robespierre was referring to. Every one of his words pierced him like a sharpened arrow. At the end he could hold back no longer and wanted to interrupt. The decree had been passed, he had no right to oppose it. His intervention was greeted by a tumult. The Jacobins wanted to hear Robespierre. When the noise had gone on for some time, Mirabeau climbed on to a chair and shouted in his powerful voice: "Will all my colleagues gather round me." He expected to see all the members gather round him to support him. Scarcely thirty did so. The others, shouting and applauding, gathered round his opponent.

This failure marked the very lowest point of his popularity, and abashed him. Order was re-established by Charles de Lameth, who was revelling in his rival's humiliation, and had no doubt that in a few months a similar experience would occur in the Assembly. Robespierre finished his speech in an awesome silence. He subsequently had it printed and sent to the provincial clubs with whom he was in contact. Everywhere those who read it expressed the same enthusiasm.

Even so, he had a setback, through the fault of his friend Desmoulins. The journalist had just married his pretty fiancée, Lucile Duplessis. Robespierre and Brissot had been his witnesses. On that day the humourist was quite moved, and even allowed himself to shed a few tears. "Cry, if you like," Maximilien said to him affectionately; but the honeymoon made him negligent. Robespierre having entrusted his pamphlet to him, was astonished to see no comment on it in *Les Révolutions de France et de Brabant*. He brought him to heel. "I would point out to Monsieur Camille Desmoulins that neither the fine eyes nor the beautiful qualities of the charming Lucile are reasons for not announcing my pamphlet on the National Guard which was sent to him." In case his old friend had lost the copy in his headiness, he sent him another one. So as to make amends, some time later Camille published an article on Robespierre that was particularly eulogistic. He criticized the people who made a point of calling him Robertspierre and added that "even if he were called Brutus or chickpea, like Cicero, the Incorruptible would always have the finest name in France". This name for Robespierre—the Incorruptible—had just appeared under a portrait of him painted by Madame Labille-Guyard which was displayed in the Exhibition of 1790.

[[·]]

Exhausted by debauchery and work, overcome by the disappointment of the ruin of his political ambitions, Mirabeau only had a few more months to live. He spent them in fighting. In one of his last struggles in the Assembly he successfully opposed a proposed decree on emigration put forward by Le Chapelier: "If you ever pass a law against emigrants," he cried, "I swear that I will never obey it." A few leftist deputies, grouped around the de Lameths and Robespierre, attempted to interrupt his sacrilegious words with shouts. With scorn he hurled abuse. "Silence the rebels. Tell the thirty to shut their holes."

He died on 3rd April 1791 at the age of forty-two in his luxurious house in the Chaussée d'Antin, which had been bought with subsidies from the Court. One of the last things he said was: "I sound the death knell of the monarchy." When he died all his critics were momentarily silenced. They only wanted to recall the services he had rendered, which were enormous. Those who had been his rivals the day before now sang his praises. Robespierre himself rendered homage to him, "to the illustrious man who, at the critical moments of the Revolution, presented such a brave face against despotism". He also voted to give him a state funeral.

7

THE TRIUMVIRATE

*"When one meddles with the direction of a revolution, the problem
is not how to make it go, but how to keep it under control."*

MIRABEAU

IRABEAU'S THREE GREAT RIVALS WHILE HE WAS STILL ALIVE—
Duport, Barnave and Alexandre de Lameth—carried on his policy. They
also wanted to stop the Revolution. They were satisfied with what had
already had been achieved, without wanting to go backwards in any way. "How,"
Le Chapelier asked Malouet, "can we restore to royal authority the energy it
needs, if we also are afraid that it might be used against us?" They were attacked
by the left, who accused them of treason, and by the right, who were out for
revenge. As far as the king was concerned, he was no more able than Mirabeau
had been to put his trust in these "factious people" who, in his eyes, had led the
nation astray. At the very most, he considered using them to bring influence to
bear on the Assembly. With Montmorin as a go-between, the Court began to have
dealings with Alexandre de Lameth.

Meanwhile Robespierre relentlessly pursued his campaign against the electora
law. On 21st April 1791 he spoke against it at the Cordeliers' Club. This left-bank
club had a number of passive citizen members, since the rather high subscription
kept them out of the Jacobins. They gave their champion an enthusiastic reception.
He reminded them that the people had not broken the yoke of the feudal aristocracy only to fall once again under the aristocracy of the rich, which was the
most intolerable of all.

A debate on the colonial problem, which opened in May, provoked his first confrontation with the Triumvirate. The problem was to decide whether or not the

principles of freedom and equality could operate in the West Indies as they did in France, since in the Antilles there was a population of whites, blacks and half-breeds, of masters and slaves.

There were two main schools of thought in the Assembly. First were those who supported slavery and carried on the slave trade, known as the Club Massiac. The others formed a group called the Amis des noirs, among whom were Robespierre, Brissot, Abbé Grégoire and Condorcet, who campaigned for the abolition of slavery and the political equality of coloured people, both blacks and half-breeds. The Colonial Committee proposed leaving it to local assemblies to frame laws for bettering the conditions of the *hommes de couleur* and freed Negroes, arguing that since they were on the spot they would know the situation better. But since they consisted entirely of white settlers, there was hardly any likelihood that they would ever carry out reforms. Robespierre had the opportunity to expose the injustice and absurdity of allowing whites to make laws for blacks. "It is as if, when it was a question in France of deciding whether the Third Estate would have equal representation with the Nobility and Clergy, a commission had been set up consisting of members of these last two orders only, to give the government its opinion on the rights of the Commons." In a second speech he protested against the use of the word "slave" by Moreau de Saint-Méry, who spoke on behalf of the settlers.

On 11th May Barnave spoke, admitting that it was no doubt "painful" to allow certain institutions, contrary to the rights of man, to survive in the colonies, but necessity demanded it lest they be ruined. Poorly planned reforms would be likely to cause trouble in San Domingo, which would benefit England and only give her the opportunity to seize these territories which she coveted so much. Robespierre brushed aside the objection with contempt. "Anyone who has any respect for the legislative body could not think that he could delude it with such ridiculous arguments." Personally he saw no reason for not applying the rights of man in the colonies as elsewhere. "Let the colonies perish if the settlers want to force us, through their threats, to decree what is most in their interests." The Assembly let itself be partially convinced. It granted half-breeds and freed blacks the same rights as Whites, but withheld these rights from slaves, and allowed the slave trade to continue.

⌊⌊ · ⌋⌋

From the tone of the debates of the last months Robespierre was convinced that the deputies—apart from a small group of extreme leftist patriots who sided with

(OPPOSITE, ABOVE) *The members of the Cordelier Club took their watchful motto seriously and felt that they, alone, were the guardians of the people* (BELOW) *The meetings and debates in the clubs were seldom orderly affairs. The constant interruptions, the private arguments, often obscured the voice of the principal speaker. It was not unusual for many of those present to learn what had been discussed only by reading the accounts published the next day*

him, such as Pétion, Buzot, Abbé Grégoire and Lepelletier—were evil citizens who were betraying the people. It was therefore in the interests of the Revolution that they should be barred from taking part in the next Assembly. The only way of ensuring this was to have the present Assembly adopt a law which forbade the re-election of its members. Naturally this meant he would eliminate himself, but it seemed to Robespierre that this disadvantage was far outweighed by the advantage of the disappearance from the political scene of people such as Barnave, Le Chapelier, Beaumetz and Malouet. He rightly thought that these men would disappear into oblivion once they returned to the provinces. As for himself, instead of returning to Arras, he would stay in Paris. He had a premonition that the new Assembly would be weak, and therefore subject to external pressures. From the platform of the Jacobin Club and through his correspondence with popular provincial clubs, he would be able to continue watching over events, guiding the people and achieving the aims of the Revolution.

He was certainly fully conscious of the difficulty involved in getting such a motion accepted by his colleagues. Most of them had developed a liking for their role, with good prospects of being re-elected—particularly the left-wing members —and they had no doubt that the country would come down on their side. On 16th May the debate on the organization of the future legislative body was opened by deputy Thouret, the secretary of the constitutional committee. There were ninety clauses, the seventh of which was the question of re-eligibility. The report, which came down in favour of it, was warmly applauded.

Robespierre was prudent and skilful. So as not to collide too violently with the majority, he must not appear to have closed the way for any re-election whatsoever. He therefore began to establish a distinction—which the Thouret report failed to establish—between the elections for the next Assembly, and the subsequent ones. He had made great progress in the art of parliamentary debate. "This question," he said, "is delicate. We can only discuss it with dignity, and above all impartiality, if we have divested ourselves of all personal interest. So as to examine it objectively we must, for a while, return to being private citizens. I therefore ask that at the moment it is passed, without prejudicing any future legislative bodies, that the members of this present one should not be re-elected."

The right welcomed these words with approval. The few members of the privileged orders who still attended sessions knew that they had no hope whatsoever of being re-elected. They had nothing to lose by adopting a law which signified the elimination of people they hated. In addition there was a vague hope of revenge. An Assembly consisting entirely of new men might possibly destroy the laws passed by the Constitutent Assembly.

On the left and in the centre, murmurs of protest arose. Robespierre's speech had at least one initial result. When he finished his explanation, Thouret asked his colleagues not to decide immediately.

This delay was useful for Robespierre in giving him the time to deliver the speech

The major benefits of the period, 1789–91, were the cutting of taxes, the lessening of enforced labour, the rise to power of the Third Estate, the abolition of the nobility and the sharing of the burden of the national debt equally among the members of all three estates

that he had prepared with extreme care, as he always did on important occasions. He began by recalling "the example of the greatest legislators of antiquity who, having given their countries a constitution, made it their duty to return to the body of ordinary citizens". At this time a reference to the Romans in relation to politics, which was fashionable and flattering, never failed to produce an effect. "Picture for yourselves," he went on, "what immense authority the sacrifice made by you yourselves would give to your constitution—in sacrificing the highest honours to which your fellow citizens can call you. How feeble the efforts of slander will be when they will be unable to reproach a single one of you, who have raised up the constitution, that you attempted to turn to your own profit the power that the mission grants its creators to prolong their authority."

One of the weightiest arguments in favour of re-election was the importance of experience acquired by the outgoing deputies after three years of practice, whereas new members, who might be political novices, would find themselves more prone to make mistakes—a forecast that events were soon to prove true. But Robespierre, with this very thing in mind, did not want too clever an Assembly.

He brushed the argument aside as being offensive to France. "We have neither the right nor the presumption to think that this nation of twenty-five million men, free and enlightened, is reduced to impotence and cannot easily find 720 worthy defenders. If this nation could, at a time when it did not know its own rights, do things that were worthy of the Revolution, and now educated by two years of political life, why should it not do still even better things?"

Robespierre was on the rostrum for two hours, heard in a religious silence. It was a far cry from the days when his words were lost in the hubbub. So persuasive did he appear to the Assembly that immediately afterwards, swept away in enthusiasm, they voted almost to the man against the re-election of members to the Legislative Assembly. A monarchist deputy proposed that "the sublime speech" of the deputy from Arras be printed.

It remained to be decided whether the measure would be applicable to all future assemblies; and the same arguments for and against would be valid. Thouret and the committee wanted the right to re-election retained. "Let us take precautions for the future of the nation that a certain number of worthy men are retained. There is only one way to do so; give them the possibility of becoming deputies once more."

Pétion made a long and confused speech against re-election for all. His general drift was that two years were quite long enough as a political career to satisfy normal ambition. Duport, one of the triumvirs, then took the floor and began his reply to Robespierre, which had been awaited with curiosity. He started by letting off a few arrows in his direction. "The same men who every day make so much noise uttering the words, 'sovereignty of the people' are divesting the people of this sovereignty. Stop insulting the people whilst you deprive them, for they will then stop believing in your supposed devotion to their cause." Like the clever speaker he was, he defended re-election, but at the same time his speech was that of a man who had lost faith in all that he had fought for until then. Realizing that the Revolution was slipping from his grasp, Duport painted a picture of the short-sighted mob who overthrew one tyrant only to raise up another, and the new one would be even more dangerous than the first if he were able to manipulate the people's acceptance of his tyranny. "I am here to protect my country from the greatest danger that has ever threatened it, so that the Revolution, as it progresses, does not turn into a dictatorship. Do you believe that the normal state for a country is one of revolution, and do you want to expose France, whose people have such a mercurial nature, to the spectacle of a revolution every two years?"

Assemblies are by nature unstable, and an eloquent speech is enough to sway them. The deputies applauded Duport as they had applauded Robespierre the day before, and also voted for his speech to be published. If a vote had been taken there and then, he would probably have carried the day; but Buzot and Rewbell were still to be heard. To the general consternation Robespierre said nothing. Improvised replies were not consonant with his kind of eloquence, and he avoided them as far as possible. There was also the probability that he did not want to speak to an audience still swayed by an opponent's speech.

The debate was resumed the next day with a speech from Larevellière-Lépeaux against re-election, then from the Duc de Liancourt, who was in favour. These two hors-d'œuvres were of little interest, only serving to whet the appetite for what was to come. There was total silence when Robespierre went up the steps of the rostrum, looking even more serious than usual, with a roll of paper in his hand. He said that he only wanted to consider one question: was re-election going to ensure that the people would be well represented? "Experience has always proved that if the citizens are lazy and easily deceived, then the people who govern them are proportionately as clever and active in extending their power and suppressing public freedom." The only means of stopping them was not to let them hold office any longer. With great force he pronounced that: "A law prohibiting re-election is the surest way to safeguard freedom."

After this he made a close refutation of Duport's argument. Duport had said that since the deputies knew in advance that they would not be re-elected, they would not therefore do their duty. Instead of being concerned for the general interest of the nation they would devote themselves to local matters and would spend the time "slandering ministers". Robespierre refused to believe in the first of these dangers, and about the second he was ironical. He saw nothing wrong in deputies slandering ministers—on the contrary, "that would at least prove that they were not subject to them, and that is very important".

He went on to say that some of his colleagues seemed to share Duport's fear that all would be lost if they were not re-elected. "I reassure myself, because I believe that France can continue to exist, even when some of us are neither legislators nor ministers." Duport had said that his speech was dangerous. He sent the ball back into his court. "I would even dare to say that such a vehement speech, which was ordered to be published yesterday, is itself a danger."

The deputies applauded, but this time they did not vote that the speech be printed. After three days of reflection there had been a clear reaction in favour of re-election. This tendency, however, which was gathering momentum, was sharply halted by the incompetence of Le Chapelier, who spoke next. The idea of being forced to give up his seat made him lose his self-control. His tone was aggressive and had an unfortunate effect. "If you pass this act, which is against the constitution, each *département* will have the right to disobey it." This call to disobedience brought indignant protests. Barère, who followed him, proposed a compromise, which would allow members of a legislative body to be re-elected, provided that they missed one intervening term, and so become eligible again. His colleagues did not immediately seem to realize the advantages of this complicated system. All the same, when the vote was taken the following day, this was the one they adopted. Even so, on the crucial issue it was Robespierre who had won. No member of the Constituent Assembly would sit in the Legislative Assembly. Camille Desmoulins, in his diary, celebrated his friend's victory: "He was more afraid for the people in the election of the Chapeliers, the Mouniers, the Dandrés and the Beaumetzs, than for his own election. There's a true patriot indeed!"

[[·]]

Robespierre was exhausted by the efforts of the last few weeks. He was ill for a while, which prevented him from attending the debates for several days. He reappeared on 31st May, to deliver the most humane speech of his career. Carefully thought out and written during his illness, it was on a subject dear to him: the abolition of the death penalty.

A great majority of the Assembly wanted the abolition of capital punishment, which they saw as a legacy from former days, along with torture and *lettres de cachet*. They thought that it ought to be retained only for political reasons, "when the leader of a party is declared a rebel by decree of the Legislative Assembly". By conviction, and throughout his life, Robespierre wanted total abolition. As a young judge on the ecclesiastical tribunal, he had been deeply affected when he had to condemn a man to death. Using examples drawn from the history of Greece, Rome and Russia, he made great efforts to show that the death penalty was always "unjust, irreparable, degrading and useless. A man who butchers a child, easily disarmed and punished, seems a monster. An accused man whom society has condemned is no more nor less, in its eyes, than a conquered and powerless enemy. He is weaker before society than a child in front of a brute. Therefore in the eyes of truth and justice, these scenes of death that society ordains with so much display are no more than cowardly murders—solemn crimes legally sanctioned not by individuals but by entire nations. The man of law who prefers death to the gentler means at his disposal outrages public sensibilities, deadens moral awareness in those he governs, just as a clumsy teacher who, by frequent use of cruel punishments, deadens and degrades the spirit of his pupils. Listen to the voice of justice and reason. She cries out to us that human judgements are never absolute enough for a society of men prone to make mistakes to be empowered to put to death a man condemned by other men."

[[·]]

At the beginning of June several leftist deputies thought about putting Robespierre forward as a candidate for the presidency of the Assembly, which changed every fortnight. He was not elected, but there had to be a second ballot, which was a very rare thing. Several deputies from the right voted for him, some so as to humiliate the triumvirs, others in the secret hope that with Robespierre as president the Assembly would go too far, which would compromise him in the eyes of the public. There is nothing to show that as far as Robespierre himself was concerned

A British invention for decapitation was endorsed by Dr Guillotin as a humane and more dignified form of execution and one with noble Roman precedents

he wanted the job. At all events he evinced no regret at his failure. Victory did not rescue his successful opponent—a good peasant called Dauchy—from obscurity. Like so many of the presidents of the Constituent Assembly his name alone survives. Brissot wrote in his paper, *Le Patriote français*: "Monsieur Robespierre, who has long deserved the honour of taking the chair, should console himself with the thought that in this way homage was paid to agriculture."

On the other hand, on 10th June Robespierre was elected public prosecutor to the criminal court of Paris, in opposition to the moderate, Dandré. Duport was elected chief magistrate, but preferred to resign rather than have to collaborate with him. Pétion took over. Robespierre, who had not been a candidate, was only partially satisfied. "The electors have just made me departmental public prosecutor," he wrote to Arras, "without my knowledge and in spite of the intrigues. However honourable such a choice might be, I can only contemplate with fear the painful work to which this important situation is going to condemn me at a time when rest is needed after such prolonged activity." Any task which would appear to compromise the one that he looked upon as the most important—namely that of advising the people—seemed undesirable to him. He resigned a few months later without ever having acted in his new capacity.

[[·]]

One of the most fateful days of the Revolution, a date which would either precipitate it or stop it, was 20th June 1791. Outwitting the guards on the Tuileries, the king and his family fled. He had sadly witnessed the erosion of his power over the past two years, but more depressing to his conscience as a practising Catholic was the religious policy of the Assembly. The Constitution being drawn up seemed a monstrosity to him, capable only of creating misery for France. He thought it his duty to put an end to it.

Robespierre had gone to Versailles that day, to explain to the local Jacobin Club his reasons for resigning as their justice of the peace (he had been appointed by the townsfolk some time before, as evidence of their admiration). His new office as public prosecutor in Paris prevented him from carrying out his duties in Versailles any longer. He heard of the king's departure the next day, at the same time as everyone else, at about 9 a.m.

The affair aroused enormous feeling of amazement and anger among the people. After all the king's declarations of goodwill, no one could think of him as anything but a hypocrite. He left a document behind which had a most unfortunate effect. The royalist, Ferrières, said: "The voluntary assent to this constitution, given so many times and against which he now protests, taints his character with weakness and falseness which was certainly apt to alienate the people, who want either breadth of vision or enormous quality." The Assembly decided to sit permanently, and the constitutionalists, who had founded their policy on loyal collaboration with the king, now found themselves extremely embarrassed. It was very hard for them to escape the suspicion of complicity or stupidity. Robespierre had no doubt about it. The king's escape could only have been organized and carried out with the connivance of Bailly and Lafayette.

The strange attitude of the constitutionalists and the Triumvirate, who talked about the "abduction" of the king, only re-enforced Robespierre's belief. They had given the order for the king to be pursued, but they wanted to put him back on the throne, and therefore he must not appear guilty. Many of the left-wing deputies thought that it was much better to get rid of a man who had deceived the nation. Then the difficulty arose as to who was to replace him. The best candidate would have been the Comte de Provence, who had sympathizers among the liberals, but he too had fled. Some mentioned the Dauphin—provided that the fugitives were caught—and others put forward the Duc d'Orléans. Finally, there were those who advocated a republic, especially the Cordeliers Club and most of the people who frequented the salon of Madame Roland.

Robespierre did not like the idea of a republic. To him it seemed dangerous for the future of the Revolution. Most of the republics until then had been ruled by aristocratic governments—in particular, the most famous of them, Venice. Even that of the United States of America, the most recent, he believed to be "founded on the aristocracy of wealth, [and was] already inclining towards monarchistic despotism." That was not what he wanted for France. It was more important, in his estimation, to put an end to the division between active and passive citizens, than to change the form of government. In the circumstances, a republic would only serve to establish definitively the power of Lafayette and the triumvirs. In the afternoon he attended a meeting at Pétion's house, where they talked about setting up a republic. In her memoirs Madame Roland tells how, when the idea was put forward, Robespierre began to sneer and bite his nails and asked ironically: "What is a republic?"

At the meeting of the Jacobins that evening, the various alternatives were considered. A former lawyer on the King's Council, called Danton, a giant of impressive ugliness, had stirred up riots in the Cordeliers' district. With his stentor's voice he proposed that Louis XVI be declared "imbecile" and given a "council of prevention". The Duc d'Orléans had many supporters. If the Dauphin were chosen, would the regency council be chosen from his relatives, or from people outside the royal family? Roederer was in favour of the last idea, and made the curious remark: "This system will have the advantage of soon bringing about the knowledge of an important truth, which is that as one would have had a very good regency without a regent, so one could also have a very good monarchy without a monarch." A man called Billaud-Varenne, who was making his maiden speech at the club that day, wanted the abolition of royalty and the setting up of a republic. The warm applause that greeted his speech showed that the majority shared his opinion.

Robespierre was quite opposed to this opinion. He saw, with great annoyance, that the idea of a republic was popular with his friends, among them Desmoulins. Most of the left-wing newspapers, *Les Annales patriotiques*, *La Bouche de fer*, *Le Patriote français* and *Les Révolutions de Paris*, preached it. But in openly fighting it at this crucial moment, Robespierre might run the risk of provoking dissension among the patriots, which would only be to the advantage of the counter-revolutionaries.

With this in mind he was forced to caution and cleverly got out of the difficulty by not saying a word on the question on which all the other previous speakers had been engaged: monarchy or republic? He began by saying that he saw that everyone was sorry at what had happened. He did not share that feeling. "The flight of the chief servant of the nation does not seem to me to be a disastrous event. This day could well be the finest of the Revolution." Among the advantages which might follow, he saw first of all an inevitable weakening of the executive power. It mattered little whether they put this humiliated and despised king back on the throne or someone else. It could then mark the elimination from public life of traitors and "renegades". "But for that, measures must be taken other than those adopted by the National Assembly."

Suddenly changing his tone, he said that a great danger threatened freedom. One point in particular worried him. Both patriots and counter-revolutionaries were all saying the same thing, which was causing great confusion. Treason was everywhere, even in the very heart of the Revolution. The most urgent task was therefore to unmask those traitors who were hiding behind the face of patriotism. The National Assembly was betraying the interest of the nation. "I know that in accusing almost all my colleagues—the members of the Assembly—of being counter-revolutionaries, some out of ignorance, some out of fear, some out of resentment, out of wounded pride, some out of blind faith and many because they are corrupt, I provoke the proud against me, I sharpen a thousand daggers, and I sacrifice myself to every sort of hatred. I know the fate that is in store for me."

The prospect of the danger to which he was exposing himself moved the Jacobins. Desmoulins tells in his account how: "When this excellent citizen spoke of the certainty of paying with his head for the truths he had just spoken, more than eight hundred people rose at once and, led on, as I was, by an involuntary movement, swore to support Robespierre and presented an admirable picture by the fire of their words, the action of their hands, their hats, their faces, and by the attitude of their sudden inspiration."

[[·]]

The king was captured at Varennes. Pages could be filled with all the blunders that were committed, each one of which would have been enough to have caused disaster. The carriage was huge and slow, and its gaudy colours attracted attention. There were too many people in the party and the king foolishly put his head out of the window at the risk of being recognized. The stationing of the fresh relays of horses was forgotten. Louis XVI showed no more skill in organizing his escape than he had in governing the kingdom. He was brought back to Paris on the 25th amid an icy silence from the people. The Assembly decided that he would be suspended from his functions until he had accepted the Constitution.

With a king who was a prisoner, France, during this time, as Desmoulins wrote, was experiencing a *de facto* republic by force of circumstance. Although Robespierre did not want a republic, nor any other arrangement which would bring the Duc d'Orléans, whom he despised, closer to power, he shared too much in the general outrage to accept the preservation of Louis XVI. In a printed article entitled: "Monsieur Robespierre's latest speech on the king's flight," which he must have delivered at the club a few days after his return, but is not dated, for the first time since the beginning of the Revolution he took the king to task personally. Until then, only the king's advisers had come in for attack. "It is impossible for a king dishonoured by perjury, of all crimes the one most contrary to French honour, a king who, in cold blood, was going to make that of Frenchmen flow, it is impossible for such a king to ascend the throne once more. The least of his subjects would think himself dishonoured."

He protested when Duport proposed that the Assembly should choose from its members three commissioners to take the statements of the king and queen. Those who had fled with them would be examined by the ordinary judges of the bench.

This discrimination seemed unjust to Robespierre. He argued that if the king were presumed innocent—which is what was implied by his "abduction"—there was no offence, no complicity, and therefore no reason to try the accomplices. If the king were not innocent, then nothing justified favourable treatment. The king must be treated like any other citizen. "The same authority responsible for part of the information must be responsible for all. Why should there be respect for the royal couple? The queen is a female citizen and the king is at present a citizen accountable to the nation. As chief civil servant, he must be subject to the law."

But the majority of the Assembly did not agree with Robespierre. The report of the three commissioners—Duport himself, Dandré and Tronchet—kept up the figment of abduction, which obviously no one believed. Louis XVI completed the comedy by saying that he had been "informed" of the journey.

This wildly exaggerated travesty of the truth made irony a simple matter. Robespierre asked Duport if he thought "that the people could think that kings were abducted like women". Then he ended, more seriously, by saying that: "When the criminal is a high-ranking civil servant, it is even more dangerous not to punish his crimes."

[[·]]

Nevertheless, some people thought that it would be basically advantageous for the Revolution to restore to the throne a monarch who was dishonoured and had lost all his popularity. Gorsas wrote: "A king who is a numbskull is better than a republican whore." Sieyès demonstrated geometrically the superiority of monarchy to republicanism. He explained that a monarchy terminated in a point, but the republican form of government in a platform. "The monarchic triangle is a much better structure than the republican platform for the division of power, which is the real road to freedom."

Doubtless the fear that the king's departure would plunge France into chaos was the principal reason for the re-establishment of Louis XVI on the throne by the

(OVERLEAF) *The most surprising aspect of the arrest of the royal family in Varennes was that, bungled and amateurish as the plan and its execution were, they had not been caught before*

Constituent Assembly. Barnave warned the Assembly of the risks in an emotional speech. For him, in addition to political reasons, there was a feeling of pity for the royal family—in particular for the queen—whom he had accompanied on the sad journey back from Varennes to Paris. "Any change at this moment is fatal, and every prolongation of the Revolution disastrous. You have done what was good for freedom and equality. You have regained and returned to the State all that had been taken away from it. If the Revolution takes one step more it will only do so at great risk. You who have regenerated the empire, follow your course without leaving the path. You are all-powerful; be wise, be moderate, for therein lies the fulfilment of your glory."

The Cordeliers Club had begun an active campaign for a republic. Before making their decision, the Jacobins were waiting for Robespierre to clarify his position. However, his speech at the club on 13th July was solely concerned with a repudiation of the charge of republicanism that had been made against him by the right-wing. "I have been accused in the Assembly of being republican. My enemies pay me too much honour. I am not. If they had accused me of being royalist they would have dishonoured me, but such I am not. I would point out that for many people the words Monarchy and Republic are only vague and meaningless expressions, which do not characterize a particular sort of government. Every free state is a republic in which it is the people who count. Republic and monarchy are not incompatible."

The form of government, to which most of his colleagues in the Assembly and the club gave so much importance, seemed to him a useless quibbling with words. The important thing was that the Revolution should go forward, and for that to happen the executive had to be weak. That is why after having said that Louis XVI was unworthy of ruling, in the absence of anyone else, he resigned himself to keeping "this weak king", on condition "that he was sheltered from intrigues and the bad influence of factious people. I say that I prefer the individual that chance, birth and circumstance have given us as king to all the kings that others might wish upon us." The terms were so contemptuous that no one could accuse him of having changed his mind.

[[·]]

In response to the Assembly's decision to put Louis XVI back on the throne the Cordeliers decided to take action. On 13th July, at their instigation, a crowd gathered round the Manège, calling for deposition. The next day a deputation went to the Assembly to ask that the matter be settled by a plebiscite, but they were unsuccessful in being received. On 16th July six delegates from the Cordeliers presented themselves, bringing an address with the same request. They wanted Pétion and Robespierre to present it. The two deputies could only tell them that they had come too late. The decree which declared Louis XVI inviolable had just been passed. It would be illegal to petition against it. The delegates then asked them for something in writing to take back to the people who had sent them, as proof that they had carried out their mission. Robespierre and Pétion wrote a letter in which they explained the dangers of such action, which could be wrongly interpreted by the enemies of the people. Later Robespierre said: "I do not know what fatal foreboding warned me, but the indications were implicit, that the enemies of freedom had long been looking for a chance to persecute the people and carry out some evil plot against the united citizenry."

The Cordeliers did not share Robespierre's prudence. They did not want to abandon their project for issuing a manifesto in conjunction with the Jacobins, demanding the deposition of the king. They chose Brissot to write it. Brissot frequented Madame Roland's salon and was personally a republican. Even so, the word republic did not appear in his text, instead the manifesto only mentioned replacing Louis XVI "by constitutional means". Danton read it out to the crowd on the Champ-de-Mars on 16th July. Some of those present objected to that phrase on the grounds that it was royalist in inspiration—that it was in effect a proclamation of the Dauphin in his father's place. But the Jacobins present, as a result of Robespierre's teaching—insisted that it be retained so as to avoid any republican interpretation of the petition.

On the same day, in a second decree, the Assembly decided that Louis XVI would be restored to the throne as soon as he accepted the Constitution. This rendered the petition illegal, and the Jacobins then declared themselves against it. Now that they no longer had their restraining influence, the Cordeliers drew up another petition in which they demanded not only that the king be got rid of, but that he be tried and "a new executive power" be set up. There was no more mention of "constitutional means". The petition, placed upon the Altar of the Fatherland in the Champ-de-Mars, was signed with some six thousand names.

Robespierre had kept well away from this enterprise, with which he did not agree, and the consequences of which frightened him, since he saw that it had little chance of success. He was told about the resolution passed by the Cordeliers and made a last desperate attempt to intervene by sending one of the Jacobins, Chevalier de la Rivière, to try and stop the printing of the petition. He arrived too late. Events then took place as Robespierre had feared and foreseen. Martial law was proclaimed, there was shooting, the crowd fled in rout, and there were dead and injured in the streets.

All the same, Robespierre was accused of having been one of the prime movers of the doomed uprising. It was true that the organizers had displayed his portrait on the Champ-de-Mars alongside the petition, with the inscription: "To the man whose country owes so much," which defined him as their leader. Moreover, morally he felt that the actual responsibility was his, since in his speech he too had demanded that the king be tried. His accusations that the Assembly was betraying the interests of the nation could be seen as incitements to revolt. At one point he

We dance the Carmagnole | What a tune, what a tune | We dance the Carmagnole | Long live the cannon's boom. | Yes, it will be, it will be, it will be | To-day we are prepared to say | Yes, it will be, it will be, it will be | In the coming glorious new day

thought that he was going to be arrested, so in his "Address to the French" he forcefully absolved himself from having had the slightest connection with the disturbance. "If anyone has dared maintain that he had actually heard me advise disobedience to the laws, even those that are most against my principles, I say that he is the most impudent and basest of slanderers."

For the time being the shootings on the Champ-de-Mars appeared to ensure the power of the moderates. It was announced that those inciting others to revolt would be prosecuted, and at this the most deeply implicated left-wing leaders took fright. Marat and Camille Desmoulins suspended publication of their newspapers and hid. Danton fled first to his birthplace, Arcis-sur-Aube, then went to England under the pretext of business. Robespierre's friends feared for his life. After the meeting of the Jacobins on the evening of the 17th, he had to cross half of Paris to get to his distant lodgings in the rue Saintonge. There were angry groups of citizens everywhere, very much against the Jacobins and the Cordeliers, and detachments of Lafayette's National Guard were patrolling the streets. A member of the club who lived in the rue Saint-Honoré, suggested that it might be wiser if he spent the night at his home. The man was an honest master joiner called Duplay. Robespierre gratefully accepted his invitation.

[[·]]

One of the results of 16th July was a split in the Jacobins. The moderates, led by Duport, Barnave and the de Lameths withdrew and founded another club in the monastery of the Feuillants, not far from Duplay's home.

Robespierre welcomed the departure of his opponents and rivals with satisfaction, but many of the members regretted it. Some of them wanted to take steps to bring about a reconciliation with the dissident members. Robespierre wanted nothing less, and while seeming to back up the plan, skilfully made it fail. At the meeting on 18th July someone proposed sending a delegation to the Feuillants. Robespierre said: "I have not come, gentlemen, to oppose the measure proposed by the previous speaker." All the same, he wanted to put forward a method which he believed to be "more apt to bring back into this club the truly patriotic members of the National Assembly". All except five of the 400 deputies had in fact left. Only Robespierre himself, Pétion, Buzot, Abbé Grégoire and Prieur were left. They proposed to send an address to the Assembly, which he had already prepared and which he read to them. It was a justification of the conduct of the club in the matter of the Champ-de-Mars petition. "When the petition was drawn up it was not illegal, since it was prior to the decrees. As soon as the Jacobins had learned of the Assembly's decision, they had withdrawn it." The text was accepted. There was no further reference to the proposed action and it was completely forgotten. In the same way he wrecked another attempt at reunion on 24th July. This time they proposed disbanding the Jacobins so that each member could make individual application to join the Feuillants. Robiespierre said: "First of all, one must decide what is really in the public interest. Those who propose that you disband so that you can then join the Feuillants, have no idea what the public interest is." The Jacobins must not jettison any of their principles. Consequently, he proposed proclaiming "that the club has been, and always will be, that of the friends of the constitution". "Then," say the minutes, "all the members stood up and swore to stay united."

This policy had great success. Not only did the Jacobins survive, when at one point it seemed probable that they would disappear, but they came out of the crisis strengthened. Immediately after the break, 400 affiliated provincial clubs came down on the side of the Feuillants. Almost all of them came back a few weeks later, having got rid of their moderate members, and deciding that "where Robespierre was, must also be the real friends of the Revolution". Many of the deputies who had joined the Feuillants—among them Barère, Talleyrand and Sieyès—feeling the tide turning, rejoined the Jacobins. The rival club had only a fleeting existence, and never had any influence.

In everyone's eyes Robespierre was the saviour. One evening when he entered the hall, to waves of applause, the former actor Collot d'Herbois, who was in the chair, got up to welcome him. He proposed "that this member of the Constituent Assembly, so rightly named the Incorruptible, should preside over the meeting". The proposal was unanimously approved.

[[·]]

In August the Assembly resumed debate on the Constitution, which had been interrupted by the king's attempted escape. All the efforts of the Triumvirate tended to strengthen the executive power, whereas during Mirabeau's lifetime they had contributed so much to weaken it. They proposed that the king once more be given the right to appoint the military commanders and the treasury officials.

Robespierre spoke time and time again in an attempt to foil them. On 15th August he opposed a motion which would allow ministers to speak in the legislative body. He said that this would be an infringement of the principle of the separation of power, and would give the government a thousand means for corruption and intrigue. On the 24th he spoke against the re-establishment of the bodyguard and on subsequent days, against the maintenance of the royal prerogative to grant pardons and the application of the title of prince to members of the royal family.

These were still only skirmishes. The decisive battle was not far off. He took the floor on 1st September to speak against the attempts by the enemies of freedom to alter the Constitution in a counter-revolutionary way. "We must forearm ourselves against all the traps that may be laid for us, against all the intrigues that may beset us in this critical passage of the Revolution. We must disconcert all of them by raising, from this moment on, an insurmountable barrier between them and us." At that moment he looked up from his notes and shouted to the Assembly: "If they can still attack our Constitution, what is there left for us to do? Take up once more our weapons and our arms."

After this there was a tumult. Duport, one of the triumvirs, rushed to the rostrum, in a state of great agitation. For some time the former parliamentarian lost all control of himself as a result of his disappointments. Confronted by a calm, cold Robespierre who was supported by the applause of the galleries, he began to shout threats and insults and shake his fist. "Mister President, I beg you to tell Monsieur Dupont not to insult me if he wishes to remain close to me." When silence had been restored, Robespierre turned towards his opponent and crushed him with a long sentence delivered in his dry voice. It was one of his best improvisations: "I do not presume that there is a man in this Assembly who is vile enough to traffic with the Court on one of the articles of the constitutional law, perfidious enough to have new charges proposed by them which shame would not allow him to propose himself, or enough of an enemy of the fatherland to try and discredit the Constitution because it would put a limit to his ambition and his greed, impudent enough to dare to admit before the eyes of the nation that he only sought in the Revolution a means of advancing and aggrandising himself."

Overpowering the jeers from some monarchist deputies at the session, these biting words were greeted by shouts of joy from the galleries who were delighted to see the collapse of the Assembly. They did not realize that they were applauding the fall of the last rampart of the monarchy. As if he had been struck down, Duport did not reply. Neither Barnave nor either of the de Lameths dared speak. The Comte de Montlosier, noted that: "The party, which had been losing credit for some time, was overwhelmed by this speech." In fact, so much so that Duport himself, in a vague hope of reinstating himself, supported Robespierre when he asked his colleagues to swear "that they would never agree to compromise with the executive power on any article of the Constitution".

[[·]]

Robespierre was provided with more opportunities to jolt the triumvirs when the debate on the colonies was reopened. The concessions made in May to the half-castes and freed blacks of San Domingo had not been kept. Alexandre de Lameth was unwise enough to open up the controversy once again by asking that the decree be annulled. When the deputies from Brest demanded that it be applied, he attacked them with misplaced violence. He too had lost his self-control.

Robespierre defended the deputies by counter-attacking: "If, in order to be heard, one has only to talk of personalities, I tell you that those who allow themselves to plant suspicions on the very concept of the matter and on the deputation from Brest, I tell you that it is those men who are betraying the fatherland." There was tremendous applause from the galleries and from one section of the Assembly. Robespierre went on: "I tell you that the traitors to the fatherland are those who seek to have the decree revoked. And if it is necessary in this assembly to attack individuals in order to be heard, I declare that I attack personally Monsieur Barnave and Monsieur Lameth."

Barnave, the young representative from Dauphiné did not lack courage. In the past he had several times matched himself against Mirabeau. His weakness now was that he was struggling against the tide. He tried to defend both himself and his friends, by asking for the strictest and most vigorous examination of all that had taken place. "Honest men must not be deluded by a cabal." Robespierre replied: "Neither must they be taken in by traitors." With these words he won the duel.

[[·]]

The drawing up of the Constitution was coming to an end. For the majority its completion should have been the culmination of the Revolution. Among them was Le Chapelier who put forward a motion on 29th September that all popular

On 14th September 1791 the king was presented with the articles of the Constitution for the first time. Despite his convictions, he accepted them and promised to abide by their conditions

societies should be closed. "We no longer have any need of these clubs because the Revolution is over. It is time to destroy the instrument that has served us so well." Robespierre protested. He said that the arrogance of the counter-revolutionaries made the clubs more necessary than ever so as to watch them and contain them. "When on one hand I see that the new-born Constitution still has enemies within and without; when I see that the words are changed but that the actions are still the same; when I see intrigue and falseness raising alarm, and at the same time causing strife and discord; when I see the leaders of opposing factions fighting less for the cause of the Revolution than to usurp power and rule under the name of monarchy; when I see the extraordinary methods they use to kill public spirit and revive prejudices and idolatry, I do not believe that the Revolution is over." It was therefore up to the citizens to be on the watch in clubs and district assemblies, and since they were giving their time to the fatherland, it was right that they should be paid. "When the representatives of the people and judges and financial administrators are paid; when the head of the executive power is paid twenty-five millions, why should those citizens who are most concerned not be paid when they sacrifice their time and livelihood."

On 30th September for the second time in little over a fortnight the king came to the Assembly to take an oath to the Constitution. It was a curious illusion on the part of the members to think that after all the humiliations to which he had been subjected that he could accept it sincerely. Marie-Antoinette wrote to Mercy-Argenteau: "Tell my brother truly to assure himself that all the apparent steps that we are forced to take are imposed by our situation, but that we do not, and cannot, hold to a constitution which causes the unhappiness and ruin of the kingdom."

The president of the Assembly delivered the traditional speech, congratulating himself on the completion of the work of the Assembly, and Robespierre seated next to Pétion, listened. The king and queen departed to the shouts and applause of the deputies. But the crowd in the galleries and the street kept their shouts for the "twins of the Revolution". "They were carried in triumph. On all sides one could hear people acclaiming the incorruptible Robespierre and the virtuous Pétion. A woman broke through the crowd with her child in her arms, and put it in Robespierre's arms. The woman and the two deputies wept over it. Robespierre and Pétion wanted to avoid the triumph and leave by a roundabout way, but the people followed them. Once again they were surrounded and they were carried along to the sound of instruments and shouts of joy."

And so the National Assembly disappeared like a worn-out object, amidst the indifference of those who had so loudly greeted it at its inception. The left-wing newspapers hurled anathemas at it. The most influential members returned to their provinces where obscurity awaited them—and also, for some of them, a few months later the guillotine. Robespierre prepared himself to carry on his activities with the Jacobins in Paris. Now that they had got rid of the moderates, their numbers were increasing. In one month they had more than a thousand new members. "For us, outside the Legislative Assembly, we will serve our country better than by returning to its bosom. We will enlighten those of our citizens who need light, and we will spread public spirit abroad everywhere."

8

THE DUEL WITH BRISSOT

"Those who are merely half-hearted revolutionaries only dig their own graves."

SAINT-JUST

ONCE HE NO LONGER HAD HIS DUTIES AS A DEPUTY, ROBESPIERRE prepared to make a journey to Arras. He wanted to see his family once more and put his affairs in order. It would also serve as a few weeks of holiday for him. After two years of hard work and nervous tension he badly needed to rest "in the bosom of his family", as he wrote to Charlotte announcing his arrival. The writer in *Le Babillard* describes him as "of pale complexion, deep sunken eyes, a wild and nervous look on his face". At times he had sharp pains.

He did not expect an enthusiastic reception from the citizens of Arras, apart from the small group of Jacobins. Arras was a reactionary town, as Augustin's defeat in the legislative elections had proved. The electors had preferred a young barrister called Densy, who showed counter-revolutionary tendencies.

Robespierre asked Charlotte to keep the news of his arrival a secret, but Augustin, who was proud to be the brother of a famous man, busily spread it around. Robespierre left Paris on 12th October and on the 15th arrived at Bapaume, where Charlotte, Augustin and their friend Madame Buissart had come to meet him. "We clasped him in our arms and tasted the unspeakable pleasure of seeing him again after two years' absence." The inhabitants of the little town did not have Jacobin feelings. They would have greeted the traveller with reserve had it not been for the presence of a battalion of the Parisian National Guard on its way to the frontier, which noisily demonstrated its joy. This gave those who were unenthusiastic pause to think. The executive council of the district and the municipality "although aristocrats", hastened out to greet him, even going so far as to organize an escort of honour to accompany him to Arras, "where an even greater crowd was waiting for him".

As he entered the town, he was met by cheering people. The citizens took the horses away from his coach and wanted to drag it, but Robespierre was against the idea and got down, "for", as he explained to Charlotte, "it is undignified for free people to harness themselves like animals to convey a fellow man". As far as the conservative municipal authorities were concerned, not only did they not put themselves out, but they tried to put a damper on the celebrations. "I no sooner got home than they sent the police lackeys with an order to extinguish the lanterns, which was not punctually obeyed everywhere."

Charlotte tells us that her brother spent only a short time in Arras, and preferred to spend a few days in the surrounding countryside, probably with the Carvin cousins, "there to enjoy the pleasures of rest and meditation". When he returned he visited Dubois de Fosseux. The reunion was hardly warm-hearted. His old friend held anti-revolutionary opinions, and they never saw each other again. On the other hand, a brief visit that he made to Béthune was a triumph. The patriotic inhabitants of the town, on horseback and preceded by a trumpet, "went to meet him, half a league from their doors". They gave a banquet for him, which was concluded by the offering of a civic crown. "The ladies", said *La Chronique de Paris*, "envied the men the honour of giving it to him, and so the men deferred to them. However, his modesty would not permit himself to have his head decorated. He put it over his heart."

Every one of the popular clubs in the town wanted to see him. He also accepted the invitation from the Lille club on 24th November. His pride was satisfied, but, more than that, the trip was politically useful. The proximity of the frontier demonstrated much more clearly to him than in Paris just how vulnerable it was. The men of the National Guard he could see were patriotic to the man, but their discipline was deplorable because of the reluctance and incompetence of the municipal authorities. He doubted their ability to stand fast in the face of an enemy army. He therefore took two decisions. The first was to put national defence (something about which he had hardly troubled himself until then) at the top of his list of priorities, and the second was to oppose with all his might any war until the people were able to defend themselves.

He also realized much more clearly how many people were emigrating. On the way to the frontier the sight of the inns full of nobles leaving France constantly worried him. Finally, the religious problem held his attention. The conflict between those priests who had taken the oath and those who had not was much more obvious in the provinces than it was in Paris, and was frequently violent. The faithful drove out those priests who had taken the oath and considered them intruders. Sometimes both sides used rather unusual methods to rout an opponent. "There has just been a miracle worked here," he wrote in one of his letters to

Duplay, "which is not astonishing, since it was caused by the Calvary at Arras which, as we know, has been responsible for so many more. A priest who had not taken the oath was saying mass in a chapel where the precious relic is situated. Some devout people were waiting for him in the usual manner. In the middle of mass a man threw down two crutches he had brought with him, stretched his legs and walked. He showed the scar still visible on his leg, and the papers which proved that he had had a serious injury. His wife arrived and asked for her husband. She recovered her senses to give thanks to heaven, and proclaim a miracle. All the same, it was decided among the council of the faithful that they would not make a great deal of the matter in the town, but rather in the country. Since then, several peasants have come to burn little candles in front of the Calvary chapel." A friend of Augustin, Abbé Joseph Lebon, a priest of Neuville-Vitasse who had taken the oath, pointed out to him the resourcefulness of the counter-revolutionary movement among the stubborn who would not take the clerical oath. It was not therefore, as he had previously thought, a question of tolerance or philosophical opinion. "I realize how little we in Paris understand the mind of the public and the power of the priests. I am convinced that the latter by their own efforts alone could restore despotism, and that the Court would only have to leave them to it for them to succeed." This letter, printed in *La Chronique de Paris*, alerted Jacobin opinion.

[[·]]

He returned to Paris on 28th November, taking with him a large dog called Brount. The same evening he went to the club. His absence had not affected his popularity. The members cheered his reappearance. "I was welcomed by the public and the club with such cordial tokens of goodwill that they amazed me in spite of all the manifestations of affection to which the people of Paris and the Jacobins had accustomed me."

One piece of news in particular made him happy. His friend the "virtuous" Pétion had just been elected Mayor of Paris to replace Bailly by 6,728 votes to Lafayette's 3,100. Paris had 800,000 inhabitants, of whom 80,000 were active citizens. Nine-tenths of them had thought that there was little point in putting themselves out to elect their most important official. Such a large number of abstentions certainly constituted a disturbing indication of civic mindedness. Robespierre did not seem to take any notice of this. He was only interested in the result. Nor was he in any way jealous. He had been offered the post, but public office held no attraction for him. What he did not know was that a considerable number of royalist votes had contributed to the success of the Jacobin candidate, through the intervention of Marie-Antoinette. She said to a *confident*: "Monsieur de la Fayette does not want to be Mayor of Paris only to become, a little later, mayor of the palace. Pétion is a Jacobin, a republican, but a fool, incapable of ever becoming a party leader."

As soon as the meeting at the Jacobins was over, Robespierre went to see the new mayor to congratulate him. "How happy we were to see one another again. How delighted we were to greet each other. Pétion lives in the superb house that the Crosnes and the Lenoirs occupied, but his spirit is still simple and pure. This choice alone would be sufficient to justify the Revolution. He has been given an immense burden, but I have no doubt that the affection of the people and his qualities will give him the necessary means to carry it. I am dining at his house tonight. These are the only occasions when we can see each other as a family and talk freely."

He was also happy about the composition of the new legislative body. He wrote to Buissart: "I find that the present National Assembly has great resources and I look upon it—contrary to the opinion of everyone else—as superior to the preceding one." This Assembly was the outcome of the elections held in the atmosphere of crisis generated by the flight to Varennes, and was markedly more left-wing. There was not one monarchist in it. The former Feuillants, of whom the most notorious was Théodore de Lameth, the young brother of Charles and Alexandre, represented the right in this Assembly. There was a fair number of independents in the centre who would have been able to dominate the Assembly had they not been divided and without a programme. There was not one reputation or talent that stood out from the crowd. It was doubtless with the independents in mind that Comte de la Mark wrote: "Three-quarters of the deputies are of no account." The small group of left-wing deputies, on the contrary, was made up of people of brilliant qualities. The leaders were Vergniaud, Gensonné, and Guadet, representing the Gironde, and Brissot and Condorcet, representing Paris. All Robespiere's hopes rested on them. For their part, their papers, *La Chronique de Paris* and *Le Patriote français*, never tired of praising him. There was also a newcomer, whom he had just met, and whom he admired from the start: a lawyer from Auvergne called Couthon, a man of pure principle and gifted with great energy. He made a mark for himself at the first session by proposing that they stop addressing the king as Sire or Majesty.

[[·]]

When Robespiere had accepted the hospitality of the joiner Duplay on the evening of 17th July he had thought that it would only be for a night or two. But he was immediately delighted in the midst of such good people, and stayed on. He kept on his rooms in the rue Saintonge for a month until he had made up his mind. He went there to pick up his letters, but any visitors who went to call on him would not find him there. After a while, giving in to the entreaties of his new friends, he agreed to settle permanently with them.

In his eyes the Duplays were the image of a virtuous and united family, just as he hoped every French family to be. They might almost have stepped out of one

398, rue Saint-Honoré, Robespierre's home.

of Rousseau's works. Maurice, the father, was fifty and proud of his title of master joiner. He was the son of a carpenter from Vézelay and had come to Paris while still young. Through hard work and care he had built up a reasonable fortune, which put him between the artisans and the middle classes. According to Jean-Jacques Rousseau, this was the most interesting category of the social structure. Duplay rented the house in Paris in the rue Saint-Honoré, but he owned several houses in the city which brought in money. He was a good husband, a good father, and no less a good Jacobin. Ever since the club was founded he had attended meetings regularly. He often took his wife there. Later the youngest daughter said of her mother: "My mother was very good but very strict."

The Duplays had five children, four girls and a boy, who created an enjoyable atmosphere. Robespierre was always serious himself, so in order to live he needed to be surrounded by happy people. The oldest girl, Sophie, was by now married and no longer lived at home. The other three were: Eléonore, then twenty-four years old, Victoire and Elisabeth (known as Betsy), who was the youngest and prettiest. She later married Philippe Le Bas. Jean-Maurice, the last child, was a schoolboy of thirteen. The last member of the household was a nephew, Simon Duplay, an orphan whom his uncle had adopted as his own. When war broke out Simon enlisted and returned from Valmy with a wooden leg. At times he acted as a secretary for Robespierre.

Robespierre's hosts admired him greatly and were affectionately prepossessing towards him which he very much appreciated. He was, according to Charlotte, "extremely sensitive to all this kind of thing. My aunts and I would have spoiled him with a host of little attentions that only women are capable of." There were four women round him at the Duplays. If, as often happened, he fell ill, they provided all the necessary treatment. There would be no more meals at the restaurant, either, for they were disastrous for his delicate stomach. We may picture him in the dining-room as his visitors sometimes saw him, "well combed and powdered, dressed in a spotless dressing gown, installed in a large chair in·front of a table laden with fine fruit, fresh butter, pure milk and fragrant coffee. The entire family— father, mother and children—tried to detect in his eyes all his wishes, so as to anticipate them immediately." He was always the person to say grace, we are told. He would not have liked to live with a family that neither respected nor mentioned the name of God. Another eyewitness, the banker Ouvrard, who had called on him in connection with business, recalled: "I found him beside two young ladies, breakfasting with coffee. He received me very well and invited me to share his breakfast."

They had given him a room on the first floor, which Elisabeth described in her diary: "It had only one casement window and one fireplace. The furniture was the simplest in the world. There was a walnut wood bed, with curtains which were made of bluc damask that had come from one of my mother's dresses. There was a very modest writing desk, a few straw-seated chairs, and also a set of pigeon holes that acted as bookshelves. The only window looked out on to the sheds."

Such lodgings would scarcely have satisfied his colleagues in the Constituent Assembly, or later those of the Convention. Even those of humble origin rapidly accustomed themselves to luxury. Now that he was master of France, the idea never occurred to Robespierre to change. As he himself wrote: "Little is sufficient for the man who has no desires." The inadequacies of the furniture were compensated for, it is true, by the flattery he received—"Homage," said one visitor, Larevellière- Lépeaux, "such as is only offered to a divinity." Another visitor, Barbaroux, has left this picture of the little study set aside for Robespierre to receive visitors: "It was quite a pretty boudoir, where his picture was repeated in all manner and forms in all the arts. He was painted on the right-hand wall, engraved on the left. His bust was at the back, and on a bas-relief opposite. There were in addition, on the tables, half a dozen Robespierres in little engravings."

Elisabeth said: "It was with pleasure that our mother watched our interest in Robespierre." He treated the girls as if he were an affectionate older brother and they confided in him. "Little Elisabeth, think of me as your best friend. I will give you all the advice a person needs at your age." "One day," Elisabeth relates, "when Robespierre was out of the house, Camille Desmoulins came and asked for him. He was carrying a book under his arm, and as he was leaving he asked me to keep it for him. When he had gone I was curious and glanced at the book. It was an Aretino, illustrated with engravings of a kind I had never seen before. When Robespierre came home that evening, he noticed that I was upset as I told him about Desmoulins's visit. He questioned me, and when he heard what I had done he said, 'Forget it. It is not what the eyes inadvertently see that sullies innocence, but the evil thoughts that one has in one's heart.'" On another occasion, when she admitted to him that she did not believe in God, he said: "You are very wrong. You will be unhappy if you do not believe in Him. You are still very young, Elisabeth. Think well upon it, for it is the only consolation on earth."

As for Eléonore, he said that she had a "Roman soul". It was commonly said that she was his fiancée, and the maliciously inclined said that she was his mistress. Charlotte, who was jealous of her brother's attachment to the Duplays, denied that he loved her. Elisabeth Le Bas, however, maintained that her sister was "promised to Robespierre". Doctor Souberbielle was guarantor of their engagement and the purity of their relationship: "As one who habitually ate at the table of this household, to which I was doctor, I swear that it was a slander. They loved each other a great deal, they were engaged to be married, but nothing immodest passed between them." Her portrait shows a plump healthy girl with dark hair and heavy features—a plain girl but not without some attraction. The most important thing for Robespierre was doubtless the fact that she shared his patriotic sentiments. But if they looked upon themselves as engaged—it is reported that one day they came into the dining-room hand in hand, which indicated that they were engaged—they agreed to put off their marriage till calmer days. "Overwhelmed with business and work as my brother was, and entirely taken up with his career how could he concern himself with love and marriage?"

When the evenings were fine, after the Jacobin meetings, Robespierre went with the girls for a walk in the Champs-Elysées. "Usually we chose the remotest spots. So we spent some happy times together. We would often watch the Savoyard children. Bon-Ami (this is what they called Robespierre) liked to see them dance and would give them money. He had a dog called Brount of whom he was very fond. The poor animal was very attached to him."

On other evenings the Duplay family assembled with a few friends, such as the painter David and the writer Buonaroti, and they made music. Sometimes Robespierre would read verses from a tragedy by Racine, or a few pages of Rousseau. "Whatever he read he invariably stirred our emotions," said Madame Le Bas. These gatherings never lasted after 11 p.m. He would then go to his room to work on his next speech. The first glimmerings of dawn often found him at his desk.

Like many of his colleagues, Brissot embraced the revolution to obscure his dubious past

[[·]]

Meanwhile the talk all around, both in the Assembly and at the club, was war. The rage for war, aroused in Paris while Robespierre was away, was everywhere. Brissot the deputy-journalist, a patriot with a solidly established reputation, extolled its necessity. The Jacobins heard him and followed.

He was a rather undistinguished individual, small and thin, with features as craggy as those of Robespierre. He wore his black hair long and unpowdered. His clothes were black, too, and visibly threadbare, giving him the look of a Quaker. It was hard to explain why he was so poor, since he moved in financial circles, and did not disdain making deals when the occasion arose, even if of a questionable honesty. His suspicious past as an opportunist was hardly a recommendation. In his youth he had lived from hand to mouth, was somewhat fraudulent and speculative and an informant in the pay of the police. He had a diploma in law from the University of Rheims—which were often to be bought. The Revolution seemed to him a way of getting out of his indifferent position, so he rushed into it as a journalist, editing *Le Patriote français*, and then got himself elected to the Legislative Assembly. He was consumed with ambition, and had a brilliant but superficial intelligence. He was imaginative, energetic, and very enterprising.

His reasons for pressing for war were various, offering a curious mixture of personal and patriotic motives. He deplored the drop in enthusiasm for the Revolution, to which the large number of abstentions in the various elections bore witness. Previously everyone had been keen to take part in the elections to the States-General. He saw war as the best way to rekindle this enthusiasm. In addition, victory would increase the value of the *assignats*, which was melting away.

"Soon confidence is reborn in the empire, credit is re-established, money regains its balance, our *assignats* flood Europe, and thus interest our neighbours in the success of the Revolution, which henceforth has no redoubtable enemies." War, bursting forth like a theatrical trick, and propagating the rights of man afar, would reveal to the world the name of Brissot, its architect. He wrote to Dumouriez "Who is Richelieu, who is Albéroni, and what are the projects that are so praised, when compared to the universal revolution which it has been given to us to unleash?"

A few months previously, revolutionary France had solemnly declared peace to the world, and now no danger threatened her. Even after Avignon had been annexed, no foreign nation showed hostile intentions towards France. Generally the opposite was true, and the Revolution was looked upon with sympathy, especially in England, where it was seen as a movement destined to make France as liberal a state as England. Emperor Leopold wrote: "There is no sovereign in the universe who has the right to take a nation to task for the constitution it has given itself. If it is good, so much the better. If it is bad, the country's neighbours will benefit." As far as he himself was concerned, he thought that it was bad, and was glad. Far from thinking of opposing it, he thought that France would be weakened in the years to come. Austria, Prussia and Russia would then be the more able to carve up Poland, a project they were even then considering. Since the Revolution served their interests, they had no reason to oppose it. If they intervened, it would not be to put an end to disorder, but rather to increase it. There were numerous foreign agents in Paris, some with orders to foster movements, others to obtain for their countries the friendship of the new leaders. Louis XVI and Marie-Antoinette could call on the solidarity of other monarchs, who certainly disapproved of the treatment they were receiving, but had no intention whatsoever of taking up arms to support them.

Brissot and his friends advanced as a reason for the war the concentrations of émigrés at Koblenz, Mainz and Turin—some 20,000 people in all, whom they denounced as offensive and dangerous for France and the Revolution. The Comte de Provence had proclaimed himself regent "during his brother's captivity", and in Worms the Prince de Condé was busy forming a small army.

They hoped that the hostilities begun against the elector, on whose territory the émigrés were gathered, would soon extend to neighbouring countries. Since this would be a war waged against kings and not peoples, there could be no question about victory. They maintained that the people, far from fighting against them, would rise up and help them as would God Himself—why not? Carra, the journalist, wrote: "The tyrants will have slaves armed with sabres and guns, and we will have free men armed with pikes and scythes. They will have the thunder of their many guns, and we will have the fire of heaven, for have no doubt but that heaven will fight for us." "War, war," shouted Bishop Le Coz, a deputy. "This is the cry that assails my ears from all parts of the empire." There was one exception to this warlike zeal of the revolutionaries, and that was Marat. He pointed out that the émigrés could not hope for help from the great powers, they represented no danger, and so there was no reason for tormenting oneself about them.

[[·]]

Such was the atmosphere at the Jacobins when Robespierre returned to Paris. On the very day that he reappeared he heard Dubois-Crancé read from the rostrum a proposal for a decree to be put before the Assembly, asking the king to disperse the gathering mobilization of émigrés on the frontiers. The speakers who followed all voiced the same opinion. Robespierre must have found himself taken unawares by these speeches. He knew what the state of the French Army was, and it seemed to him that war could only be a dangerous adventure. All the same, either he decided not to provoke an impromptu head-on collision with the prevailing consensus, or else he had not organized all his arguments. When it was his turn to speak he did not oppose the motion. The people listening might even have thought he approved of it. There were two points in his speech. He criticized the form of the motion and pointed out that the Assembly should not "ask the king" to act but should tell him what he was to do. Instead of threatening such insignificant people as the electors of Mainz, Trier and Köln, they should deliver an ultimatum to the emperor himself. They should say to Leopold: "You are violating the rights of a free people in allowing the assembly of a few rebels whom we fear not in the least, but who insult our country. We call upon you to disperse them by a certain date, or we will declare war on you in the name of the French people, and of all nations who are the enemies of tyrants."

By naming the emperor as the enemy—in other words, the whole of Germany— Robespierre possibly wanted to force the people who wanted war to reflect what a difficult task it would be. Ten days went by before he spoke on the subject again. What he saw and heard in this interval was more than enough to disturb him.

At the Jacobin Club the most admired speakers—Carra, Réal and Roederer— between them continued to increase the pitch of their warlike speeches. They talked only of "forcing the king to put his armies into the field". Brissot and his friends spoke enthusiastically about "the crusade for freedom". Yet France was still in a state of turmoil and from an internal point of view the Revolution was still not yet secure. Robespierre saw it as: "The folly of a person who was running to put out the fire in a neighbour's house whilst his own house was ablaze." In addition, the Court, the king, Lafayette and the Feuillants also wanted war. On the right only de Lameth's little group of friends was against it, realizing that it would either cause a reaction or increase the power of the extremists. As far as Robespierre could see, all those people simply wanted to use the war as a means of fighting the Revolution. He was not mistaken. At that very moment Louis XVI was writing to Breteuil: "Instead of being a civil war, this will be a political war, and things will be very much better as a result. The physical and moral state of France make it impossible to support a war during a semi-campaign. I must have the room to devote myself to it, as I would have done in former times. My conduct must be such that in the nation's misfortune the only possible course of action open to us is the one throwing itself into my arms."

Louis XVI had good reason to be satisfied. In starting the war the revolutionaries were doing him the service of forcing the other monarchs to give him the help he had vainly sought from them. If by chance the emperor refused, in spite of everything, to enter into the conflict, and the princelings of the Rhine showed themselves incapable of sustaining the shock of the French Army—even a weakened army— victory would give him renewed popularity and the chance to make a show of strength. This was the plan of the war minister, the young Comte de Narbonne, who was counting on making a name for himself with a few easy successes. All the same, was one to think that the emperor would allow his vassals to be crushed? Sooner or later he would intervene with force. A delighted Marie-Antoinette wrote to Mercy-Argenteau: "The fools, they can't see that they are serving our interests. For if we start, all the powers will have to be involved in the end." It did not escape Robespierre's attention that the king had refused to sanction the decree on emigration. Therefore it was not against emigration that he wanted to fight. The Court was setting a trap for the patriots.

The patriots, however, rejoiced more and more in their visions of victory. Brissot wrote in *Le Patriote français*: "One can already imagine the tricolour hoisted on the palaces of emperors, sultans, popes and kings." Couthon himself wrote in a letter: "The majority is for war. Possibly the Revolution needs the war to consolidate itself." He added: "I think that this is what is best." On 9th December, from the rostrum of the Jacobin Club, Carra accused Louis XVI of intrigue with Leopold to strengthen his throne. Amidst a thunder of applause he demanded the mobilization of the nation's entire forces and an immediate declaration of war against the emperor. Then, to the surprise of everyone, Robespierre spoke. He said he doubted that the emperor was getting ready to support his brother-in-law's cause with arms. In Robespierre's opinion the foreign powers: "Had more the intention of frightening us than attacking us". One had to be wary of "succumbing too confidently to this imagined coalition." He greatly feared, on the contrary, the consequences of a declaration of war, which would put the armed forces of the nation in the hands of the king, the Court and aristocratic generals, and would leave Paris at the mercy of all the counter-revolutionaries.

[[·]]

Meanwhile, the Court busied itself putting into effect the plan which had so innocently been provided by Brissot and his friends. On 14th December Louis XVI appeared before the Assembly accompanied by de Narbonne. He announced that an ultimatum had been sent to the elector of Trier to disperse the groups of émigrés in his country. If he refused "he [Louis] would have nothing other to do than propose war". After the king departed, the minister informed the Assembly of the state of the French Army. Within a month France would have 150,000 men on the frontiers, in three armies, commanded respectively by Lafayette, Lückner and Rochambeau. The Assembly applauded his martial declaration. The condition of success was obviously that the elector should not submit. Of course there was always a possibility that he would take advantage of the opportunity to get rid of the émigrés who were such an embarrassment. Through Breteuil the king asked the emperor to advise the elector to reject the ultimatum.

[[·]]

The king's initiative had the immediate result of renewing his popularity. This was assumed as an indication that he had taken sides with the Revolution. That same evening a man called Biauzat affirmed his belief in his good faith. Consequently the club should stop debating the question of the war. Robespierre took this as one of the Court's counter-revolutionary intrigues in an attempt to stop him speaking. He vigorously opposed it. "I will discuss the question of peace and war as my conscience dictates, because freedom is the dominant passion of my life."

He was to struggle, almost alone, throughout the succeeding weeks, against the club's best speakers. Brissot opened fire on 16th December to a packed session of the club. "Which of us, sirs," he began, "would not be indignant that these rebels and their protector should be allowed to breathe for so long?" Now that the government showed itself ready to act, it seemed surprising to him to hear some people proposing to "hang up the sword". Yet the situation had not changed. What had altered was the attitude of the Court, and this change disturbed him. Certainly he did not deny that it was only natural that the actions of the Court should give rise to suspicions. He shared them himself, up to a certain point. But that was exactly why they had to destroy the very cause of these doubts, and the reason lay in Koblenz. "Where do our aristocrats get their insolence from? They believe in the army of Koblenz. Where does the opinionated fanaticism of our dissidents come from? They call upon, they pay, the army of Koblenz. Finally, what is the origin of the domination of our moderates and intriguers, who want to dominate and do dominate everywhere? From the fear that Koblenz instills. Do you wish to destroy at one single blow aristocrats, malcontents and dissident priests? Destroy Koblenz. Once Koblenz has been destroyed, all will be calm within and all will be calm without." Robespierre feared that the leaders would turn traitor. Brissot brushed aside his objection. "In a free country they cannot possibly turn traitor," a thousand pairs of eyes were on them, and death dogged their steps. Another objection was the suspect attitude of the executive power. Robespierre wondered how anyone could commit the defence of the Revolution to elements which, by their very nature, were hostile to it. Brissot replied that this was exactly why war would provide an excellent and conclusive test for them. If one of them turned traitor, "the fatherland will soon pass judgement on him".

Truth to tell, Brissot's speech abounded in curious contradictions. For example, having just denounced the intrigues of Vienna and Berlin, he admitted that neither capital wanted war. This was a surprising conclusion, and yet another reason for declaring war on them. "I say that so as to unmask those who do not want war and yet pretend to want it, we must have war." It was agreed that Robespierre would reply at the next session, on 18th December. There was a crowded programme that day, including the reception of an English delegation, and the delivery by a deaf-mute sculptor of busts of Pétion and Robespierre. After this a sword of honour, the gift of a Swiss citizen, was presented to Deputy Isnard, who was in the chair. He brandished it above his head in a theatrical gesture. "Here it is, gentlemen, this sword which will ever be victorious. The French people will utter a great shout and all the other peoples will reply. The earth will be covered with fighting men and all the enemies of freedom will be struck off the roll of free men." He was going to carry on in the same manner when Robespierre's dry voice interrupted him. "We are busy discussing a matter of great importance. I beg the Assembly to stop these eloquent motions which might lead opinion on at a time when it ought to be controlled by the calmest possible discussion."

The first speaker on the list was Roederer, who spent an hour delivering an inflamed harangue for war. It was truly a clarion call. "We must sound the attack. Those who hesitate are our enemies." His call inspired such warlike enthusiasm in his listeners that to have opposed it head-on would have achieved nothing. Therefore Robespierre, who followed him, began very cleverly with a concession to the mood. "I am just as much for the war as anyone else, but it must be a war that the nation really needs; a war in which we will crush our enemies at home; then we will march against our enemies abroad, if any still exist; but the nation must reject any idea of war that is proposed in order to annihilate freedom and the Constitution under the pretext of defending them."

He saw clearly an alliance against these ideals consisting of the Court, the ministers and the aristocrats, the very people to whom Brissot proposed giving command of the Army. "Patriotic legislator, to whom I now reply, what precautions do you propose to prevent these dangers, and to confront this alliance? None." Brissot did not distrust enough, which he described as "a shocking state of affairs". "Patriotic legislator, do not slander distrust. Whatever you say, distrust is the guardian of the people's rights. It is to the passion of freedom what jealousy is to love."

Brissot had given as his principal reason for not fearing betrayal the fact that "the people were there". Was he therefore making an appeal for insurrection, asked Robespierre. Insurrection only rarely constituted a remedy, and one that was uncertain and extreme. In order for it to succeed there had to be a combination of circumstances that was extremely rare. Since the people had representatives, the business of mounting guard fell to them, and not to it. "Are you not there, too, representatives? What are you doing if, instead of foreseeing and confounding the plans of the oppressors you can only abandon the people to the right of insurrection? Before running to Koblenz, put yourself into a position of being able to make war. The seat of the trouble is not at Koblenz, it is in the midst of us, it is in our bosom. Before anything else, we must make the tools of war immediately. We must arm the National Guard and the people, even if it is only with pikes. We must adopt new and more severe measures against ministers whose negligence endangers the security of the state. We must support the dignity of the people and defend its rights, which are all too frequently neglected."

The distrust that he felt, he said, "was the fruit of three years' experience of perfidy and intrigue". In fact, it came from his temperament, and his political activities had only heightened it. Up to a point he succeeded in making his listeners understand it. There was no longer any doubt in the minds of the Jacobins that the Court was busy in treason, and some even began to suspect Brissot of personal motivation. But on the question of the war itself, he had not convinced them. The glory and the advantages of it seemed to them greater than the dangers.

[[·]]

Brissot spoke again at the Jacobins on 30th December. His speech was full of characteristic sparks, but sadly superficial in its argument. He developed the idea that great betrayals are always fatal for the traitors. If Louis XVI, therefore, intended treason, the war would discredit him and bring about his downfall. With a certain amount of perfidy, Brissot accused Robespierre "of having degraded the French people by comparing them to a nation groaning in slavery. Who has not been shocked to see a defender of the people speak against the cruel catastrophe of the month of July?" In concluding he made a few ambiguous statements about riots: "Since this time we have seen as our leaders the Pétions, the Roederers, the Robespierres and that ingenious Desmoulins, who has exhausted all his spirit and all his learning to support the arguments of the aristocrats. If they are leading us now, it is in place of the people who used to be there."

Robespierre replied on the 2nd and 11th January. Some of Brissot's remarks had hurt him, and his tone was therefore more bitter. To begin with he protested about the title "defender of the people". "First of all, know that I am not the defender of the people. I have never aspired to this glorious title, I am of the people, I have never been anything but that, and I never want to be anything but that. I despise whoever has the pretension to be anything more than that." Of course, unlike some, he did not know how to flatter the people "so as to confound them", but the actual evidence of his respect for the nation was to arm it against its own faults, for even the people had faults.

The substance of Robespierre's speech was a reiteration of his previous one, namely, that it was dangerous to entrust the defence of the Revolution to its natural enemies, the Court generals. "At least come forward National Guards, you who are specially devoted to the defence of our frontiers. What? Are you still unarmed? What? You have been asking for arms for two years and you still have not been given them? What can I be saying? You have been refused uniforms, you have been condemned to wander from place to place, despised by ministers, mocked by insolent patricians who review you to enjoy your distress. That does not matter— we will melt down our fortunes in order to buy arms, we will fight naked, as the Americans do. Shall we wait to overturn the thrones of the despots of Europe? Shall we wait for the orders of the ministry of war? Shall we take counsel for this noble enterprise from the genie of freedom or from the mind of the Court? Shall we be guided by these same patriots, the eternal favourites, in a war declared in our midst between the nobility and the people? Let us march ourselves to Leopold. Let us only take counsel with ourselves alone. What! Here are the warmongers stopping me. Here is Monsieur Brissot telling me that Monsieur le Comte de Narbonne must direct the affair, that we have to march under the orders of Monsieur le Marquis de la Fayette, that it is for the executive power to lead the nation to victory and freedom. Ah! Frenchmen! That one word breaks the spell."

One passage in particular in Brissot's speech was to be the object of Robespierre's sarcasm. "Your generals," he had said, "are to be missionaries of the Constitution." No one, retorted Robespierre, likes armed missionaries. "Never has a more extravagant idea sprung from the head of a politician than to imagine that one people has only to enter another's territory, with arms in its hands, to make the latter adopt its laws and its constitution." Before the influence of the French Revolution could be felt abroad, it must be well and truly established at home. "To expect to bring freedom to foreign nations before having achieved it ourselves is a certain path to slavery, both for France and for the world. The Declaration of Rights is not like the sun's rays, which in a moment light up the whole world. It is not a thunderbolt to topple a thousand thrones. It is easier to inscribe it on paper or to engrave it on bronze than it is to write it out character by character in the hearts of men."

From the applause that the Jacobins gave to this speech, Brissot realized that he was not equal to the task of replying to Robespierre. He was a threat to his ambitions and resolved to bring him down by other means. At once a campaign of insinuation against the Incorruptible was mounted in the Brissot press. Robespierre opposed the war because he was in the pay of the Court. There was talk of collusion between him and the Austrian party and even of an interview between him and Marie-Antoinette at the Princesse de Lamballe's.

At the Jacobins he was going to make his friends plunge into realms other than that of war. At the same time, to keep up the deception, Brissot indulged in a hypocritical little farce of reconciliation. He said that he deplored "the attacks on the purity of his soul which spoilt Monsieur Robespierre's speeches". If he had made a mistake, it was in good faith, "out of human weakness". He urged Robespierre to put an end to their quarrel that was "scandalous and fatal for freedom", and which could only help the counter-revolutionaries.

Most Jacobins wanted nothing more than to restore good faith among the members of the club. One old member, Dussault, who was respected by everyone because he had been a friend of Rousseau, got up and called on the two men to be reconciled by a fraternal kiss, which was at once performed amidst cheers. Although Robespierre had given Brissot a kiss, he deemed it necessary to state immediately afterwards that his gesture in no way signified that he had given up fighting against Brissot's opinions whenever they were against his principles. "I have just fulfilled a brotherly duty and satisfied my heart. I still have a debt that is more sacred to pay to the fatherland."

This precaution was by no means superfluous. The very next day *Le Patriote français*, in describing the scene, let it be understood that Robespierre was giving up his opposition to the war. He had, said the newspaper, "invited the assembly to concern itself further with the question of the war so as to consider the measure necessary to assure success in battle, and made one hope that Monsieur Brissot and he would easily agree on this point".

[[·]]

Towards mid-January Robespierre was visited by a curious character who was stocky, broad in the shoulders and bow-legged. He had a steep, low brow, a broad aquiline nose and a pale complexion. He was carelessly dressed, untidy, with a dirty scarf tied round his head. It was Marat. The editor of *L'Ami du peuple* had a unique position in the Revolution. His mother was from Geneva and his father was an Italian of Spanish origin. He was born at Boudry in the principality of Neuchâtel, whose sovereign was the King of Prussia. Thus North-Swiss by nationality, and having failed to become a British citizen, he finally settled in France. First he practised medicine, in the service of the Comte d'Artois, and in his spare time he studied scientific problems. In particular, he was concerned with disproving Newton's theories. Then, like so many others, he launched himself into the Revolution. Unlike them, however, he never tried to form a party for himself or have followers. In his isolation he flattered himself with the saying that "geese go in flocks". The vehement denunciations he made recalled the curses of the Old Testament prophets. In Marat's eyes none of the revolutionaries had anything to recommend him except for Robespierre, whom he never attacked. He loved the people, but at the same time he thought they were stupid and incapable of knowing where the best course lay. Consequently, he wanted a dictatorship set up. In spite of the fact that he obviously thought himself the most suitable person for the post, he would not have been displeased if Robespierre had assumed it, so great was his regard for him.

Until the winter of 1792 the two men had had no dealings whatsoever. Robespierre had mixed feelings about him and avoided him. He who was always so correctly dressed, was repelled by the negligent dress of the journalist. His incitements to murder disturbed him, since they might bring the Revolution into disrepute. All the same, their ideas frequently coincided. Marat had even on occasions anticipated Robespierre in his denunciations. On the matter of the war they thought alike.

The conversation turned around public matters, about which Marat spoke in despair. It seemed to him that the Revolution was in danger. He had come to see Robespierre to talk to him about the ways of saving it. "You are the man," he told him, "whom I respect most in the world, but I would respect you even more if you were less moderate as far as the aristocrats are concerned." Robespierre replied: "I make the opposite reproach against you. You compromise the Revolution. You make yourself hated by demanding heads. The scaffold is a terrible expedient, and always fatal. It must be used soberly and only in those serious cases where the country is headed for ruin. Your constant calls to violence destroy the salutary effect that your paper used to exert."

All the same, so as to make his reproaches less severe, Robespierre suggested that inwardly Marat doubtless repudiated these exaggerations which discredited

'Poor Marat was the victim of toppled tyrants
But glorious Marat led them to their graves'

his principles. Marat burst forth: "My credit with the people comes not from my ideas but from my daring, the impetuous outbursts of my spirit, my shouts of anger, despair and fury. Yes, if I had had the people's arm to guide after the decree against the garrison of Nancy, I would have decimated the deputies who passed it. After the decision on the events of 5th and 6th October, I would have had all the judges burnt at the stake. After the massacre on the Champ-de-Mars, if I had had two thousand men with the same feelings as I had, I would have marched at their head and stabbed Lafayette in the midst of his battalions of brigands, burnt the king in his palace and butchered our atrocious representatives in their seats."

Robespierre was frozen with terror. He turned pale. The little man opposite him only filled him with horror. He said nothing for a moment and then broke his silence only to tell Marat that he did not agree with him. "You do not understand me," replied Marat. With three words Robespierre terminated the interview: "That is possible." Marat left. He retained all his respect for Robespierre—that of a wise senator—but at the same time regretted the fact that he had neither the daring nor the capabilities of a statesman.

[[·]]

On 25th January the Assembly passed a vote on an ultimatum to the emperor, to which he was to reply before 1st March, "if he intended to live in peace and good understanding with the French nation". Silence or a reply in the negative would be regarded as a declaration of war. That evening at the Jacobins, Robespierre took up once again the arguments of his previous speeches against the war, amplifying some and compressing others. Once again he voiced his doubts about the nature of the intentions of the king, the ministers and the aristocratic generals. He stressed the country's lack of preparation and ended with a very sombre allegorical picture of the future. "I see a crowd of people dancing in an open plain, covered with grass and flowers, waving their arms about and filling the air with shouts of joy and songs of war. Suddenly the ground caves in under their feet; flowers, men and weapons disappear. I only see an open gulf, full of victims. Flee, flee, whilst there is still time; before the ground on which you stand collapses under its covering of flowers."

After this he made known his intention of making another speech at the next session on the same subject. In spite of their admiration for him, the club began to be somewhat tired of the discussion, which was going round in circles and getting nowhere. One of the members, Lasource, protested, pointing out that one of the aims of the club was to look at the questions on the agenda of the Legislative Assembly, and therefore they should consider the payment of taxes. But Robespierre stuck to his guns. One could rely on the "lights and experience of the patriots of the legislative body", to talk about taxes. It was for the Jacobins to discuss "deeper questions, which are for all times and all occasions, and directly concern society". Rather oddly he maintained that the problem of the war "had never been sufficiently illuminated, nor sufficiently developed". This was a difficult claim to support after two months of discussion, and therefore when Lasource's motion was put to the vote, it was carried.

This defeat mortified Robespierre, who was not used to such a thing, and so he did not speak for a fortnight. Even so, during this time the Jacobins did not go without references to the war. In the absence of Robespierre, Billaud-Varenne delivered a long and weighty harangue. Be that as it may, Robespierre took the floor again on 10th February with a speech "on the means of saving the State and freedom".

There were four propositions. The first concerned the Army, which had to be purged by the expulsion of the aristocratic officers. Soldiers such as the "heroes" of Châteauvieux, who had been expelled for indiscipline, ought to reinstated, or better still formed into special legions "who would be the people's sweetest hope and the staunchest rampart of freedom".

The second point was the security of Paris. Patriotic legions were to be kept in the capital instead of allowing them to be sent far afield under the pretence of defending the frontiers. There was an aristocrat plot intended to deprive Paris of its defenders. The permanence of the Sections had to be ensured also, to watch over the public spirit, "as in the finest days of the Revolution".

Under the third point he looked at the ways of ensuring the union of Paris and of the rest of France. To do so he put forward the idea of a new civil and fraternal confederation of all the national guards in the kingdom, a repeat of the Festival of the Federation, in which the representatives of the *départements* would come and repledge their oath of "Freedom or Death".

The fourth and last point was to enumerate the ways of awakening public spirit, by tearing the people away from their growing indifference to the Revolution, which Robespierre described as "political death". These means—"great and simple measures"—consisted of organizing national festivals, games, on the lines of the sublime institutions of the peoples of Greece, in which artists and poets "received, in front of the most magnanimous of all people, the prize for their talents and their service, crowned by the hands of their old men, or, which is perhaps better, by the hands of beauty". The theatre could also become a school of civic virtue, by staging "the prodigious men of freedom, such as Brutus, William Tell and the Gracchis".

For a moment, nevertheless, one might have thought that the war which Robespierre so feared would not take place. Emperor Leopold died on 10th March 1792. His son, Francis II, was believed to be better disposed towards the Revolution. In fact, he was much more hostile to it, dreaming of conquests and glory. He replied to the Assembly's ultimatum by demanding the return of Avignon to the papacy and guarantees for the princes in possession of Alsace.

Momentarily, however, Robespierre shared the general illusions about the peaceful intentions of the new emperor. He spoke at the Jacobins on 26th March, and pointed out that Providence, in striking down Leopold, had intervened to the advantage of France more usefully than the wisdom of statesmen. The word Providence was rarely mentioned at the club, where atheists were in the majority. Coming from Robespierre it had even more effect, and some of his supporters were incredulous and amazed. A friend of Brissot, the Girondin deputy Guadet, thought that it was a good opportunity to teach him a lesson in public, and as a result his prestige would be diminished. He asked indignantly: "How could the Incorruptible conspire to put the people under the slavery of superstition once more?" Robespierre, as a disciple of Rousseau, hated atheists, and regarded them as immoral, aristocratic people. He replied with a vibrant testimony of faith in the Divinity. "There is nothing superstitious in using the word Providence. I personally believe in the eternal principles on which human weakness is based before beginning its search for power."

Thereupon the club fell into an uproar and cries of "Order" were heard on all sides. The cries came more from his friends than his enemies, for they wanted to have him silenced in case he compromised himself. But Robespierre was not the sort of man to buy popularity at the price of denying his convictions. Without worrying about the protests round about him, he demanded silence: "No, Sirs, you will not stifle my voice. There is no point of order that can stifle this truth." There was silence. He then proceeded to deliver a tirade, on that occasion an improvised one, setting out his reasons for believing in a God who protected the feeble and the oppressed. "How could I have continued to do work that is beyond human strength, if I had not lifted up my soul?" Not only did this God sustain and comfort him, but better still he watched with solicitude over the future of the nation. "Of course, I recognize the fact that the French people have played their part in the Revolution. Without them we would still be under the yoke of despotism. But when I saw so many enemies created against the people, so many faithless men, employed to overthrow the work of the people, when I saw that the people themselves could not act and that they were forced to abandon themselves to faithless men, then more than ever I believed in Providence."

[[·]]

The criminal tribunal of Paris, to which Robespierre had been elected public prosecutor, finally organized itself, after a rather long delay. To the general amazement, on the day before it was due to open, Robespierre sent in his resignation. People were even more astonished because some time previously, at the Jacobins, he had described at some length how he intended to carry out his task. He explained: "I abdicated rather in the way that one throws away a shield so as to fight more easily against the enemies of the public good. I abandoned it and I deserted it as one deserts the trenches to go in through the breach." That meant that he could only have carried out his duties as public prosecutor to the detriment of another role which for him had come to take first place in his list of priorities, that as guide of public opinion. Even so, his supporters regretted the fact that his resignation made possible the election of a notorious Feuillant as his successor, Duport-Dutertre. He could not be relied on to suppress counter-revolutionary intrigues. The Brissotin press naturally did not avoid the opportunity of criticizing Robespierre. With all his fine words, he was nothing more than "the hornet of the patriotic hive". They insinuated that he had sold his resignation to the Court because he needed capital for his newspaper *Le Défenseur de la constitution*, the first issue of which came out shortly afterwards.

In fact, by resigning he was giving up a considerable amount of revenue, but money matters did not interest him. From the time when he no longer received the salary of a deputy, it is difficult to see where his money came from. No doubt the Duplay family gave him his board and lodging free. They were well rewarded merely by having such a guest. In contrast to himself, Robespierre pointed out that the Brissotins were notable in the way they sought lucrative situations for themselves and their friends. He enjoyed underlining the difference that existed on this point between himself and them. "I swear that I do not want any situation. We have all proved this, we, the friends of liberty. We have avoided ministries. I want no situation and there is no situation suitable for me. Unless it be the one in which I can fight faithlessness and machiavellianism conspiring against the rights of the people. I will be always at this post. Whatever bayonets the tyrants might surround me with, they will not frighten me. If they want to murder me, that is where they should come."

$$[[\cdot]]$$

At the beginning of March the king appointed General Dumouriez Minister of Foreign Affairs. He was said to be a friend of the Brissotins. Dumouriez was not without talent or merit. He was a soldier and a diplomat, and had seen his first action during the Seven Years War. When the Revolution opened the door to talent, it seemed to him a means—as it did to many others—of hoisting himself up to the front rank. His plan, in common with those of Mirabeau and Barnave before him, was to reconcile the monarchy with the new institutions. "If I were King of France," he said one day to Monsieur de Montmorin, "I would outmanoeuvre all the parties, by putting myself at the head of the Revolution." It was a wise piece of advice. All that was wrong with it was that it referred to Louis XVI.

Shortly after Dumouriez's appointment, several of Brissot's friends became ministers such as Clavière, Roland, Grave and Lacoste. Public opinion might well have been led to believe that the king had suddenly been converted to Jacobinism. Mirabeau had once advised him to choose ministers among the Jacobins, and explained that: "A Jacobin who was a minister would not necessarily be a Jacobin minister." In Mirabeau's estimation, it was a case of buying consciences with positions, so as to take advantage of their popularity. Unfortunately the intention of Louis XVI was quite different. He wanted to destroy their public esteem by showing them to be inept. He would then get rid of them and they would not be heard of again. Apart from Dumouriez, in fact, the new ministers were far from being luminaries. Roland was an old man who had once been a factory inspector. He was sententious and pedantic and brought to the direction of matters of State all the capacities of a shopkeeper. In addition he allowed himself to be guided by his wife, who was certainly clever, but erratic—all passion and impulse. The Brissotins had wanted war, which was about to break out. They would take the responsibility for the inevitable defeats. This subtle game needed a much better brain than that of Louis XVI to carry it off.

All the same, revolutionary opinion welcomed the new set of ministers—except, that is, for Robespierre and Marat. It seemed to them that an alliance between the Court and the Jacobins was unnatural. They concluded from it that following the example of Mirabeau, Barnave and de Lameth had let themselves be bought. All at once they found their vigilance faulty; the king's intrigue completely eluded them. The sole intention of the Brissotins was to betray the cause to the Court. In his usual way, Marat made known his thoughts in *L'Ami du peuple*, without mincing words. Robespierre decided to keep quiet for the time being, though still watching their behaviour.

So as to gain the support of the Jacobins, Dumouriez indulged in a little piece of play-acting which, for a time, was totally successful. On 19th March he went to the club wearing a red cap. He was a member, but until then had rarely attended the meetings. "My brothers," he said, "I have a very heavy burden, and one which is very difficult to support. I need your advice. Give it to me publicly in your newspapers. I beg of you the truth, no matter how brutal." Such talk was quite a novelty from the mouth of a minister. It was greeted with unanimous applause. Many members complimented him on his attitude. Robespierre did not like military men. He suspected them, since he saw them as potential dictators. Even so, Dumouriez's declaration touched him. Possibly he was half convinced, for he allowed himself to say a few friendly words: "I am not one of those who think that it is absolutely impossible for a minister to be a patriot, but Dumouriez will have to prove with actions that he really is for the Revolution. Only then will I be prepared to give him all the praise he will merit. Until then, let him come to the club like an ordinary member to prove his fellowship and to receive advice."

As for the general, he scarcely felt any sympathy for the Incorruptible. He knew that he could not induce him to serve his ends, and that if he came to suspect the Brissotins he would be faced with an enemy. He therefore had at the same time to allay his suspicions and make the public believe that he respected Robespierre. When Robespierre left the rostrum, he threw himself into his arms. The onlookers loudly applauded this gesture, which seemed to them an alliance between the minister and the people. Dumouriez had achieved his purpose.

Robespierre allowed himself to be embraced, unmoved, but he did not quite repell him. All the same, he did not seem at all pleased that the general had arrived wearing a red cap. He never wore one himself, but only had a tricolour cockade in his buttonhole. How could he put such a covering over his powdered hair that was so carefully combed? In his eyes it was dishonouring the people to encourage them to give such importance to such a symbol in which counter-revolutionaries could rig themselves up to dupe the people. Even so, the cap had great success with the Parisians and members of the club, the majority of whom wore it. Brissot extolled enthusiastically in his paper: "This hat, which covers the head without hiding it, heightens its natural beauty and grace and lends itself to all sorts of embellishment." At the end of the session one of those present tried to put one on Robespierre's head. No doubt he was an admirer and he did not want his idol to appear to disadvantage alongside Dumouriez. Robespierre immediately snatched it off and threw it to the ground. From anyone else but him the gesture would have seemed a sacrilege. Even so, no one protested. In fact, for a while fewer red caps were seen at the club.

[[·]]

When the imprisoned soldiers who had mutinied in Nancy and Châteauvieux had been pardoned by the Assembly and arrived in Paris, it seemed for a moment that Robespierre and the Brissotins were reconciled in their hostility to Lafayette. In their eyes he was the butcher of the Champ-de-Mars, and they suspected that he was organizing a *coup* to take over power. The ceremonies organized by the popular clubs to "feast" the general's victims could be used to foil his plan.

The released soldiers were welcomed on 9th April by the Legislative Assembly, and they then went to the club. Vergniaud was in the chair that day. He complimented them and embraced them. Collot d'Herbois suggested that they would like to hear Robespierre "who had been so concerned about their fate". He thereupon took the rostrum and praised the services they had given the cause of freedom. He asked that they be assimilated again into the army from which they had been unjustly expelled.

But he especially took advantage of the opportunity to attack Lafayette, in particularly violent terms: "I have denounced this man by despising him. Even so, I see that it is more dangerous to denounce the Marquis de Lafayette than all the kings of the earth. I am surrounded by enemies and murderers, but the day on which the daggers reach my chest will be the one on which I will denounce him again to the public scorn with all my energy."

The ceremonies in honour of the mutineers took place on 15th April, with the usual parades and march-pasts in the streets. This was known as the Festival of Freedom. The opposition called it the Festival of Robespierre. In fact, his name was loudly cheered by the *sans-culottes*.

A reflection of the state of the relationship between Robespierre and the Brissotins is found in his dealings with Madame Roland, the group's inspiration. At the start, the similarity of their ideas had brought them close together. During the term of the Constituent Assembly she had received in her salon in the rue Guénégaud deputies and "advanced" journalists such as Pétion, Brissot and Buzot. Robespierre sometimes went there, and although she deplored his unadorned language and monotonous way of speaking, she forgave him because of his great love of freedom. She felt only slightly affronted that he did not pay her court as the others did. He suspected that her salon had aristocratic tendencies. He thought that they busied themselves more with intrigue than with the cause of the people. All the same, for some time they hid their disagreements under a veil of mutual deference to each other's patriotism. In March 1792 Madame Roland returned from a visit to the country and once more lived in Paris, at the Hôtel Britannique. Her husband had just been called to be minister. A letter from her at this time to Robespierre has been found. She was happy, she told him, to have had news of him and hoped that he would soon come and see her. Obviously her intention was to renew cordial relations between Robespierre and her friends with kindly flattery. "I maintain a simplicity here which will, I hope, make me worthy of your respect, despite the fact that I have the misfortune to be the wife of a minister. I cannot hope to contribute anything useful, unless good patriots help me with their ideas and their attention. You are at the top of the list. Please come quickly. I am eager to see you and tell you once more of my esteem for you—an esteem that nothing can alter." Robespierre seems to have accepted the invitation, but we do not know what they said to each other. The interview does not seem to have gone as Madame Roland had hoped. There is a curious note from her on the subject to her friend Bosc. "I am at home to Robespierre, who asked me for an appointment." She was the one who had asked for it. Doubtless she did not want to seem to be making advances towards one of her friends' opponents.

When she wrote to him again, on 25th April, relations with Robespierre had deteriorated considerably. All the same, she made a last attempt to meet him and bring him round to her husband's policy—in other words her own—but he declined to come. She expressed her regret: "I wanted to see you because you have a burning love of freedom and devotion to the public commonality."

[[·]]

Discussion about the war went on in the press. From the Brissotin side it was a matter of more and more attacks on Robespierre, most often by insinuating that he aimed at a dictatorship. The fashion was for echoes of Antiquity, and Gorsas's *Courrier des quatre-vingt-trois départements* recalled a remark of Brutus, about Cicero: "A real patriot does not have this excessive love of domination. He does not display virtues. He does not use intrigue to throw them into relief." Then he asked his readers the insidious question: "Is the original of this picture still alive?" Robespierre was infuriated and wrote a long letter of protest to Gorsas; unable to get it published in the newspaper he complained to the club.

Judging by the number of speeches they made there, one might think that the Brissotin dominated the club. In fact, although they formed a small and active group, they were definitely in the minority. The majority was for Robespierre.

Louis XVI announced the declaration of war against his brother-in-law Joseph II, Emperor of Austria, to the unanimous and enthusiastic acclaim of the deputies

They must have realized that they would have to support him on the day that Réal attempted to reply. Amidst the shouts and protests that drowned his voice he had extreme difficulty in making himself heard. So he reproached Robespierre "for exerting a tyranny over the club that weighed heavily on every free man within its walls".

[[·]]

Despite this, the warlike policy of the Brissotins won the day. On 20th April Louis XVI came to the Assembly to propose a declaration of war against the King of Bohemia and Hungary, which was a curious way to refer to the emperor. It was carried unanimously. Nevertheless, it was far from being a display of national unity in the face of the enemy. Each party hoped to win its own victory from this war, together with the destruction of its adversaries. All were mistaken. War brought about their ruin, and brought to power the one man who had opposed it.

Any semblance of courtesy had now disappeared in his diatribes against the Brissotins. "No one," wrote Robespierre, in allusion to the deputy-journalist's past, "has ever accused me of having exercised a dishonourable profession, or of having sullied my name in scandalous procedures." Brissot replied: "There are three current opinions about Robespierre: that he is mad, that his conduct is the result of wicked pride, and that he is in the pay of the Court."

The Brissotin tactic in this struggle, which aimed at dominating the Jacobins, consisted in allowing no quarter. After Réal, Guadet took up the accusation of tyranny. "I denounce him for always talking about patriotism, then deserting the post of Public Prosecutor to which he had been elected. I denounce him for seeking to become the idol of the people. I draw his attention to another who would die rather than desert the post of duty. I mean myself." Clearly, Guadet was not guilty of excessive modesty. Robespierre replied with a long explanation of his political action. "I know that I am criticized for making so many speeches, but I do it to guarantee freedom, establish equality and dispel intrigue." When these aims were fulfilled, he assured his listeners, he would gladly retire into private life. He recalled his efforts in defence of the people's rights in Artois, and the enthusiasm inspired in him by the first days of the National Assembly. Proof of his lack of ambition was the fact that he had voluntarily excluded himself from the Legislative Assembly. He had even been asked to ostracize himself and go into exile. Which despot would agree to grant him asylum? How, in any case, could he abandon his country in this serious crisis? "Heaven has given me a heart full of passion for freedom."

Brissot followed. He had not been heard at the club for some time. As usual, he showed considerable skill. His entire speech was against Robespierre, but he did not name him. He complimented himself, he said, on the existence of the new minister, and did not understand how anyone in the club who did otherwise. Jacobins should only be delighted to see Jacobins in power. "May it please Heaven that all should be Jacobins, from the throne to the meanest servant." Desmoulins was heard to shout: "He's clever—the slut." With a reference to Greek history, he fired this last shot: "Remember that Aristides and Phocion did not always bombast the assembly or the public, but were at their posts in the field and in the assemblies."

Pétion was still commonly looked upon as the man of politics closest to Robespierre. In fact he began to disassociate himself from him, because he was jealous of Robespierre's popularity, and because of his friendship for Brissot, who, like himself, was from Chartres. In a letter to the club he deplored the "hideous human passions" that divided and ruined the common cause. "We have lost the energy of free men. We shout like children and madmen." There was nothing to upset Robespierre, but then later he attributed the cause of the quarrels "to a frustrated ambition", which might lead one to suppose that the Incorruptible was jealous of his mayoralty, or of the Brissotin ministerial posts. Some days after he repeated the insinuations at the club. Robespierre did not reply. However, when Doppet proposed that henceforth denunciations should come before a special committee, and stop the club from losing time in personal quarrels, Robespierre objected: "I believe, along with many others, that there ought to be a limit to the zeal of good citizens in making denunciations. But if this club were to forbid my replying to warmongers who plot against me, I should resign and go into retirement."

9

THE FALL OF THE KING

"I will forget whom the Constitution has put in the seat of power, if only to keep an eye on the scoundrels who surround him."

ROBESPIERRE

ROBESPIERRE, AS WELL AS DANTON, WAS ONE OF THE FEW REALLY popular politicians who did not have his own newspaper. Since the beginning of the Revolution, the number of journals had considerably increased. Consisting of two or three sheets, they needed no special talent to start publication, nor experience, and moreover not much capital outlay. Doubtless, Duplay put up the money to pay for paper and the printing of Robespierre's. The editor's name was enough to guarantee a wide number of readers.

The new newspaper appeared under the title *Défenseur de la Constitution*, as a tribute to the official name of the Jacobins. There were twelve issues from May to the end of August 1792, succeeded by *Lettres à mes commettants* from October 1792 to April 1793, of which there were twenty-two issues. Robespierre's journalistic adventure then stopped, and in that area he was much less successful than Desmoulins, Marat or even Fréron. He was much more preoccupied with other business.

In the prospectus he declared: "Reason and public interest began the Revolution; ambition and intrigue have stopped it." He said that the object of his publication would be "to educate good patriots".

Most of the time his articles were simply literal reprints of his speeches to the Jacobins. The first issue, entitled "Explanation of my principles", justified the title of the newspaper. Robespierre did not deny the faults of the Constitution—he recalled the fact that he had strongly opposed some of its provisions—but when confronted by the efforts of the counter-revolutionaries to destroy it, "so as to erect on its ruins a royal tyranny or a sort of aristocratic régime", the Constitution had to become the rallying point for patriots. Internally rather than externally the war against the aristocracy, injustice, treason and despotism had to be carried on. Thinking about Lafayette, his *bête noire*, and possibly also about Dumouriez, he put his fellow citizens on their guard against the ambition and intrigue of the generals "in case there rises up in France a citizen strong enough to make himself our master one day, either to hand us over to the Court and govern in its name, or to crush both king and people and build on their ruin a legal tyranny, the worst of all tyrannies." He could not possibly have known that in a garrison at Valence there was at the time a young lieutenant called not Lafayette, but Bonaparte.

In the next issue, he praised himself. Defence of his own conduct was for him the same thing as a defence of the Revolution, with which he identified himself. "From the moment I announced the intention of opposing the factious, I have seen men [readers recognized the Brissotins] who, until a short time ago, still had a reputation for patriotism, declare a war on me more serious than the one that they pretended to make against despots. I saw them use all the means that one never lacks when one has put public fortune in the hands of one's friends and when one shares, in different guises, in all kinds of power, sometimes as a royalist, sometimes as an ambitious tribune."

On another occasion he dealt with the question of the choice between a republic and a monarchy, becoming more and more controversial, as he avowed that Louis XVI was not really the ideal monarch to apply the Constitution.

> I am a royalist, yes, as a man who for three years has struggled almost alone against an all-powerful Assembly to oppose the excessive extension of royal power; as a man who, braving all the slanders of a faction that today is entangled with the one that is hounding me, demanded that the fugitive monarch should be subject to legal justice; as a man who, certain that the majority of the Assembly would put Louis XVI back on the throne, freely exposed himself to the vengeance of this king to demand the rights of the people; as a man, finally, who will defend the constitution to the peril of his life against the Court and against all factions. I am a republican, yes, I want to defend the principles of the freedom of the sacred rights which the constitution guarantees to the people against the dangerous systems of those who intrigue and who look upon it as the instrument of their ambition. I would prefer to see an Assembly representative of the people and of free citizens than of a people enslaved and vilified under the rod of an aristocratic senate and a dictator.

Finally, in another issue, he dealt with a subject close to his heart, the status of the soldier in a free country, where he is both a man and a citizen. While not denying the necessity for discipline, he set limits to it. Therefore, if the soldier missed roll-call, a parade or a manoeuvre, if he left his post or refused to obey orders, he deserved to be punished. On the other hand, if the officer attempted to prevent him from seeing his friends; from attending clubs permitted by law; if he meddled with his correspondence or his reading matter, he was overstepping the limits of his authority. In fact, Robespierre distinguished between two sorts of discipline. The first, which he repudiated, was the absolute power of leaders over all the actions and the person of the soldier. The second established their legitimate authority, restricted to what was related to military service. One was founded on prejudice and servility; the other drawn from the very nature of things and reason. The first turned soldiers into so many serfs destined to follow blindly the caprices of one man; the second made them willing servants of the country and the law, and allowed them to be men and citizens. "The first is suitable for despots, the second for free men. With the first one may conquer the enemies of the State, but at the same time enchain and suppress the citizens. With the second, one triumphs more surely over foreign enemies and defends the freedom of one's country against internal enemies."

Suddenly events proved Robespierre right. The Brissotins had been truly mad in declaring war with the Army in a state of disintegration. When they had barely heard the sound of the approaching enemy, Dillon's column had fled to Lille, and he was killed by his own men. Biron's army, also seized with panic, fled from Mons without a fight. Soldiers talked about the generals' treason, while the generals accused the troops of lack of discipline. A large number of officers deserted. Grave, the Minister of War, was overwhelmed by the disasters and resigned.

The king realized that the time had come to take advantage of the defeats that he had foreseen and to get rid of the Brissotin ministers, according to his plan. He could no longer put up with Roland's pedantic ways, and his sermonizing. In particular, he refused to sign two decrees presented to him. One was intended to set up a camp of 20,000 reserve soldiers in Paris, and the other decreed the deportation of refractory priests. The Civil Constitution of the Clergy had continually troubled his pious religious conscience ever since its establishment (in July 1790). At the beginning he had not showed his opposition in the hope that the Pope would oppose it. When the Pope condemned the Constitution, Louis hesitated no longer. Religion gave this apathetic man some energy. On 13th June Roland, Servan and Clavière were dismissed. Dumouriez accepted the post of Minister of War. His respectful attitude pleased the king, who had no doubt that the man was sincerely devoted to him. Unfortunately Dumouriez's plan to make the king more popular by making him lead the Revolution required, as a start, that the king should sign the decrees. Louis XVI could not agree. Dumouriez then resigned, knowing that by staying at his post he was compromising himself to no end. But he did not give up his plan. The king was sad to see him go, and apprehensive also, feeling that he was losing a friend.

In the Assembly, where the Brissotin influence was dominant, a motion was passed expressing "its regret at the departure of the patriotic ministers".

Robespierre scarcely felt himself affected by the dismissal of those people in whom he had no confidence. He did not hesitate to let the fact be known. "Our security does not depend on the fate of a minister, but on our fidelity to principles, on the progress of the civic spirit and the wisdom of our laws. The public safety rests not on the character of the ministers whom the Court may dismiss as often as it pleases, but on the energy and patriotism of the National Assembly. We ought to be less occupied with Monsieur Servan than with trying to get freedom respected, and in supporting the unfortunate people who are persecuted."

Most people were expecting a show of strength from the Court. In fact, ever since it had been deprived of the support of the monarchist nobility who had fled, the Court was incapable of carrying this out itself. As for the liberal nobles—the people who had first launched the Revolution—the king was too repelled at the thought of putting himself into their care to accept their help. He sharply refused Lafayette's offer to take him to Compiègne under the protection of his army. He was counting on a foreign victory to restore all his lost powers. As for the Sections, under the influence of the Brissotins, they were organizing a rebellion to overthrow the king unless he agreed to reinstate the patriotic ministers and sign the decree. Robespierre disagreed with these popular movements, since he feared what the consequences might be if the Revolution had a luckless failure. He recalled the shooting of the Champ-de-Mars and the events which had ensued. He was not far off the mark in suspecting the treachery of those who promoted the massacre.

He was expecting Lafayette to attempt a *coup d'état*. In fact, the general was considering such a move, but made the arrant mistake of revealing his intentions in a threatening letter to the Assembly, calling upon them to defend the king against the tyranny of the clubs. While Danton and Pétion were talking of taking the Tuileries by assault on the 18th (June), Robespierre denounced the general. He demanded that the Assembly dismiss him, and that he be prosecuted. As for the projected insurrection, he tried to stop it, or at least to delay it. Chabot tells how "some of Robespierre's friends went to beg the people to wait for the arrival of the men from Marseilles to overthrow the throne, and to content themselves with a simple petition sanctioning the decrees that were useful for the people". It seems, in fact, that Chabot himself was sent to the Faubourg Saint-Antoine to beg for clear-headedness. But it was already too late. Columns of people from the faubourgs were marching on the Tuileries.

Robespierre's fears had been justified. For hours the people marched past the king, who drank a glass of wine to the health of the nation, wearing a red cap, but who refused to promise to sanction the decrees. In fact, his courage and good nature won for him the sympathy of the rioters. At the end Santerre, the activist

(OPPOSITE) *The angry mob that invaded the Tuileries was calmed by the king's affability when he donned the cap of freedom and toasted them with wine. However, he refused to approve decrees establishing a military force in Paris and exiling anti-revolutionary priests*

brewer, was heard to murmur "the whole thing is a mess". When an insurrection fails (which is what Robespierre had foreseen) it inevitably produces a reaction. The American Ambassador, Morris, wrote in his diary: "The Constitution, I think, has today breathed its last." The invasion of the palace horrified many people. Protests came from seventy-five departments against "the attempt on the royal person". Roederer explained that: "A vast movement was brewing in favour of the king amongst the majority of the inhabitants of Paris. General indignation arose against the factious as a result of the impressions of the 20th June that were spread about." A royalist petition received thousands of signatures in Paris.

Louis XVI was unable to turn this sudden change of opinion to his advantage. Rather than accept the help of people they did not like, Marie-Antoinette and he were ready to die. Lafayette was no less keen to carry out his *coup d'état*. The two conditions for success were secrecy and an army. He had already made his intentions known, and came alone to Paris, having left his army at the frontier. On the 28th he appeared at the bar of the Assembly, applauded by the Feuillants, while the left remained silent. In his speech he recalled his earlier letter in which he had denounced the behaviour of the clubs—in particular the Jacobins, "a sect that has usurped national sovereignty, tyrannized the citizens, and whose public debates left no doubt about the heinous nature of the projects of their leaders". He threatened the intervention of his eighty-thousand soldiers if the Assembly did not take steps to re-establish order and legality. But these soldiers were far away. That evening at the Jacobins, Brissot, Guadet and Robespierre demanded that a decree be issued for the arrest of Lafayette. To both the king and queen he was the symbol of the insurrection and their semi-captivity and was coldly received at the Tuileries. His last chance was the National Guard, over which he still had a great deal of influence. He intended to raise it during a review. But the queen warned Pétion, who had the review put off. Only one hundred and fifty volunteers responded to Lafayette's appeal.

[[·]]

Robespierre's authority was considerably increased by these events. He was the wise man who had twice seen things clearly for what they were. Although he was pleased that Lafayette had failed, the failure of the uprising of 20th June pleased him less. "What difference does it make if the ghost known as the king has disappeared and depotism remains? What will freedom have achieved if intrigue and ambition still hold the reins of government?" At the beginning of July even worse news came from the front. In the Assembly Vergniaud denounced the king's conduct in insolent terms, and demanded that he be deposed.

The date of 7th July marked a change in Robespierre's opinion about the war. One of the reasons why he had opposed it was his belief that it would put arms into the hands of the counter-revolutionary generals. He had been scarcely affected by the recent defeats, believing that victories would only have made the generals more dangerous. The disappearance of Lafayette seemed a good omen. If other "traitorous" generals were in turn dismissed and replaced by patriots, it would become possible to drive back the enemy victoriously. These were the ideas put before the *Fédérés* who had come to Paris for the celebrations of 14th July. On that day the king received no cheers and the Mayor of Paris triumphed—"Pétion or

The threat of invasion by the Prussians and Austrians, presumably to restore Louis to his royal privileges, was one of the chief causes of the king's ultimate downfall

Robespierre appealed to the rabble of Marseilles not to be suborned by fine dinners and wines.
In the Champs the drunken mob set about slaughtering a troop of French Guards

death." But the celebration took place in an atmosphere heavy by comparison with the high spirits of 1790.

The crisis (of a general insurrection) was precipitated by two events on 30th July. One was Brunswick's Manifesto, threatening Paris with destruction if the king were not re-established in all his authority, and the other was the arrival of the Marseillais. "Frenchmen ready to play the role of Brutus", Robespierre called them in a letter to Buissart. "If they leave Paris without saving the country, all is lost. But all of us intend to sacrifice our lives in the capital." The men from Marseilles in common with the other *Fédérés*, were showered with attention by the counter-revolutionaries, who tried to win them over with gestures of friendship, parties and banquets. Robespierre put them on guard against the dangers of seduction.

"Avoid treacherous embraces, loaded tables where in golden cups one drinks the poison of the moderates and and forgetfulness of the most holy of duties."

Robespierre now believed the uprising to be essential, and the presence in Paris of twenty-thousand armed *Fédérés* guaranteed its success. "Great ills require strong remedies. The State must be saved by any means at all. Nothing is unconstitutional except that which leads to its ruin. Deprived of public confidence, Louis XVI is no longer anything on his own, and royalty has become prey to all the ambitions of its despoilers."

One further reason for his change of mind was that the Brissotins opposed the uprising. Brissot and his friends had, in fact, just realized that if the Revolution took one more step it would be beyond their control. They in their turn made desperate efforts to halt an uprising. Whereas a few weeks previously they had openly wanted the downfall of the king, they now wanted to keep him on the throne. Using the painter Bose as their emissary, they warned the king that a new revolt was on the way. The only way to avoid it, said the memorandum delivered by Bose and signed by Guadet, Gensonné and Vergniaud, was to recall the patriotic ministers. But how could Louis XVI believe that these men, whom he had always known to be republicans, really wanted to preserve his crown for him? Paradoxically the Brissotins abandoned their republicanism at the very moment when the republic was about to be founded. Brissot tried to reassure the king, but unfortunately had no effect upon him. To others what he said smacked of treason. "If there are any men who are now striving to establish the republic on the debris of the Constitution, the sword of the law ought to strike them down just as it struck the conspirators of the two chambers and the counter-revolutionaries of Koblenz." When they heard about this, there was only one explanation as far as the *sans-culottes* were concerned: the Brissotins had in turn sold themselves to the Court.

As for Robespierre, he had now decided for the republic. On 1st August he unveiled his plan. As soon as the king was overthrown, the Assembly, which he thought to be unworthy of trust, must be dissolved. There would then be an election of a National Convention by universal suffrage—no more distinction between active and passive citizens. The members of the two preceding assemblies would be excluded from the Convention. The new assembly, which would be elected for one year, would be entrusted with the task of framing a new Constitution. Then in an alarmist speech on 5th August, he communicated some serious news to the club. The Tuileries was full of drunken Swiss guards, each armed with fifteen cartridges. Louis XVI would certainly try to escape; and it was the duty of every good citizen to be on his guard to prevent this happening.

Pétion, now allied entirely with the Girondins, visited Robespierre on 7th August. Since their enstrangement they had had no contact, but Pétion thought that he could influence Robespierre because of their previous friendship. As far as Robespierre was concerned, a man who had abandoned the just cause could no longer be his friend, no matter what his past might have been. For an hour the Mayor of Paris talked to him about the dangers of an insurrection, begging him to use his influence "to put off the resistance to oppression". He said that the Assembly should be left to discuss the deterioration of events calmly, and should not take any action until a pronouncement had been made.

But all that Pétion had to say was useless. They parted on a note of coldness. On 8th August a rumour went round Paris that the Assembly might transfer itself to Rouen or Orléans. The Jacobins were worried about this rumour, but Robespierre reassured them. They should not let gossip distract them from the principal question, namely the dethroning of the king.

The same evening he wrote to his friend Couthon, who was ill and away from Paris:

Here we are approaching extremely important events. The fermentation is on the boil, and everything seems to point to intense commotion here in Paris this very night. We have come to the climax of the constitutional drama. The Revolution is going to move at a faster pace—unless it is overwhelmed by military and dictatorial despotism. In the present situation it is impossible for a friend of freedom to foresee and direct events. The destiny of France seems to abandon her to intrigue and chance. What is reassuring is the strength of public spirit in Paris and in many of the *départements*. The Sections of Paris reveal an energy and wisdom worthy to serve as a model for the rest of the State.

In the sequence of events of 10th August there is no trace of Robespierre's having played any active part at all. It did not suit him to be in the midst of the hubbub—unlike Danton, who liked noise and movement. Marat said about him: "He avoids any group where there is unrest, and pales at the sight of a sabre." The leader of an insurrection must ride a horse and brandish a pistol. Robespierre was incapable of doing either of these things. He was a man for the study and the council chamber, and once the preparations had been made, he thought that his part was over, and wisely left it to others more suitable than himself to put it into action: the butcher Legendre, or Santerre, the brewer from the Faubourg Saint-Antoine. Later the Girondins made fun of his absence, maintaining that he had hid himself in a cellar,

On the 10th of August, the Men from Marseilles threatened the Swiss and National Guards.
The soldiers panicked and fired into the mob. The Marseillais scattered, reformed and charged
the Palace. A bloody massacre ensued

Archives N aler

N°. 688.

DÉCRET
DE L'ASSEMBLÉE NATIONALE.
Du Dix Août 1792.
L'An Quatrième de la Liberté.

L'Assemblée Nationale, considérant que le
danger de la Patrie sont parvenu à leur comble ;
que c'est pour le corps législatif le plus saint des devoirs
d'employer tous les moyens de la sauver ; qu'il est
impossible d'en trouver de efficace tant qu'on ne
s'occupera pas d'étarir la source de ces maux ; —
Considérant que ces maux dérivent principalement
des défiances qu'a inspiré la conduite du chef du
pouvoir exécutif dans une guerre entreprise en son
nom contre la constitution et l'indépendance
nationale ;

Que ces défiances ont provoqué de diverses parties
de l'Empire un vœu tendant à la révocation de l'autorité
déléguée à Louis Seize ;

ready to flee to Marseilles in the event of failure. It was an unfair accusation. He simply stayed in his room, and friends came to tell him the news.

In the evening, when it was all over, there was a meeting at the Jacobin Club. Robespierre was present, as usual, to explain his thoughts on the situation. It was extraordinary that he did not say a word about the king. For the majority of those present, the question was still whether there was to be a republic or a monarchy, with the Dauphin on the throne and the Duc d'Orléans as regent. For Robespierre the form of the state was of only secondary importance—that problem could solve itself, logically, later. He had no doubt that it would be a republic. What mattered for the moment was to prevent the Brissotins from seizing power. For this reason he demanded that the Legislative Assembly be replaced by a National Convention. Commissioners should be sent to the provinces to explain what had happened. The *Fédérés* should write home to those who had sent them to the capital. In Paris the Sections should inform the Assembly of the wishes of the people. Finally, steps should be taken without delay to secure the liberation of all imprisoned patriots.

[[·]]

As far as Paris was concerned, the insurrection on 10th August had the effect of transferring power over the city to a new Commune. As a representative of the Piques section where he lived, Robespierre belonged to the Commune. Between 10th and 26th August he attended meetings regularly, but then stopped doing so while he concentrated his efforts on the election for the Convention.

This fortnight gave him a determining influence on the course of events. The Legislative Assembly was in total disarray, abandoned by two-thirds of its members, and incapable of resisting the injunctions of the Commune. Robespierre was the person behind most of these injunctions. On 12th August he headed a delegation which came to demand the abolition of the *directoire* of the Department of Paris, a reactionary assembly that had in the past approved retention of the royal veto. It seemed unlikely that a newly elected council would be any different. In this event it would be better to keep the old council, which was already discredited, and limit its role to the handling of finance. The rest of its functions would pass to the Commune. "The general council of the Commune needs to retain the power given to it by the people on the night of 9th/10th August to safeguard the public safety and freedom." On 14th August a delegation from Robespierre's section, and led by him, came to demand the demolition of the statue of Louis XIV in the Place Vendôme, and the erection on the site of a monument to the glory of the citizens who had fallen on 10th August. In time a statue of Liberty appeared on the site, later to be replaced by the column with the statue of Napoleon.

(OPPOSITE) *Immediately after the events of the morning of the 10th of August a decree was issued suspending the rights of the king signed by Danton in the name of the Nation*

The next day another delegation demanded the setting up of a special criminal tribunal to judge the guilty ones (of 10th August). These would include those people who had attempted to defend the Tuileries, and in particular, the Swiss guards. "The serenity of the country depends on their punishment," said Robespierre, "and yet you have done nothing to touch them. Your decree is insubstantial: it mentions only the crimes of 10th August, yet crimes of the enemies of the Revolution extend well beyond that date." The tribunal was to be made up of representatives from the Sections, "with the jurisdiction to judge absolutely and without appeal". At first the Assembly refused, but against the threat of a direct insurrection it yielded. The Sections received a mandate to choose the judges for the tribunal. Robespierre headed the list of those elected. It was commonly believed that he should also be the president of the tribunal, but for the second time—to the surprise of all—he refused on the excuse that "the carrying out of judicial functions was incompatible with that of a member of the Commune". It was a bad reason, for he would soon no longer be a member. Another excuse, which he later offered, was more human: "I could not judge people whom I had opposed. I had to remind myself that if they were the people's enemies, they were also my own."

A new government had been formed, comprising the former Brissotin ministers, and so realizing Robespierre's fear that they would only profit from a course of events by seizing power. It also included Danton as Minister of Justice. The Girondins, who could barely tolerate his brutal manner, hoped to use him as a kind of screen against extremist threats. According to Condorcet, he was "the man whose ascendance would enforce the utterly contemptible instruments of a useful, glorious and necessary Revolution". Danton was, nevertheless, superior to his colleagues, and soon became the master of the cabinet. Robespierre received a letter from him on 14th August in which he asked "his dear friend" to become one of the four members of the judiciary committee. At this time Robespierre and Danton were on very good terms. Robespierre's friend Barère and Collot d'Herbois would also be committee members. The work would have taken up only four mornings a week, but Robespierre refused. This time he could not claim inability or any moral excuse. Even in a secondary capacity, he did not want to collaborate with a Brissotin government.

Meanwhile, tension between the Commune and the Assembly increased. The Assembly announced its intention to dissolve the Commune and to reinstate the municipal authorities it had displaced. The Commune instructed Robespierre to

(OPPOSITE) *Three days after the uprising at the Place du Carrousel at the entrance to the Tuileries where the uprising began a scaffold was erected surmounted by a guillotine for the express purpose of executing the enemies of the state and conspirators against the Nation. Many members of the Swiss and National Guard who defended the Palace were beheaded*

ask Pétion to co-operate with them in maintaining order and in preventing a counter-revolution. The Mayor of Paris did not share the same feelings as the new council, and after 17th August he stopped attending the meetings. He took exception to Robespierre's supremacy seeing that his own authority was unrecognized. In view of the state to which their lack of common understanding had fallen, nothing could have come of their meeting. Since the Assembly persisted in its determination not to recognize the insurrectional Commune, the idea of organizing a popular demonstration against it was discussed. Robespierre put forward another way of appealing to the people, which had the advantage in his eyes of being more legal: "We ought to withdraw into our Sections; explain our situation to them; ask their feelings about the things we have done; hand back to them the powers they have given us, and if they want us to continue in our own work, ask them for the means of sustaining us at our posts, where we shall die if need be." There was no need to have recourse to this second investiture of the elections. The Legislative Assembly had in the meantime capitulated, and the Commune simply continued to function.

Among Robespierre's papers there is a letter from Pétion dating from this period. It seems that the mayor had intended a reconciliation with him. "You know, my friend, what my feelings for you are. You know that I am not your rival." It was, however, clumsy on his part to reproach Robespierre for being susceptible to jealousy, and insinuating that he was jealous of the title of mayor. Robespierre replied in severe terms: "Do you imagine that the applause of a few *sans-culottes* could make me lose my head so far as to betray the cause of freedom and equality? You maintain that I flatter the mobs, but you do not say that there is much more advantage in flattering the rich and the well-born."

[[·]]

The elections for the Convention were to take place in two stages, a fact which Robespierre regretted but accepted because of circumstances. In his eyes the most important thing was that the distinction between active and passive citizens should disappear. Nine hundred delegates would be given the task of choosing the twenty-four deputies for Paris. Although there was universal suffrage, these elections were neither free nor general. In fact, the opposition did not have the right to make itself heard. As a preliminary to the campaign the Assembly had decreed on 11th August that all royalist newspapers were to be suppressed. The only ones to remain were those of the Jacobins, the Brissotins and the Cordeliers. The number of people actually eligible to vote was hardly one-tenth of the seven million registered for the whole of France.

The nomination of electors took place in Paris from 26th August to 7th September. On the 27th the Piques Section adopted Robespierre's proposal that the electoral assemblies would vote publicly. Of the sixteen delegates Robespierre was

The royal family were herded from the Tuileries to the Temple. 'Naughty beasts,' says the sans-culotte, 'we fatten them with our blood and they ask us to slit our throats.' The turkey (Louis) appeals to Lafayette, the wolf (Marie-Antoinette) moans that her plans are upset

elected first: and among the sixteen was his friend Duplay. Robespierre was also nominated by the Section Halles-au-Blé.

The Bishop's hall, where the meetings of the Parisian electoral assembly were to take place, proved to be too small; and Robespierre and Collot d'Herbois were instructed to ask the Jacobins to lend their hall. In this way, discussions and voting would take place under the scrutiny of the public in the galleries. On 4th September the committee was organized with Collot d'Herbois as President. Robespierre was content to be Vice-President. Their first proposal was to deny the right to vote to all those who had belonged to "uncivic" clubs, such as the Monarchist Club, the Sainte-Chapelle Club and the Feuillants. As a result about 200 of the 990 members were eliminated. Then in an excess of caution, so as to guarantee "good results", it was decided to have the nominated deputies scrutinized by the Sections, so that "the majority would have the means of rejecting those who were unworthy of the people's confidence".

Robespierre's objective was to assure the success of the Revolution, and he had learned from Rousseau that: "The spirit of the people may reside in an enlightened minority, who consequently have the right to act for the collective advantage." It seemed normal to him that only the most virtuous citizens should be called upon to express the general will. On 5th September he was elected by 338 votes out of 525, against his opponent Pétion. The mayor took his defeat very badly. In fact, it

was a painful insult for a man whom, a few weeks earlier, the Parisians had so warmly acclaimed and whom they had affectionately named King Jérôme. In a time of revolution, popularity is soon exhausted. Robespierre, in his *Lettres à ses commettants*, said that one could "see his face change colour during the counting of the votes".

The Paris elections marked the fall of the Brissotins, although in the provinces it is true that they later recovered their popularity. Brissot himself received only seven votes. When the first round failed to produce a conclusive result, Robespierre intervened on behalf of Desmoulins, who had opposed Roland's friend, Kersaint. He wrecked Tallien's candidacy because he doubted the purity of his principles, and reproached him for being "strong when the people were strong, and weak when the people were weak". He was unable to fend off the candidacy of Philippe Egalité (as the Duc d'Orléans now called himself), which was supported by Danton. He gave his support to the patriotic butcher Legendre, and to Marat in opposition to the English chemist Priestley, who had had the curious idea of putting himself up for election. "Doctor Priestley writes away in his study, but what need have we of men who only produce books? We need patriots who have had experience of revolutions, who have fought man to man against despotism. As for myself, I confess, I prefer a man who in order to fight Lafayette and the Court would hide in a cellar for a month."

[[·]]

News (received on 26th August) of the surrender of Longwy, the siege of Verdun, and the threat of a Prussian invasion of the capital reached the anxious city at the same time as word of royalist uprisings in the Vendée. For several days bloody events had also been taking place in Paris. Between 13th and 29th August some three thousand suspects—priests, nobles and others—had been arrested. The rumour was current that conspiracies were hatching in the overpopulated prisons. Notices signed by Marat were posted on the walls, encouraging volunteers not to leave for the frontiers before having "carried out the justice of the people on traitors". Several Sections passed similar proposals, after which the killers went into action. On 2nd September three hundred priests and debtors were put to death at the Carmelites, and blood flowed at the Abbaye. Following instructions from Maillard's tribunal, thieves, priests and debtors were put to death indiscriminately at Châtelet, and young delinquents at Bicêtre. Only the dregs of Paris, one ought to point out, took part in these murders—less than a thousand people. The small number makes it hard to understand why the authorities did nothing to stop them—neither the Commune nor the Assembly. Théodore de Lameth said that:

(OPPOSITE) *During the night armed bands of patriots roamed about, shouting slogans and beating drums. They ferreted out traitors and even invaded their homes*

"During this time they made painful dissertations on insignificant things." When Roland's secretary asked Danton as the Minister of Justice to intervene, he replied: "I do not care about the prisoners. They will have to take care of themselves." Later he claimed credit for the initiative, perhaps out of boastfulness, when the event seemed to him to have a ring of grandeur in its monstrousness. "I looked my crime straight in the eyes and committed it." Danton liked bombasting.

In public Robespierre remained as imperturbable as if the massacres had happened on another planet. One might have thought that he did not even know that they had taken place. He blamed no one, but on the other hand, he did not encourage or excuse, unlike Billaud-Varenne, who went and actually congratulated the killers. Souberbielle maintained that he always spoke of the events in horrified terms, and Charlotte said that he reproached Pétion for not having tried to do anything. Pétion is supposed to have replied: "Nothing in the world could have saved the prisoners." At least the mayor went to harangue the crowd in one of the prisons, but to no avail, it is true.

As for Robespierre's moral responsibility, he had previously said something which sounded like an encouragement to massacre: "Bear in mind that the courage and energy of the people alone can save freedom. The people are enslaved as soon as they relax. They are despised as soon as they are no longer feared; they are con-

Several days of carnage began on 2nd September when mobs invaded the prisons of Châtelet and Bicetre. Regardless of the crime or guilt of the prisoners more than 800 people were slaughtered before any attempt was made by the authorities to restore order in the city

quered as soon as they forgive those enemies whom they have not crushed." On the night of 2nd September Robespierre was at the Commune denouncing Brissot and his colleagues: "So no one dares to name the traitors? Well then, for the safety of the people, I will name them. I denounce Brissot, the murderer of freedom, and the Gironde faction. I denounce them for having sold France to Brunswick and for having been paid that money before their betrayal." The Brissotins had, in fact, some time previously in their papers proposed the absurd idea of putting either the Duke of Brunswick or the Duke of York on the throne of France. It seems, however, that they did not really have a plot, but simply wanted to try and blackmail Louis XVI in some way.

On hearing Robespierre's denunciation, the Vigilance Committee of the Commune ordered the arrest of Brissot, Roland and other important Girondists. The mandate of arrest against Brissot was opportunely altered to an order of investigation, which came to nothing. In the committee's opinion Roland was well and truly caught, but Danton intervened. In spite of his lack of esteem for him, Danton could not let one of his fellow ministers be arrested in this way, and doubtless subsequently murdered. Robespierre agreed to go with Danton to the town hall to ask for Roland's release. He met Pétion there. *Le Moniteur* reproduced the interview, which was their last.

"Robespierre, you are causing a lot of trouble. Your denunciations, your alarms, your hatred and your suspicions are stirring up the people. Now then, explain yourself. Have you any proof? Have you any facts?"

"You are surrounded by gossiping sycophants. You allow yourself to be led astray. People turn you against me. You consort with enemies. You daily see Brissot and all his party."

"You are mistaken, Robespierre. No one is more on guard against prejudice than I. Nonetheless I see Brissot but rarely. But then you have not known him, as I have, since childhood. I beg of you, let us explain things to each other. Tell me frankly what is on your mind; what is it that you know."

"I believe that Brissot had sold himself to Brunswick."

"How wrong you are. Would not Brunswick be the first to cut off his head?"

[[·]]

Among the Paris deputies to the Convention was Robespierre's brother, Augustin. His friends called him Bon-Bon, but he had failed in all his ambitions in Arras, both at the bar and in politics. It would have been hard to find someone more different from Maximilien. He was a handsome man, fond of gaming, good food and women. He could hardly be said to seem the model of virtue that a representative of the people was meant to be in the eyes of the Incorruptible. Basically he lacked ideas, and out of affection he adopted those of his older brother, for whom he had the greatest and sincerest admiration.

When they arrived in Paris, Charlotte and Augustin lodged in the Duplay house. Over the years Charlotte had become a rather shrewish spinster, possibly because of her thwarted marriage to Fouché. She directed all her affection towards her brothers, and that affection was exclusive, as happens all too often. It was only with jealousy that she could look upon the loving care which Maxmilien's friends bestowed upon him. "When I arrived from Arras in 1792, I stayed with the Duplay family, and I noticed the influence they had on him, an influence that was not founded on intellect—since my brother had more of it than Madame Duplay—nor on great services rendered, since the family with whom he had been living for such a short time had not even rendered him any. But, I repeat, this influence took its source, on the one hand, from the easygoing nature of my brother, if I may put it so, and on the other from the ceaseless and often importunate caresses of Madame Duplay."

At least she saw it this way, thinking that the privilege of lavishing attention on her brother was hers by right. "I resolved to get Maximilien out of her clutches." As if he had been a victim. Even so, she did not properly understand him, for she saw his influential position as some sort of social role. The joiner's house did not seem a luxurious enough setting to her. The first person in the Republic owed it to himself to live on a more lavish scale. This reasoning meant nothing to Robespierre but all the same he finally gave just to put a stop to her reproaches. He agreed to take an apartment for all three in the rue Florentin. "Madame Duplay was very angry with me. I think that she continued to hate me for it all her life." But Charlotte's triumph was to be of short duration. After the happy family atmosphere of the Duplay's house, life with this rather prickly person can hardly have been very pleasant for Maximilien. Immediately he regretted the move. He was promptly stricken with one of his frequent complaints which Madame Duplay was so good at treating—Charlotte much less so. "We had been living together for some time—my brother and I—when he fell ill. No one had told Madame Duplay about his illness. When he was better, she came to see him and made a great fuss of the fact that no one had told her. She began to say very disagreeable things to me. She said that my brother had not had all the necessary treatment, that he would be better cared for at her house, that he would lack nothing, and there she was pressing Maximilien to go back to her house."

Truth to tell, he asked for nothing better, to Charlotte's great indignation. She could not understand why he found the company of strangers more agreeable than her own. "In spite of my complaints, Robespierre finally decided to follow her. 'They like me so much,' he said. 'They are so good to me that it would be ungrateful to rebuff them.' He must have thought that his preference for Madame Duplay affected me. Should he have sacrificed me to her after the disagreeable things she said, after reproaching me for having let my brother go without treatment?"

Henceforth, in order to see him, Charlotte had to go to the rue Saint-Honoré. But then, she said, Madame Duplay received her "in a disgraceful way". Soon the two women quarrelled. Rather than risk meeting her, Charlotte got into the habit of sending a servant to find out the news. "One day when I had told her to give my brother some pots of jam, Madame Duplay said to her, angrily, 'Take that back, I don't want her to poison Robespierre.' My servant came back in tears to tell me Madame Duplay's dreadful blasphemy." Charlotte silently swallowed her anguish and indignation.

At least she had Augustin. Their household seems to have got along somehow. Some months later when he left for the Alpes-Maritimes on a mission, she decided to follow him. It was partly to distract herself, but also to spy on him, because she was very jealous of his women friends. Another deputy, Ricord, and his wife accompanied Augustin. At first Charlotte amused herself with things that were new to her. She rode and let herself be wreathed in the flattery that was naturally paid to the sister of a member of the Committee of Public Safety. But that did not hide the fact that the young and pretty Madame Ricord wanted to seduce Augustin. The drama exploded.

On his return, Augustin in turn spurned the rue Florentin and went to live with the Ricords. Charlotte took this new insult badly, all the while failing to understand how exasperating it was for a young man who liked to amuse himself to be watched over. Reproachful letters that became more and more bitter were exchanged. The last began in this way: "Your aversion for me, my brother, far from diminishing— as I had flattered myself it had done—has turned into implacable hatred, to the point that the sight of me fills you with horror."

Augustin had no difficulty in convincing Maximilien that all the wrong was on Charlotte's side. Robespierre himself knew only too well the drawbacks of her character. Since she persisted in making their life impossible, the only solution was to send her away. As it happened their friend Joseph Lebon was returning to Arras after a short stay in Paris. They begged him to take Charlotte with him. Lebon was now unfrocked and had become the terrorist of the region. Charlotte was very frightened of going with him, convinced that her brothers had given her such a travelling companion to ensure that she would be guillotined on arriving in Arras. Along the way she fled from his entourage. Naturally he had not considered such a thing for one moment. He was happy enough to be rid of her.

10

THE CONVENTION

"Remove the word republic. I see that nothing has changed. Everywhere I see the same vices, the same scheming."

ROBESPIERRE

O N 21ST SEPTEMBER THE CONVENTION TOOK OVER FROM THE Legislative Assembly. The elections had taken place in a climate of the greatest indifference. Hardly one-tenth of the electors had voted. When this happens the extremists usually win the day. The new assembly was therefore distinctly more left-wing, younger, and from a lower social stratum.

On the right now was a numerous group—the Girondins—who were very active, but who lacked cohesion. Alongside Brissot, Vergniaud, Gensonné and Guadet they had as principal members Barbaroux, a fiery Marseillais who was handsome and slightly plump, and whom Madame Roland saw as a re-incarnation of Antinoüs; Louvet, a bald little man who had written a successful novel, *Faublas*; Isnard, another southerner who was vehemently eloquent. "If the fire of heaven were in the control of men, one would have used it to strike down those who make attempts on the freedom of peoples." Their Montagnard opponents accused them of federalism—in other words of wanting to make France a collection of independent little republics. They denied this, maintaining that they were simply opposing the dictatorship of Paris—the city that had rejected them—by reducing it to the status of a department. This attitude certainly held dangers since the assembly sat in Paris under the pressure of the tribunes and the threat of the Sections. They all tried to control the Revolution, but it had already outstripped them.

(OPPOSITE) *Royalty was abolished at the first meeting of the Convention in the first year of the Republic*

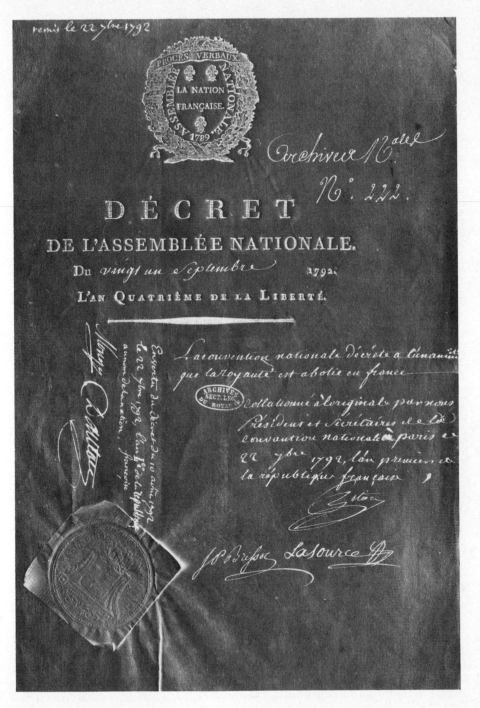

remis le 22 7bre 1792

DÉCRET

DE L'ASSEMBLÉE NATIONALE.

Du *vingt un Septembre* 1792.

L'AN QUATRIÈME DE LA LIBERTÉ.

La convention nationale décrète à l'unanimité
que la royauté est abolie en France

Collationné à l'original par nous
Présidens et Secrétaires de la
convention nationale à Paris le
22 7bre 1792, l'an premier de
la république française

The Montagnards—so called because they sat on the upper benches—formed the left-wing of the Convention. They were led by the elected Jacobins of Paris. No less than the Girondins, they were for the most part of provincial origin. Robespierre and his brother were from Arras. Danton was from Arcis-sur-Aube. The gloomy Billaud-Varenne was from La Rochelle, and Marat from Switzerland. Couthon and Saint-Just appeared as Robespierre's lieutenants. Couthon was from Auvergne and had sat in the Legislative Assembly. He had a pleasing and friendly appearance and was the sort of barrister who gave free consultations to poor people. A contemporary said of him: "He distinguished himself by his gentleness, the politeness of his forms of address, and his keenness to oblige." He had recently been struck by a cruel illness which had paralysed both legs and kept him fixed to his chair, in a state of perpetual exasperation. Robespierre had occasion to reproach him "for giving way to the first stirrings of a sensitivity that was far too unpolitical". He could certainly not have made such a remark to his other friend, Saint-Just, an implacable young man of feminine features, with long hair, rings in his ears, and holding his head above a huge cravat. Author of a licentious poem, *L'Organt*, and something of a thief, he had been in prison, and the Revolution had given him an aim—the reform of society. He went into the Convention with the intention of supporting Robespierre to whom, during the period of the Constituent Assembly, he had written the warmest of letters. "I do not know you, but you are a great man. You are not only the deputy of one province, but of humanity and the Republic."

The great majority of the assembly formed an undecided group known as the Plain (*la Plaine*), and on other occasions disdainfully the Swamp (*le Marais*) or the Belly (*le Ventre*). Various moderates sat there, such as Cambacérès the man of law, Sieyès, one of the members of the Constituent Assembly—Robespierre called him the mole of the Revolution—and Boissy d'Anglas. They were wise and skilful people who knew how to survive the storm and end their political lives with honours under the Empire.

[[·]]

The very day that the Convention met, just when nothing seemed to be able to stop the Prussian troops from reaching Paris in a few weeks, the guns at Valmy halted the foreign invasion by a sort of miracle. Few battles have made so much ink flow. Was victory to be attributed to the enthusiasm of the young volunteers; to the rain, which immobilized the enemy artillery; to the fact that Brunswick's soldiers had dysentery; to Austria's jealousy; or to corruption? Did Danton buy the general with money or with promises? He had been mentioned as a candidate for the throne. Narbonne had had offered him the command of the French Army. No less surprising was the conduct of Dumouriez, who did not want his retirement disturbed, as if a secret pact had been agreed upon. Robespierre did not forget it.

Be that as it may, Valmy saved the Revolution. But the end of external danger did not re-establish peace among the parties. Having been driven out of Paris by Robespierre, the Girondins returned full of bitterness, determined upon revenge. Since they seemed stronger by virtue of their number, the Marais joined forces with them. Pétion was elected President of the Convention, and there was not one Montagnard among the Secretariat.

Rebecqui, a friend of Barbaroux and a deputy from Marseilles, opened hostilities on 25th September. "I denounce by name the leader of the party that aspires to dictatorship. It is Robespierre." The Incorruptible immediately got on to the rostrum to reply, saying that he gladly welcomed this opportunity to defend not himself, but the fatherland. "Citizen, you had the courage to accuse me of wanting to be my country's enemy, in the face of the people's representatives, in this very place where I defended their rights. I thank you. I recognize in this deed the citizenship that characterizes the famous city that has sent you." Robespierre then began to undertake his own justification, recalling in detail his record in the Constituent Assembly. He described himself as "the most persecuted of the defenders of the people". When Robespierre talked about himself he never stopped. The panegyric was too long, and caused at first murmurs of impatience and then protests. "Cut it short," people shouted at him. One of the deputies charged him "to give in four words a frank explanation". He drew himself up, looking those who were interrupting him straight in the eye. "Well then, I am going to force you to listen to me." He then went into the attack and reverted to the theme of a Brissotin intrigue to put the Duke of Brunswick on the throne of France. He accused his opponents of federalism, which he defined as "the intention of turning the French Republic into an assemblage of federal republics which would always be at the mercy of internal disorders or foreign attacks". He ended by saying: "Let us declare that the Republic is one, under one system of constitutional laws. Only the certainty of the most solid union between all the parties of France can enable us to fight off our enemies with energy and success."

Robespierre's first speech to the Convention made a good impression. He had cleverly placed the discussion on a terrain of which the majority approved. The provincial deputies had arrived—as a result of the September massacres—full of prejudices towards Parisian representatives but no less concerned for the unity of the country. They thought that Robespierre was right. Barbaroux felt that the assembly was changing its mind and intervened. He had been an impassioned Jacobin two months before, but had been turned into a no less intransigent Girondin by Madame Roland. Robespierre had admired his patriotism at first sight, and never forgave the group's Egeria for having swayed him. Barbaroux told how he had been at the Duplays on the eve of 10th August when Panis had expounded to him the necessity for setting up a dictatorship "designating Robespierre as the most virtuous man, destined to become the dictator of France". Panis denied having held this opinion, but Rebecqui swore under oath that he had heard it. In these circumstances it was impossible to know the truth. Some of the *sans-culottes* had thought of putting absolute power in Robespierre's hands, but he could not be held responsible for such ideas. Panis's accusation miscarried, so Brissot tried to deflect the discussion by charging Robespierre with wanting to have him arrested during the night of the 2nd and 3rd of September. Marat replied. He was not bothered by the virtual unanimous hostility of the Convention, whom he was addressing for the first time, and he took upon himself the responsibility for the police visit to Brissot on that night, and haughtily claimed responsibility for the idea of a dictatorship.

[[·]]

After this debate Robespierre was quiet for a time in the Convention. On the other hand, he spoke every evening at the Jacobins. He had all the Brissotins driven out of the club and Brissot's own name was struck off the list on 10th October. In this way, from its foundation until 9th Thermidor (27th July), Robespierre asserted his control of the club by successive purges. On 28th October he read a curious essay on the role of slander in the Revolution. Above all he denounced the Convention. For the third time the national institution of representation had not fulfilled his hopes. Of course he recognized that the new assembly had in it a number of "pure and patriotic" members, but the "intriguers' party"—a party "more criminal in its ways than all the factions that preceded it"—prevented it from acting, for: "How can one be concerned with public welfare when one is only putting Parisian patriotism on trial?"

Among Girondin "intrigues", there was one that seemed to him especially "perfidious", a projected law that would punish with death any provocation to murder and civil war. It would then no longer be possible to denounce "the factious". Robespierre appealed to the Parisian Sections, and so, to protect themselves, the Girondins had new volunteers brought in from the provinces. Soon there were 16,000 of these young people. Sometimes they mounted guard in front of the Convention, sometimes they paraded through the streets chanting a song whose words demanded the heads of Marat, Robespierre and Danton. But Pache, the Minister of War and a good *sans-culotte*, cleared the capital by sending most of them off to the frontier. The others were not long in falling under the influence of the Jacobins and became propagandists among their fellow countrymen. Through its affiliated clubs also, who regularly received accounts of the meetings, the parent Jacobin Club was able to influence provincial opinion. An example of its evolution is well illustrated by some letters that Robespierre received from a man called Aigoin from Montpellier. In June 1792 he was still a partisan of Lafayette and Brissot. A few months later he vehemently denounced the "manoeuvres of the moderates", calling for the creation of new newspapers to fight Girondin propaganda.

The municipal elections in Paris made the Girondins lose all hope of regaining their influence in the capital. The extremists sought Robespierre's support and won a decisive victory. Chaumette was among them, a former president of the Insurrectional Commune and a man who embodied a strange mixture of pure idealism and ferociousness. There was also Hébert, editor of a bizarre paper, written in filthy language. At this time he was a keen Robespierre supporter. He wrote: "In my eyes Robespierre is better than all the treasures of Peru." Chambon was the new mayor.

Even so, their defeat only increased the Girondins' determination to fight. The session on 25th September had only been a prelude. They realized that if they did not quickly strike down Robespierre they would be beaten down by him.

A new offensive against him was launched on 29th October. For its success they needed the support of the Marais, and to win this they had to arouse its anxieties. Roland, Minister of the Interior, came to the rostrum of the Convention to describe the situation in Paris which he painted as being threatened by anarchists. After that he read a letter from a person called Mercadier, a sort of journalist and former Vice-President of the Criminal Tribunal. In this letter Mercadier described an interview that he maintained he had had with a notorious Septembrist, Fournier l'Américain (in fact he was from Auvergne).

According to Fournier, the September massacres had not been sufficient: Robespierre wanted to reintroduce them. The letter ended with this sentence: "I think that it is time to dam the springs of evil by taking severe measures against those who provoke murder. It is only Robespierre they want to hear and talk about, and they maintain that he alone can save the fatherland." The scene had been prepared in advance. At his name the groans of the Girondins broke out "Oh, the villain."

Robespierre rushed to the rostrum. Guadet, who was in the chair, wanted to prevent him from speaking. His weak voice was drowned by the tumult. But Danton came to his aid and overpowered it. "Now let the orator speak. And I demand to speak after him—it is time that all was cleared up."

Finally Robespierre was able to make himself heard, but again he was interrupted by hostile shouts:

"At least listen to what I want to say."

"We don't want to hear it."

"What, sirs! Do I not have the right to tell you that from time to time you have been given reports directed to only one end, and this end is to oppress the patriots who do not please?"

"To unmask imposters."

Clutching the balustrade, Robespierre went on.

"If you do not want to hear me, if things that do not please you are reason for interrupting me, if the president, instead of having the votes and the freedom of principles respected, himself uses pretexts that are more or less specious . . ."

There were more interruptions. When the noise had died down he went on.

"Since I have been speaking I have continually heard around me shouts of malevolence. I see that with perfidious insinuations they have been busy designating as factious that group of men who have deserved well of the fatherland, and although I by no means have this honour, nevertheless they do me the honour of always including me among the men they want to defame.

"What, when there is not a man among them who dares to accuse me to my face by enumerating any positive facts against me, when there is not one who dares to step on to this rostrum and open a calm and serious and well reasoned discussion with me . . ."

At that moment a little man came forward in front of the rostrum. He looked at Robespierre.

"Yes, Robespierre, I propose myself against you. I accuse you."

It was Louvet, who that day was making his début on the rostrum of the Convention. He had been preparing his speech for a month, and somewhat emphatically the Girondins called it the Robespierrides. He had gladly read passages from it to a small committee of friends with visible satisfaction.

This theatrical effect, which had been so well engineered, aroused curiosity. Louvet began in total silence: "It is a question of knowing whether there are factions of seven or eight members in this assembly, or if it is the 730 members of the assembly who are themselves a faction. You must emerge from this extraordinary struggle conquerors or in disgrace. You may go on producing partial measures in vain if you do not attack the evil in the men who are the authors of them. I am going to denounce their plots."

Louvet's argument consisted in claiming for the Girondins credit for 10th August, but keeping for Robespierre the responsibility for the September massacres. He said that the Commune, inspired by Robespierre, had only intervened subsequently, so as to sabotage the Girondin national policy. He had definitely excluded Girondin electors from voting because he was aiming at a dictatorship. "Why were the massacres not prevented? Because Roland spoke in vain, because the Minister of Justice, Danton, did not speak. Because Santerre, in command of the Sections, was waiting; because municipal officers were presiding over these executions. Because the Legislative Assembly was dominated, and an insolent demagogue came to the bar of the house to dictate the Commune's decrees, and threatened it with sounding the tocsin if it did not obey."

At these words all eyes turned to Robespierre. There were shouts of "Robespierre to the bar. Accuse Robespierre."

"Robespierre, I accuse you," went on Louvet, "of having ceaselessly slandered the purest patriots. I accuse you of having spread these slanders in the first week of September, which is to say during days when these slanders were dagger blows. I accuse you of having degraded and proscribed the representatives of the nation. I accuse you of having constantly produced yourself as an object of idolatry; of having allowed people in your presence to designate you as the only man in France who could save the nation, and of having said it yourself. I accuse you of having obviously aimed at being the supreme power."

[[·]]

Robespierre asked for a week to prepare his reply. The session was arranged for
Monday, 5th November. Meanwhile, at the Jacobins, where messengers hourly
brought news from the Convention, indignation rose. "It is not possible," shouted
butcher Legendre, "that in a free country virtue should succumb to crime."
Augustin talked of plots and assassination and brought feelings to their pitch.
"Citizens, I am much afraid. I think that murderers are going to stab my brother.
In the Convention itself I heard it loudly said that Robespierre would appear only
to die at their hands."

Amidst the tumult caused by these words, one member, Deschamps, was heard
to accuse another of having said "If Robespierre was not surrounded by brigands,
we would have got rid of him long ago." He went on: "This assassin, this traitor
is in our midst, in this room. I name him, it is Baumier." The man strongly denied
having held such opinions. A violent altercation arose between the two men.
Baumier's expulsion was about to be pronounced when Augustin spoke. As a sign
of sympathy for his brother, he said, there had to be a general reconciliation in
the club.

The danger which threatened their idol gave the Jacobins the idea of organizing
his protection. Laplanche, a former Benedictine, suggested "that in future the
galleries of the Convention should be better filled." They also decided to give
Robespierre a secret bodyguard of volunteers. A strong man from Les Halles came
forward, then the printer Nicolas and the locksmith Didier, two friends of Duplay.
Each morning one of them, armed with a large stick, went to wait at the door in
the rue Saint-Honoré, then discreetly, without being seen by Robespierre,
accompanied him to the Convention.

[[·]]

Robespierre's speech, announced in advance, was impatiently awaited by the public
in the galleries, as if it were some theatrical performance. Camille Desmoulins
described how: "A crowd of citizens had spent the night at the doors of the hall so
as to be first in." Dulaure told how: "There were individual quarrels between the
supporters of Robespierre and others which happily did not come to anything. The
terrace of the Feuillants was no less crowded. Two or three men had a piece of
tripe. They held it up and shouted that it was soaked in acid and that it was going
to be eaten by Robespierre's and Marat's enemies. The people applauded."

Desmoulins again tells how Robespierre went to the rostrum "bearing his
head in the most calm manner". Louvet's speech had only been a literary exercise
in effects. Basically it was rather hollow, with unproven accusations following one
another at random. Robespierre was going to take them methodically, one by one,
so as to refute them logically as a barrister defends a client. Was it possible, he asked

paris le 12 brumaire l'an I de la republique

mon ami, je n'ai pas oublié un instant ni l'armée
du rhin, ni nos deux commissions. j'ai pressé toutes
les mesures nécessaires, et j'ai lieu de croire qu'aucune
n'a été négligée. le comité a adopté un plan
qui me paroit très bien conçu, et dicté par le même
esprit que celui qui a si bien réussi pour l'armée
du nord. ce plan est plus vaste
et plus hardi, que celui qui consiste à défendre
les différens points du territoire, avec différens
corps d'armée: il est plus sage et atteint
seul le but. carnot qui nous en a présenté l'idée
vous a déja écrit, pour vous le développer.
nous vous enverrons ce collegue, dans peu de jours
pour mieux vous
expliquer nos idées, si vous ne les avez pas
entiérement saisies. nous comptons beaucoup
sur l'energie que vous nous communiquez à l'armée
et sur l'activité que vous deployez. pour moi, je
ne doute pas du succès, si vous l'appliquez, à
l'execution de notre plan. au surplus les ordres sont
donnés, pour procurer à l'armée tous les renforts qui
sont à notre disposition. adieu, je vous embrasse
de tout mon cœur Robespierre

Robespierre's letter of instructions to a general of the Army of the Rhine

first, that he had envisaged dictatorship? "You will agree that if such an idea was criminal, it was even more rash, for in order to carry it out not only would the throne have to be overthrown, but the Legislative Assembly annihilated, and above all not replaced by a National Convention. How, then, does it happen that I have been the first in my public speeches and in my writings to call the National Convention the only remedy for the ills of the fatherland? Only a madman could think that without arms or money the trust he enjoyed in Paris could be extended to the eighty-two *départements*." The argument, which was very reasonable, made its effect. For the elections, he went on, he had done nothing apart from what the rules allowed. In any case the Revolution justified illegal measures in other circumstances; in particular arrests. "You may as well condemn the suppression of royalist newspapers; the disarming of suspects, and the purging of deliberating assemblies. All these things were as illegal as the taking of the Bastille."

He disdainfully brushed aside the accusation of complicity in the September massacres. "Those who have said that I played the smallest part in the events of which I speak are either excessively credulous men or excessively perverse." He was devoting all his time to the electoral assembly or to the Jacobins, and knew nothing about what was going on in the prisons. Or at least—he corrected himself—he had been one of the last to learn. The general council, of which he was a member, tried to stop them without success. The indignation at the number of the victims of 10th August, the feelings caused by the approach of the enemy and the desire of the people to take its vengeance on the prisoners made any intervention useless. "What, then, is the relevance of the blood that was shed. Posterity will only see in these events their sacred cause and their sublime result. Citizens, do you want a revolution without revolution? What is this spirit of persecution that wants to revise, as it were, the one that broke our fetters?"

He left the rostrum amidst applause, much of which came from the Marais who, a week earlier, had applauded Louvet. Robespierre's speech was calm and precise, and made a strong impression. With their clumsy attacks, his adversaries had just opened up the way for him to dominate the assembly. In times of revolution one often becomes what opinion believes one to be. By aiming its blows at Robespierre, the Girondins made him out to be the leader of the Montagnards. One deputy asked that his speech be printed and sent to the *départements*. The Girondins felt themselves at such a loss that the majority of them added their votes to those of the rest of the assembly. The Convention went on with the agenda for the day, and did not allow either Louvet or Barbaroux to reply. More than one Girondin had a vision of the fate that awaited him in a few months' time. When he went home that evening Louvet said to his wife: "We would do well to get ready to go into exile or to mount the scaffold."

He published in pamphlet form the second speech that he was unable to deliver, with the title: 'To Maximilien Robespierre and his royalists." But the real reply was a humorous article by Condorcet which appeared in *La Chronique de Paris* on 9th

November 1792. It is certainly worthy of being quoted, if only in part:

> One wonders why there are so many women who follow Robespierre, to his home, to the Jacobins, to the Cordeliers and to the Convention. It is because the French Revolution is a religion and Robespierre one of its sects. He is a priest with his flock, but it is obvious that all his power is on the distaff side. Robespierre preaches, Robespierre censures. He is furious, serious, melancholic, exalted without passion. He thunders against the rich and the great. He lives on little and has no physical needs. He has only one mission—to talk, and he talks almost all the time. He harangues the Jacobins when he can attract some disciples there; he keeps quiet when he might damage his authority. He refuses positions where he could help the people and chooses posts in which he thinks he might govern them. He has given himself a reputation for austerity which borders on sanctity. He climbs on the benches, he talks about God and Providence. He has himself followed by women and weak spirited people, he soberly receives their adoration and their homage. The reproach of dictatorship was therefore clumsy, and the proposition of ostracism absurd. Robespierre is a priest and will never be anything but that. It was like taking Hercules' club to crush a flea that will disappear in winter.

Between 5th and 30th November Robespierre was not seen either at the Convention or the Jacobins. This absence would seem to correspond to his illness at the time of his stay with Charlotte in the rue Saint-Florentin. The day he reappeared at the club, he had his friend Duplay demand the removal of the bust of Mirabeau, which had presided over their proceedings since his death. An iron safe had just been discovered, disclosing the correspondence between him and the Court that had existed at the end of his life. Robespierre denounced "this traitor". Mirabeau, he said, had been nothing more than an "intriguer", a "political charlatan", and did not merit an honour that ought to be kept for "the true friends of the people". "I see only two men who are worthy of our homage, Brutus and Rousseau." Therefore they should remove his bust, along with that of Helvetius, "for Helvetius persecuted Rousseau and would now be a counter-revolutionary". The two busts were thrown to the ground, and since they were made of plaster, they broke. The fragments were scornfully kicked aside.

Some people remembered that at the beginning Robespierre had been one of Mirabeau's colleagues. Despite the fact that they had subsequently had differences of opinion, Robespierre had spoken Mirabeau's funeral oration. In *Les Révolutions de Paris*, Prudhomme wrote that it was Robespierre's idea that his body be deposited in the tribune's Panthéon, defying him to prove that Mirabeau was less honest than Pétion or Manuel. It was an inopportune reminder. Robespierre did not like to admit that he had been wrong. He felt himself even more embarrassed by the fact that he had not neglected to reproach others for having had dealings with Mirabeau. He thought it necessary to produce a long reply, justifying himself. It was not him, but the Directoire of Paris—that counter-revolutionary assembly—who had proposed the Panthéon. He disapproved of the idea, as he disapproved of Mirabeau. He gave his support all the same, because he saw that public opinion wanted it. If he had made a mistake he hoped that in the light of his political career as a whole, and the persecutions he had endured in the name of freedom, he would be forgiven.

[[·]]

During the three weeks of Robespierre's absence, the Convention began the debate on Louis XVI's trial. Saint-Just said that the ex-king was guilty simply by virtue of having reigned and ought to be put to death by decree and not by judgement. It was a political act. The other speakers were more indulgent and talked in terms of prison or exile. Then the discussion had dragged on and eventually stopped. The Girondins tried to smother the matter, out of pity for the man. Nevertheless they dare not openly declare their intention of saving him for fear of being taken for moderates, and so were therefore content to let time go by. But in this matter, as on almost all questions, they revealed their divisions. Barbaroux, one of their most influential members, wanted the death penalty.

The same day that he returned to the assembly Robespierre, who suspected them of wanting to put the king back on the throne and reign in his name, took the rostrum to propose what he described as "an efficacious measure to confound forever the enemies of the National Convention. I demand that the last of the French tyrants, the chief tyrant, the conspirators' rallying point, be condemned to the supreme penalty for his misdeeds. As long as the Convention puts off the decision about this important trial, it will arouse the rebellious and uphold the hopes of those who are partisans of royalty."

His proposition embarrassed the Girondins. They were already suspect in many peoples' eyes since the discovery of the iron safe, and could not oppose the trial without being accused of being royalist. For their own security they had to seem to be in favour of it. On 3rd December Barbaroux proposed "that Louis should stand trial".

All the same, Robespierre took up the argument of his friend Saint-Just. There was no need for a trial to condemn the king, because it had already been done. The Revolution had passed judgement. "Louis XVI is not an accused man. He has been condemned by the institution of the Republic. For if he were pardoned, it would be the Revolution, and all those who carried it out, who would be condemned." The rigorousness of this argument made it irrefutable. "You are not judges. You have no sentence to give for or against a man, but a measure of public safety to adopt, a national act of providence to carry out." If the nation had judged the king by what had happened on 10th August, it was not for the Convention to question the sentence, but only to carry it out. There were no legal formalities to be observed.

"The nation does not judge as legal courts do, it throws a thunderbolt." A public debate might cause fratricidal quarrels among the patriots, to the joy of the factious, "for all the ferocious hordes of despotism are once more ready to tear at the breast of the fatherland in the name of Louis XVI. Louis is still fighting us from the depths of his prison."

> "I demand that this memorable event be preserved as a monument intended to nourish in the hearts of peoples the feeling for their rights and horror of tyrants, and in the souls of tyrants the salutary terror of the justice of the people. I demand that the Convention declare Louis from this moment a traitor to the French nation and a criminal towards humanity. I demand that he set an important example to the world in the very place where, on 10th August, the noble martyrs of freedom fell.
>
> "'It is a weighty business that must be judged wisely,' you say. What is there in it? Is it his actual person? In the eyes of freedom he is only more vile because of it. In the eyes of humanity he is only more guilty. What importance does the miserable individual of the last of the kings have for the people? The representatives of the people's wishes ought to do their duty. These wishes demand the Republic, they founded it, and still Louis lives.

The struggle between Girondins and Montagnards went on throughout the whole of the month of December with increased vigour. On 7th December, at the Jacobins, Robespierre once again denounced "the Girondin faction. It has done nothing for the people, yet it sets the provinces against Paris and creates obstacles to the king's trial." Even so, he did not propose that violent means should be used against them "for although insurrection is the most sacred of obligations, there must be no repetition of 10th August". But public opinion must be enlightened and patriotic deputies must not let themselves be reduced to silence. "Let us swear at the rostrum rather than yield our place when they refuse to let us speak." A dozen of the deputies present at the meeting undertook to die alongside Robespierre the next time that the Convention interrupted his speeches. The butcher Legendre made a more practical suggestion. His colleagues should be earlier risers, so as to get to the sessions. They were negligent in this respect, "for their adversaries are already in their places, ready to begin, whilst the patriots' seats are still empty".

On 12th December Robespierre attacked in particular Roland, whom he accused of having used his post as Minister of the Interior in an attempt to destroy the club and its affiliated societies—"This man, who originated the plot to steal all the jewels in the store house." He then put forward a rather unexpected proposition. He had learned at college that there were two ways of educating the mind— by reading good books and by reading bad books. In future the club meetings should be opened by a recitation from the two worst Girondin newspapers, Brissot's *Le Patriote français* and Condorcet's *La Chronique de Paris*. He knew that this would be a good way of maintaining the wrath of the Jacobins.

[[·]]

Meanwhile the assembly had, under the influence of the Girondins, decided that the trial of the king would take place; but Marat had an amendment which stated that the votes would be cast on the rostrum, as each name was called, thus ruining their hope of avoiding the death penalty by a secret vote. On the 13th, a deputation from the Commune presented itself at the bar of the Convention to demand that when the king's lawyer, de Sèze, went to visit him in the Temple, he should be searched with the utmost rigour, "even in the most secret places". The reason given was fear that he might be carrying letters to Louis from his supporters. Murmurs of disapproval greeted the proposition, but Robespierre defended it. He said that plots were being formed to save the king, so precautions had to be taken. As usual, there was applause from the galleries. Even so, no decision was taken on this question. On the 16th the Girondins made one of their clumsy attempts to divert attention by proposing that citizen Egalité be exiled. Robespierre had little sympathy for the person whom he suspected of intrigue. In fact, he thought it would be a good thing if all the members of the royal family were exiled. They could live in England at the expense of the Republic. But if the assembly decided on the expulsion of Orléans, this might be taken as a precedent for the ostracism of true patriots. He therefore opposed it as "a Girondin plot, aimed at distracting attention".

There was a curious debate at the Jacobins on 23rd December on the respective merits of Marat and Robespierre. Each received his share of praise. Among those who took part, the journalist Robert put forward the reasons that made him prefer the Incorruptible: "Robespierre is wise and moderate. Marat is exaggerated and has none of Robespierre's wisdom. It is not enough to be a patriot. One must be wise in the means used to achieve the ends, and in that Robespierre is manifestly superior to Marat." Dufourny, another member, expressed the opposite opinion that Marat was "one of these strong heads which are needed in time of revolution". There was no definite decision about the superiority of either one, but it was finally decided that a circular should be sent to the affiliated provincial societies "giving in detail the resemblances and the dissimilarities between the two men, so that good citizens might make a separation between two names that they wrongly think they ought always to link with one another." It was certainly not done to displease Robespierre that he was named Friend of the People, and homage rendered to him.

[[·]]

During this time the king's trial took place. Louis appeared before the Convention. De Sèze made his speech for the defence on 26th December. It was then that several Girondin deputies—Salles, Buzot and Rabaut Saint-Etienne—proposed an appeal to the people. The French people would be called to basic assemblies to ratify the Convention's sentence. The argument put forward was that only the people could take away the inviolability that the Constitution had given the king. Without the sanction of the people any act of this sort by the people's representatives constituted an attack on the sovereignty of the people. The Girondins had no doubt that the death sentence would be rejected by the people. They could therefore vote for it without any remorse, thus escaping the threats of the Parisian Sections, and taking away from their opponents the advantage of seeming to be more patriotic than themselves.

Robespierre did not let the purpose of this manoeuvre escape him. He also foresaw that the result of an appeal to the people would be the rejection of the death penalty. He said that the assembly was to be on its guard against "movements of sensitivity. Clemency that colludes with tyranny is barbarous. It was not so much Louis XVI who was on trial as the staunchest defender of freedom. It was against him and his party that the basic assemblies would give their decision." His fears were justified, since calling upon the people ran the risk of putting into question the entire work of the Revolution. "Was it not tantamount to declaring permanent civil war by summoning the forty thousand basic assemblies of the Republic?" When the people elected their representatives it was up to them, and not the people, to take responsibility for the decisions. Bad citizens, aristocrats and Feuillants would not fail to turn up in their droves to influence simple men and corrupt base minds with money. It was giving the royalists the means of meeting and assessing their strength. Intriguers would rush to the basic assemblies. But would the ploughman leave his fields or the workman his work? He returned to the idea that the people had shown their wishes on 10th August and then delegated power to its representatives. There were therefore no grounds for consulting the people. Those who proposed such an appeal were nothing more than divisive. "There is a plot to discredit the Convention and dissolve it, possibly through this interminable affair. It thrives not amongst those who energetically press for the principles of freedom, not amongst those who are dupes of a deadly intrigue, but among twenty or so scoundrels who control all its machinations." He ended: "I demand that the National Convention declare Louis guilty and worthy of death."

The Girondin leaders reacted, sending the ball back into Robespierre's court, but did not name him, since the parliamentary method of speaking at that time restricted people to generalities. Birotteau said: "The Convention crushes all these pygmies stuffed with pride. Like the frogs in the swamp, they force us to notice their existence by their noises." Vergniaud said: "Each breath that these men draw is an imposture because of their very nature, as it is in the nature of the snake only to exist through the distillation of poison." Gensonné said: "It is only too true that love of freedom has also its deception and its cult, its talebearers and its hypocrites. In the field of political economy there are as many charlatans as there are in the field of the art of medicine. . . ."

But the galleries applauded Robespierre and howled down his contradictors. On the next day, the normal agenda of the Jacobins was set aside so that he could repeat his speech. He read it in his monotonous voice, with even more pauses than usual, so as to give the journalists time to take down his words exactly, amidst a religious silence. Even so, on this subject provincial opinion differed from that of Paris, even in the Jacobin milieu. During the following week countless protests arrived at the rue Saint-Jacques, inveighing against the positions of Marat and Robespierre. Some even demanded that they be expelled from the club.

[[·]]

Voting began on 14th January. It lasted almost a week, since most of the deputies thought that they should give their reasons in quite long speeches. There were three questions. The first was about Louis's guilt, and received an almost unanimous reply in the affirmative, apart from some abstentions. Then the proposal for a plebiscite was rejected by 424 votes to 283. On the 16th the vote was taken on the sentence. The Girondins were expected to vote against death, but they did not dare to do this. Mailhe, the first, pronounced the word, then Vergniaud, who, only the night before, had said that he would not vote for it, even if he were the only one. When they capitulated, most of their colleagues did likewise. Obviously all the Montagnards voted for the death penalty, including the Duc d'Orléans, who did not abstain, and this upset Robespierre. As far as he himself was concerned, his logic allowed him no other verdict: "I am inflexible where oppressors are concerned because I have compassion for the oppressed. I do not recognize the humanity that slaughters people and pardons despots. The feeling that drove me to ask—in vain—that the Constituent Assembly should abolish the death sentence is the same one that today has forced me to demand that it should be exacted of the tyrant of my fatherland and the royalty itself in his person. I vote for death."

Next, before the results were announced, the President read a letter from de Sèze, demanding to be heard. He must have hoped through a final appeal to obtain banishment only. Robespierre opposed permission to speak. He said that the assembly should stick to its vote. "The nation has condemned the king who was oppressing it, not only so as to carry out an act of vengeance, but also to give a strong example to the world."

On the 18th the sentence was read. There were 361 votes for death and 360 against. Several Girondin deputies made a last attempt to save the king's life by proposing a stay of execution. Robespierre fought it. Humanity itself, he said ordered a speedy execution. In any case, a delay constituted a danger for the peace of the State.

Should Louis be kept as a hostage, to talk terms, if need be, with the despots allied against the Republic? "Ah! What Frenchman would not shudder at this idea? If we gave only the merest thought to a compromise with tyranny, we would find ourselves as a people already defeated. Our freedom would be flawed or

out voté

12

130 Robespierre —— La mort.

131 Danton —— La mort.

132 Collot d'Herbois —— La mort

Manuel —— La détention dans un fort ailleurs qu'à Paris jusqu'à ce que l'intérêt public permette la déportation.

133 Billaud-Varenne —— La mort dans 24 heures

134 Camille Desmoulins —— La mort.

135 Marat —— La mort dans 24 heures.

136 Lavicomterie —— La mort.

137 Legendre —— La mort.

138 Raffron —— La mort dans 24 heures

139 Panis —— La mort.

140 Sergent —— La mort.

141 Robert —— La mort.

Dusaulx —— Le bannissement à la paix.

142 Fréron —— La mort dans 24 heures

143 Beauvais —— La mort.

144 Fabre d'Églantine —— La mort.

145 Osselin —— La mort.

146 Robespierre, jeune —— La mort.

147 David —— La mort.

148 Boucher —— La mort.

149 Laignelot —— La mort.

Thomas —— La détention jusqu'à la paix, et la mort dans le cas d'un arrivement du territoire français de la part de Puissances étrangères.

appel nominal des 16 & 17 janvier 1793.

150 L.J. Égalité —— La mort.

151 Carnot —— Pas de ....

152 Duquesnoy —— La mort.

153 Lebas —— La mort.

Thomas Payne —— La détention : le bannissement à la paix.

Personne —— La détention : le bannissement à la paix.

154 Guffroy —— La mort dans le délai de la loi, sçavoir

Culart —— La déportation dans une de nos îles pour y être détenu, et le bannissement de toutes les terres de la République à la paix.

155 Bollet —— La mort.

annihilated by this shameful trait of thraldom and pusillanimity." The reprieve was finally defeated by 380 votes to 310.

Louis XVI mounted the scaffold on 21st January. That day Robespierre remained shut in his room. He had had the shutters closed and the gate of the house, too. Because the children were surprised by this, he said to them: "It is because something is going to take place today that you should not see."

(OPPOSITE) *The voting on the question of the king's fate was vocal. This part of the roll-call begins with delegates 130 and 131, Robespierre and Danton. The king's cousin was 150, and the Anglo–American pamphleteer, Thomas Paine appears, numberless, after Leban 153. The writer declared for imprisonment and then banishment when peace had been declared*

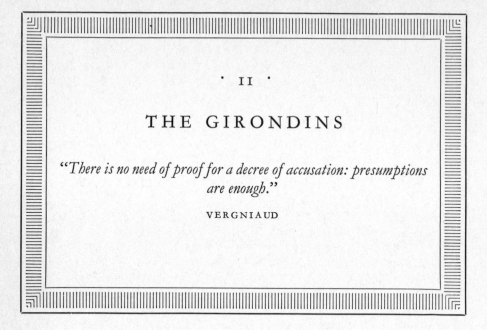

IN HIS *Adresse aux départements* OF 23RD JANUARY, ROBESPIERRE explained to his readers that acquittal of the king, or even a stay of execution, would have ensured the success of the counter-revolutionary plots. It was obviously the Girondins to whom he was referring. Urgent measures had to be taken against them. Barère pressed for severe punishment of anyone found hiding émigrés, and Robespierre seconded him. But above all he demanded an examination, "with republican severity", of the use to which Roland had put public money. Old Roland certainly had made no attempt to make personal financial gain from his position, but used part of the funds to which he had access to subsidize party newspapers. One point, however, is worthy of note. In the same speech Robespierre expressed the hope that, now that the tyrant was no more, the assembly would abolish the death penalty.

The Girondins had suffered a political defeat with the condemnation of the king, but undeniable military successes made up for it. The victory of Valmy had been followed by a series of triumphs on all fronts. In two months Nice, Savoy, Mainz and Belgium were successively conquered. Brissot's prophecy was being fulfilled, that the peoples of the occupied countries would welcome the French.

Internally, however, they had to face a disastrous economic situation. Paris was full of unemployed artisans and domestic servants. As a result of emigration, and the disappearance of a market for luxury goods, the people were hungry, as in years of famine, and began to murmur: "When we had a king we were not so unhappy as we are now, when we have 750 (kings)." In January troubles broke out because of a dearth of sugar. The Jacobins swore not to use any more until it was in plentiful supply again. Roland, overwhelmed by disappointments, and aware of the fact that he could not remedy the lack of provisions, resigned. The popularity of the "virtuous" Roland, for whom the people had risen on 20th June, was quite finished. In *L'Ami du peuple*, Marat denounced the "capitalists, profiteers, monopolists, luxury dealers, tools of chicanery and ex-nobles", and demanded the guillotine for them.

For Robespierre also, the solution lay in the punishment of the conspirators. He saw a counter-revolutionary plot as the source of the troubles. It seemed to him that economic difficulties were "the inescapable inconveniences of a great revolution". Its conquests were well worth a few material privations. A nation which put considerations about "food" first was quite unworthy. Only political questions ought to be worth worrying about.

Nevertheless, in the Sections, and in particular those in the poor districts most affected by privations, a new wave of revolutionaries began to appear who advocated social reforms above all. They were known as the Enraged (*Enragés*). Their leaders were very young people such as Leclerc, Varlet, and a former priest called Jacques Roux. They demanded an immediate taxation of food-stuffs and then an agrarian law—in other words, nationalization of land. In their wild talk these new comers showed hardly any respect for their predecessors.

Robespierre was too much the disciple of Rousseau to accept the classic concept of the right of property "to use and to abuse". He agreed that there ought to be fixed limits by subjecting it to the "right of the community over all". Too great an inequality in the distribution of goods led to political inequality, and from there to the destruction of freedom. But making goods communal did not seem a desirable move to him. Politically, moreover, it would have been a mistake. At a time when they were trying to rally the peasants to the Revolution by selling them the confiscated property of the Church and the émigrés, one could not tell them that they would not own this property. He denounced the ideas of the *Enragés* with a certain amount of violence, not only because of his opposition to their doctrine, but because he could not concede that anyone could claim to go further than himself as far as the Revolution was concerned. He thought that these people wanted to compromise the Revolution by extremism. Under their disguise of *sans-culottes* they were basically only counter-revolutionaries. "This agrarian law, about which you have spoken so much, is only a phantom created by rogues to frighten imbeciles. Doubtless the extreme disproportion of wealth is the source of many of the ills and many of the crimes, but we are not convinced that equality of income is any less a chimaera. For myself, I believe it even less necessary to private happiness than public felicity. It is much more a question of making poverty honourable than of proscribing wealth. Fabricius's cottage has no reason to envy Crassus's palace."

On 12th February Jacques Roux appeared at the bar of the Convention. "It is not enough," he said, "to have declared that we are French republicans. In addition the people must be happy. There must be bread, for where there is no bread there is no more law, no more freedom and no more republic." These sacrilegious words unleashed Marat's wrath. He was also unable to admit that anyone could appear to be more of a revolutionary than himself. He denounced the petitioners as "counter-revolutionaries in the pay of aristocrats and foreigners". Robespierre said that those who organized riots and raids on bakeries could only be treacherous people who wanted to harm the State.

Ten days later, on 22nd February, a delegation from the Quatre Nations Section, led by Jacques Roux and Varlet, came to the Jacobins and demanded measures against the monopolists. Augustin showed them the door. "These over-repeated discussions about food supplies alarm the people." On 25th the assembly began a debate on the food problem. Tallien proposed sending troops to Lyons, where fairly serious riots had taken place. Robespierre supported the measure, and it was adopted. "What is this," he shouted indignantly, "they have the Republic, and they ask for bread? Only tyrants give bread to their subjects. What the Constitution owes to the French people is freedom, cemented by humane laws. It is the enjoyment of the sacred rights of humanity and the exercise of all the social virtues that the Republic develops." He proposed to increase the repressive measures against émigrés as a remedy to the economic problems.

However, that evening at the Jacobins he made a few corrections to his speech. If the leaders of the movement seemed evil-intentioned counter-revolutionaries to him, the same was not true of the people who followed them. The disorders were due to the natural resentment of the poor. "The people are suffering. They have not yet harvested the reward of their labour. They are still persecuted by the rich." Two letters from Augustin to Buissart, dated 21st February and 6th March, express Robespierre's thoughts on the matter well. He was too busy, so left it to his younger brother to keep up his correspondence with his friends. "You have made the head of a tyrant fall, they tell us, and you could make the people happy. These specious reproaches chill the people's confidence in the Montagnard deputies." In the other letter: "We are going through a critical time. The *sans-culottes* of Lyons have the worst of it and, from the news, the counter-revolution has made headway in that town. They want to do the same thing in Paris. Food supplies are hoarded and prices rise suddenly. They push intrigue to such an extent that they steal the bread from the bakeries and the people are unable to find any to buy. The object of this is to turn the wrath of the citizens against the Jacobins."

The military situation underwent a complete change during the same month. After Belgium, Dumouriez undertook the invasion of Holland. He unwisely threw himself into the attack with reduced forces, since the majority of the volunteers had gone home. On 13th March he suffered a crushing defeat at Neerwinden and began to retreat.

The event gave the enemies of the Girondins a new weapon which they seized immediately. As soon as the news reached Paris, Robespierre went to the Bonne-Nouvelle Section with Billaud-Varenne. He spoke about the dangers the fatherland was exposed to, and exhorted those present to take arms and rush to the frontiers. Both of them [Robespierre and Billaud-Varenne] resolved to keep watch in their absence that the counter-revolutionaries did not take over at home. Did this mean that there would be another September? Brissot at least interpreted it in this way, complaining in *Le Patriote français* that Robespierre had made a call to "anarchy". The same day, in the Convention, Robespierre absolved the soldiers of any blame for the retreat. As was his custom, he attributed it to the incompetence of the generals. However, Dumouriez was not included in his criticism. For one thing he had approved his plan for the invasion of Holland, since he imagined that it would have been followed by a revolution in England, and then he thought that Dumouriez would have been goaded on to win more victories for his own personal glory. In this Marat was more perspicacious than Robespierre, since from the start he said that the general's objectives were a *coup d'état* and restoration of the monarchy. In fact, Dumouriez had begun negotiations with Coburg, the Austrian Commander-in-Chief. There was to be an armistice which would allow him to march on Paris with his army to dissolve the Convention and restore the monarchy in the person of the Dauphin, in whose name he would govern.

However, the Convention also began to be suspicious. Two of its members, Danton and Delacroix, were sent to Belgium to sound out the general's intentions. There have been many conjectural reconstructions of their conversation. Danton was by no means incorruptible, and he may have been bought off by Dumouriez. It is also possible that the very short time he spent in the headquarters did not allow him to see the truth. Be that as it may, when he returned to Paris, Danton defended Dumouriez before the committee. He said that he was a good general. He might well have made one or two stupid mistakes, but the responsibility for them lay with the ignorant and flatterers in his entourage. Personally, Danton believed him to be a man of no ambition. What they should do was to leave him in charge, but to watch him. Robespierre was astonished at this. In the recent past his mistrust of the general had grown. He now sought his dismissal, and he said so, but the committee was largely Girondin and did not agree. From then on Robespierre suspected a plot.

Events were to prove him right. On 29th March the Minister of War showed the assembly a letter from Dumouriez, full of threats. He made the same mistake as Lafayette by revealing his intentions before carrying out his *coup*. The Convention replied by summoning him to the bar of the house.

But it was fated, it would seem, that the Girondins were to make only mistakes. Instead of abandoning Dumouriez, they continued to support him in their newspapers, and so they deprived themselves of any excuse that they were being deceived through ignorance. Even on 2nd April *Le Patriote français* published an article in praise of him. This gave Robespierre his chance to denounce him. "This morning Dumouriez's crimes were unmasked. A letter has been read in which he

Representatives of the Convention went to Dumouriez's home to arrest him. As they left with their prisoner, they were surrounded by another party and themselves arrested

declares war on the Revolution. Dumouriez is a traitor and he has accomplices here, in Paris, in the government, in the courts—everywhere. The only remedy is a reconstruction of the government."

In the Convention the disarray of the Girondins was revealed by a proposition from Vergniaud that anyone who wasted the time of the House on trivial matters should be declared an accomplice of Dumouriez. This absurd motion was greeted with applause. Robespierre spoke on 4th April. His speech was a long act of accusation against the Girondins in a tone of irony. He rarely used this device, and it was therefore an even more efficacious weapon. "I dare not say that you ought to strike with the same decree such patriotic members as the gentlemen Vergniaud, Guadet, Brissot and Gensonné. I dare not say that a man who corresponds every day with Dumouriez ought in the least to be suspected of complicity, for surely this man is a model of patriotism and it would be a sacrilege to ask for a decree of accusation against Monsieur Gensonné." After this he turned his attacks against the Committee for General Defence, which had refused to dismiss Dumouriez. "It is time this comedy ended. The Convention must take revolutionary measures. But I must say that they will never be promulgated by the Committee for General Defence, for

principles hold sway in this committee that freedom frowns on." At these words shouts arose from the Girondin benches. "You are criticizing one of the committees of the Assembly." Robespierre replied: "I declare that I do not regard myself as a member of that committee any longer. I no longer want to be a member of a committee that has more similarity to a council of Dumouriez than to a committee of the National Convention." He went on, in the midst of protests: "I cannot hide from you my surprise that the people who, from the beginning of the Revolution, have not ceased to slander this side—which was and will always be the party of freedom—should now stay silent about Dumouriez's crimes, and that we should be the only ones, the people who have been slandered so much, to lift up our voices on the perfidy of this traitor."

The Girondins felt the sting, and in particular Brissot, who interrupted the speaker. "I demand to speak after Robespierre." It would have been better had he kept quiet. His words gave Robespierre the chance to specify his attack by concentrating it on him. "Since Brissot demands to speak so as to blast me, I am going to apply to Brissot what I have just said." He recalled the praise of Dumouriez that had appeared the month before in *Le Patriote français*. Then came the implacable conclusion. "I declare that the first measure of public safety that is to be taken is to decree the accusation of all those who are suspected of complicity with Dumouriez, and in particular Brissot."

The effect of this speech on the Convention was seen the following day, 5th April, when the Committee for General Defence was replaced by the Committee of Public Safety with nine members: Danton, Cambon, Barère and Delacroix included. There were no Girondin members. At the Jacobins Augustin, as his brother's spokesman, demanded the people's intervention against the Girondins. "All good citizens must unite in their Sections and must direct public opinion better than they have done so far, and they must come to the bar of the Convention to force us to arrest the disloyal deputies." The call was heeded. On the days that followed, several delegations came to the bar to demand that the Girondins be arrested.

Robespierre delivered a long speech to his colleagues on the theme of Girondin intrigues as part of an international plot that he called "the foreign conspiracy". He told them that he was going "to lift a corner of the veil". "A powerful party is plotting with the tyrants of Europe to impose a king on us, with an aristocratic constitution and a false system of representation, with two chambers."

To achieve their goal they were using: "War outside and factions inside." He named Pitt as the mind behind the plot, and his accomplices the middle classes, who were afraid for their possessions, and the nobility who hoped to recover their privileges. These counter-revolutionaries had posed as champions of the people as long as they needed the people's support, but now that they had achieved their objective, they were abandoning them.

[[·]]

Despite the fact that they were unrepresented on the Committee for Public Safety and weakened in the cabinet by the loss of Roland, Clavière and Lebrun, the Girondins determined to fight on. In the Convention they still influenced quite a large number of right-wing and centre deputies, which gave them a majority. It was of course an uncertain majority, for these were deputies ready to abandon them if it became dangerous to support them. Moreover, quite cleverly, they had succeeded in depriving Robespierre of some of his supporters by sending quite a number of Montagnard deputies to the provinces under the pretext of supervising the enrolment of volunteers. But Robespierre increased his attacks. One of his methods was to repeat the same thing incessantly. In this way his ideas took root; without having to furnish proof, doubts became certainties. On 10th April he listed in a long indictment the Girondin "crimes". They had opposed the removal of the king in July 1792. They had intended putting the Dauphin on the throne. They had supported, in succession, Lafayette and Narbonne. They had had war declared. They had had six millions voted in secret funds for Dumouriez. They had slandered the Paris commune of 10th August. They had wanted to transfer the assembly to a provincial town. They had stirred up division at the heart of the Constitution. They had voted for a referendum. They were Dumouriez's accomplices. They were factious, intriguers and moderates.

This terrible speech left Brissot dumb, whereas until then he had been the chief Girondin spokesman in their struggle against Robespierre. From that day on he was heard no more, as if he had suddenly been convinced of the inevitability of defeat. Vergniaud took over. The barrister from Bordeaux had the advantage of not being embarrassed by a troubled past. It was only Madame Roland's opposition that had prevented him from leading the party. He was very eloquent, but unfortunately the sort of speaker who let himself be carried away by his sentences. On that particular day he made the mistake of defending himself by excusing himself, maintaining that he was tired—a very slim justification for a politician. "Amidst the anxieties that roused me during the fight that the friends of freedom had with despotism, perhaps I may be excused for not having been infallible." The arrows that he aimed at Robespierre, and which had been used too frequently, had blunt points. "At least Monsieur Robespierre, who at that time wisely buried himself in a cellar, should not be so hard on me for a moment of weakness." He denied having thought of taking the assembly outside of Paris. "I am astonished that this imputation should come from Robespierre's lips, who himself wanted to flee to Marseilles." If the Committee for General Defence had not been able to take the necessary measures, the fault was Robespierre's, since he refused to collaborate. The peroration is well known: "You call *us* moderates! I was not so on 10th August, Robespierre, when you were hiding in your cellar. But if, under the pretext of revolution, to be a patriot one must declare oneself the advocate of murder and plunder, then I am a moderate."

Pétion took the rostrum on 12th April. His old friendship for Robespierre had changed into a hatred that clouded his mind. "It is impossible," he shouted, "to tolerate such slander any longer. Robespierre must be branded at last as slanderers were before. I will not be happy until I have seen these men who want to confound the Revolution lose their heads on the scaffold." Such a declaration, by its violence, could only anger the members of the Marais. Robespierre had his chance to protest. "We are the ones they want to slaughter." David, the Jacobin artist, who had a flair for dramatic scenes, rushed into the middle of the hall baring his chest. "Strike, I propose my own murder. I, too, am a virtuous man."

It was now Guadet's turn to strike his blows. He was intelligent, cold, and knew how to use irony with skill. He was clever enough to ignore Robespierre and attack Marat, claiming a decree of accusation against him. He was sure to be listened to if he attacked a man whom everyone hated. His fall would weaken the Montagnards and cause a reaction against Robespierre. Robespierre fully realized the plot, but he disliked coming openly to the defence of the Friend of the People, since he did not want to seem to approve of his extremism and his plan for a dictatorship. He therefore did so with reticence, emphasizing that he did not share the "errors" of "this accused person who was not my friend", but at the same time recognizing that he regarded him as a good citizen and a zealous champion of the people's cause, and innocent of the accusations made against him. He criticized the

After a stormy and dramatic trial for treason Marat turned the tables on his accusers and was acquitted. The delighted deputies and gallery covered the victor with garlands

assembly's speed in hounding him, whereas they had failed to indict Dumouriez. "It is not against Marat alone that they want to bring the decree of accusation, but against me." However it is significant that he refused to sign a Jacobin manifesto for the defence of the Friend of the People got up by Desmoulins and Dubois-Crancé.

The incidents at Marat's trial, his triumphal acquittal and his return to the Convention, carried by the people, girded with laurel and almost hidden by garlands of flowers, only exacerbated the struggle. At the request of Robespierre, Camille Desmoulins wrote the most biting of his pamphlets—'Jean-Pierre Brissot unveiled'—against the Girondins. He wanted to convince opinion that not only were they counter-revolutionaries, but scoundrels and thieves. Brissot was a "villain", Buzot a "hypocrite", and Guadet a "corrupt man". The people must demand that "they be vomited out of the Convention". This was then the subject of an address written by Robespierre to which the General Council of the Commune gave its support, and which was presented to the assembly on 15th April by thirty-five Sections.

On 26th April Robespierre was at the Jacobins after having been absent for ten days. He had been ill once more. Nothing else could have kept him away at this critical time. It even seems as if he still had a fever on that evening, for contrary to his usual practice of prudence, he gave a call to revolt: "I invite the people to riot in the National Convention against the corrupt deputies." In his normal condition he would never have spoken the following sentence. It shows at least to what degree in his subconscious he identified himself with the Revolution: "I declare that, having received from the people the mission of defending their rights, I regard as my oppressor whoever interrupts me or refuses to let me speak, and I declare that I will launch a revolt against the President and all the members in the Convention. I declare that I will punish traitors myself, and I promise to look upon any conspirator as my enemy, and to treat him as such."

[[·]]

The month of May was to be decisive. It began with a demonstration by the young supporters of the Girondins, crying: "Down with the Montagnards. Long live the law." Many *sans-culottes* thought that they were shouting: "Long live the king [*roi*, instead of *loi*]", which was a plausible mistake, and they were naturally indignant. Robespierre had no hesitation in supporting the rumour, which helped his accusation of royalism against the Girondins. He added that some of the demonstrators had even worn the white cockade.

The notice on the door leading to a room of one of the Revolutionary committees firmly announces that the familiar form of address is to be used and please close the door

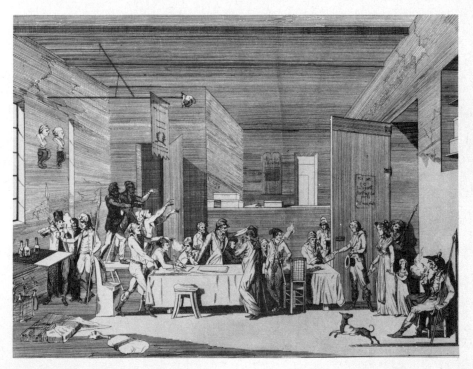

On 8th May he made a speech at the Convention about the defence of Paris, with a eulogy of Paris in it, which was an indirect way of getting at the Girondins. More than 50,000 men from Paris had taken part in the fight against the coalition of despots and foreign enemies. There was certainly a counter-revolutionary army in the Vendée, but the one in the capital was even more dangerous.

On the evening of the same day, Robespierre spoke at the Jacobins and put forward the measures that he thought ought to be taken against the army in the capital. A revolutionary army should be created and recruited by the Sections; all suspects should be arrested; the *sans-culotte* who enrolled were to be paid by the State; an arsenal for the manufacture of arms should be set up, and all slanderers of the Republic and traitrous generals were to be punished. On 12th and 13th May, he repeated these proposals.

The Girondins replied on the 18th by setting up a commission of twelve members to investigate the acts of the Commune. They also ordered the arrest of Hébert, Varlet and several other extremists. On 28th May in the Convention Robespierre denounced Brissot as a royalist. During the previous weeks his nerves had been subjected to too severe a tension. That evening, at the Jacobins and on the eve of victory, he succumbed to defeatist talk. "I am no longer capable of prescribing for the people the means of their own safety. It is a task that is well beyond the strength of a single man, certainly beyond mine, exhausted as I am by four years of revolution and the sight of the triumph of tyranny and all that is vile and corrupt. It is not for me to indicate the measures to be taken, whilst I am burnt up with fever."

One can well imagine the consternation that these words produced on the assembly. At the thought that their guide was going to leave them, protests were heard on all sides. Applause gave Robespierre back his energy. In any case, for the moment his role in the struggle against the Girondins was ended. The movement had been set in motion by him, and he could now leave the final direction of it to others.

[[·]]

As on the eve of 10th August, when Brunswick's manifesto had been made public, something was needed to ignite the anger of the people of Paris. A vehement Isnard did this with a declaration in which, almost in the same terms as the Prussian general, he threatened the capital with destruction: "I announce to you in the name of all France, Paris will be annihilated. Soon they will pore over the banks of the Seine to see whether Paris ever existed." The Sections replied to this provocation by appointing an Insurrectional Committee. On 31st May the Convention met to the sound of tolling bells and drums beating the alarm. The Girondins were there, ready to give final battle, but for several nights most of them had not slept at home for fear of being arrested. The first speaker, Tarbais Barère, a master of *volte-face*, suggested that the Commission of Twelve members be suppressed so as to calm the people. A fortnight earlier he had supported its institution.

Couthon the invalid spoke up demanding "the heads of the traitors of the commission". Robespierre took the rostrum. He was obviously exhausted and stopped after each sentence. "I will not take up the Assembly's time with the flight and return of those who deserted its sessions. . . . One does not save the fatherland by paltry measures. . . . There is one that I adopt, and that is the suppression of the Commission of Twelve. . . . But do you believe that that is sufficient to satisfy friends anxious for the safety of the fatherland, . . . No, we must follow the measures that the people who have made their petition have just presented . . . we must . . . we must . . ." It was then that Vergniaud made his famous remark: "Conclude then." It had the effect of a whip on Robespierre: "Yes, I am going to conclude, and against you. Against you, who after the revolution of 10th August wanted to send to the scaffold those who brought it about; against you who never stopped urging the destruction of Paris; against you who wanted to spare the tyrant; against you who plotted with Dumouriez. My conclusion is the decree of accusation against all Dumouriez's accomplices and against all those who have been named by the petitioners." As Brissot had been, Vergniaud was silenced.

All the same, that day the Convention only voted to suppress the Commission of Twelve. This was insufficient to strike down the Girondins. The Insurrectional Committee immediately went into action to tell the deputies what they were to do. At its instigation, on the next day, new delegations presented themselves at the bar, demanding in threatening terms the arrest of twenty-six members of the Gironde. During the night of the 1st/2nd June, Clavière and Madame Roland were taken to prison. The threatened deputies met to dine at a house in the rue de Clichy. Even at such a juncture, they did not lose a taste for heroic sentences. Vergniaud said to Pétion: "Let us drink to life and death. Let us not worry about ourselves, but about the fatherland. This glass of wine will be my blood that I would drink to the health of the republic."

Meanwhile, the Insurrectional Committee gave the order to Hanriot, Commander-in-Chief of the National Guard, to occupy the Convention with his men. Even some of the Montagnards felt that an insult had been made to national representation. At the suggestion of Barère, the assembly decided to leave "to go and debate in the midst of the armed force". They were obliged to stop in front of Hanriot's guns, and came back under the ironic gaze of a little group that had remained behind. "Citizens," said Couthon, "all the members of the Convention ought to be reassured about their freedom. You have gone to the people. Everywhere you have found them respectful towards representatives, and implacable against conspirators." He decided that the deputies who had been denounced should be arrested at home, where they would stay "under the safe keeping of the French people, the National Convention, and the loyalty of the people of Paris". The guillotine did not yet threaten them. It was simply a matter of eliminating them politically. They would not be brought before the tribunal until they fled, and the departments rose in revolt.

[[·]]

"Nothing will ever separate us," Robespierre had written a year previously [February 1792] to Pétion. In a few weeks the former mayor of Paris would be nothing more than a fugitive pursued by the police, and soon to die of cold and hunger in the snow. His body was found half eaten by wolves. So ended a friendship.

Another, however, was being strengthened. Danton, returning from his second mission to Belgium in February 1793, found that his wife Gabrielle was dead and had been buried for a week. He was a man of violent impulse in grief as in action, and had the coffin opened so as to embrace her for one last time. Robespierre wrote to him on 16th February: "If in the few moments that can shake a soul such as yours, the certainty of having a tender and devoted friend can offer you a consolation, I present it to you. I love you more than ever, and until death. Do not shut your heart to the voice of friendship that shares all your pain. Let us weep together for our friends, and let us soon make the effects of our pain felt by the tyrants who are responsible for our public and private griefs. My friend, I would have sent these heart-felt words to Belgium; I would have come to see you before now if I had not respected the first moments of your real affliction. Embrace your friend."

THE JACOBIN DICTATORSHIP

"If the peril is such that the apparatus of law is an obstacle to protecting oneself from that peril, then one appoints a supreme leader who silences the law and suspends for a moment its sovereign authority."

JEAN-JACQUES ROUSSEAU

THE FALL OF THE GIRONDE HAD THE LOGICAL CONSEQUENCE OF the Jacobins taking over power. Among Robespierre's papers there was a memorandum dating from this period which outlines his political programme:

> There must be one single will. It must be either republican or royalist. For it to be republican, there must be republican ministers, republican deputies and a republican government. The inner dangers come from the middle class. To conquer them the people must be rallied. Everything had been set to put the people under the yoke of the middle class, and to send the defenders of the Republic to the scaffold. The middle classes triumphed in Marseilles, Bordeaux and Lyons. They would have triumphed in Paris without the present intervention. The present insurrection must continue until the measures necessary for saving the Republic have been taken. The people must join with the Convention and the Convention must save the people. The insurrection must spread itself on the same lines; and the *sans-culottes* be paid and stay in the towns. They must be given arms, they must be roused and enlightened. Enthusiasm for the Republic must be exalted by all possible means.

So as to rally the masses to Jacobin doctrines, three laws inspired by Robespierre were to give them substantial advantages. The law of 3rd June set up the sale of the possessions of émigrés in small lots, with a period of ten years for payment to be made. This made it possible for the less wealthy peasants to buy land. The law of 10th June provided for the subdivision of communal property in equal portions. The law of 27th July abolished without any indemnity the seigniorial rights and dues founded on ancient charters. The people who benefited from these measures could hardly fail to support the Republic. A return to the *ancien régime* would have meant for them the loss of these advantages. Finally, to cushion the effect of rising prices coupled with the depreciation of *assignats*, there was a general increase in the salaries of civil servants.

All the hacks who sang the praises of the Girondins at the height of their powers now began to lavish homage on their new masters with the same zeal. Even so, some of them were afraid lest they be unable to make people forget their past conduct. One of them, Granville, editor of *Le Moniteur*, wrote to Robespierre to excuse himself: "We were forced, at the risk of being denounced, at the risk of losing the confidence of our subscribers, to publish the most absurd diatribes of the imbeciles or the intriguers of the right wing."

Like so many others, he was a thurifer of the Incorruptible until 9th Thermidor.

[[·]]

One of the victors' first measures was to appoint a special committee to put an end to the Constitution. The Girondins's idea, which had been the work of Condorcet, gave an essential role to the executive power. It was badly received by the Assembly, and discussion of it had been interrupted. Robespierre referred to it as an "insidious plan laid by intriguers". The political battles had not allowed the debate to be resumed. There were five members of the committee: Hérault de Séchelles, Ramel, Mathieu, Couthon and Saint-Just. The last two were in effect Robespierre's surrogates. Five days were sufficient to finish their work. Robespierre presented the project to his colleagues in these words: "One need only read the preamble to give heart to the friends of the people and to make their enemies despair. All Europe will be forced to admire the finest monument of human reason."

Robespierre dominated the debates which lasted until 23rd June. Naturally he experienced some defeats on points of detail. For example, he was unable to have quashed an article setting up parliamentary immunity. Instead it was put to one side. He spoke on the freedom of the press, not so as to ask—as he had done in the Constituent Assembly—for total freedom, but limited freedom, in the interests of the Revolution. It was a question of being able to strike at "the authors of public writings directed against freedom". The most curious of his propositions related to taxes. Until then he had, along with many others, thought that only the rich ought to be taxed. But the article decreeing that no citizen should be excluded from the honourable duty of sharing in public expense made him change his mind. Exempting the poor from taxes was tantamount to offending the purest sector of the nation, and establishing a distinction between rich and poor was destructive to freedom. All the same, there was the question of those totally without means

The denunciation of the leaders of the Girondin drove many of their colleagues to beg for mercy at the feet of their enemies. Many saved themselves from death only by flattery

who truly could not pay. He suggested that a special amount be given them by the State, which they would then pay as taxation, by way of a contribution.

Article Four provoked a lively debate. It decreed that the French people would never make peace with an enemy occupying their territory. Mercier, a Girondin and the author of *Tableaux de Paris*, posed the question: "Do you flatter yourselves that you will always be the victors? Have you made a treaty with Victory?" Basire, the Montagnard, yelled his reply: "We have made one with Death." The sentence meant nothing, but it had a martial air that drew applause. Even so, it did not satisfy Mercier, a sensible man, who made yet another insidious remark: "You do not have a true notion of freedom, and yet you pretend to compare yourselves to the Romans."

This brought Robespierre to the rostrum: "I would never have thought," he shouted, "that a deputy of the French people would dare to pronounce in this place such vile words, or to cast doubts on the Republican virtue of the people he represents. Where has this man discovered that we are inferior to the Romans, or that the constitution we are drawing up is unworthy of that despotic senate that never knew the Declaration of the Rights of Man?"

When the time came for voting, some of the deputies of the centre remained seated, which wrought indignation among the Montagnards. Robespierre did not want the Plain to join forces with the remaining Girondins, and so extended a protecting hand over them. The acceptance of the Constitution had put him in a good mood, and he permitted himself a joke: "If some members did not get up," he said, "I would assume that they were paralytic rather than bad citizens." When the people were asked to ratify it, the Constitution was accepted by 1,800,918 votes to 11,610. This meant that there were 4,300,000 abstentions. When it became law there was a celebration. The official copy of the Constitution was engraved on tablets, enclosed in a cedar chest which was then ceremoniously placed in front of the president's desk in the Convention. It was destined to stay there without anyone worrying any more about it. As Robespierre explained, its application required new elections, "which risked replacing the purged members of the present Convention with the envoys of Pitt and Coburg". The elections ought therefore to be deferred until there was peace. "The aim of constitutional government is to preserve the Republic. That of revolutionary government is to found it."

[[·]]

On 13th July 1793 Marat was assassinated by Charlotte Corday, who believed she was avenging the Girondins. The *sans-culottes* revered him as a martyr. He was invoked in a sort of canticle *O cor Jésu, o cor Marat*—"O Heart of Jesus, O heart of Marat." On this occasion Robespierre had great difficulty in hiding the disgust with which Marat filled him. There was also a kind of jealousy that the assassin's blows had been directed at someone else, since he had so often said that he was

*Immediately after she had stabbed Marat Charlotte Corday was arrested and swiftly tried.
Her doom was pronounced in no time and she was trundled to execution*

stalked by death. "The honours of the dagger are reserved for me also. The priority was only decided by chance." The evening of 14th July at the Jacobins, where, one after another, all the speakers praised the Friend of the People, must have been most disagreeable for Robespierre. Why should they talk so much about Marat, he protested, and not about the safety of the fatherland. When the fatherland is saved it will be time to honour Marat as he deserves. "We ought not to provide the people with the spectacle of a state funeral today." While he scorned the proposal to bury Marat in the Panthéon, as Mirabeau had been, a friend of the dead man, Bentabole, shouted: "Yes, Marat will be buried there, in spite of what is said by those who are jealous of him." The apotheosis took place, and Robespierre could not avoid being there. An eye-witness, Merlin de Thionville, said: "He was forced to preside over the ceremony, but looked more like someone taking the coffin to the refuse dump than to the Panthéon." At least he had got rid of a rival, who could have become dangerous. There is a letter from Augustin,

Notes on a sketch of Robespierre at the Convention read: eyes green, complexion pale, green striped nankeen jacket, waistcoat blue with blue stripes, cravat white striped with red

in which there is no doubt that he is expressing his brother's opinion, suggesting that the death of the Friend of the People would finally be to the advantage of the Republic.

[[·]]

Robespierre became a member of the Committee of Public Safety in two stages. The first was the elimination of Danton, who was not re-elected when his term of office ended on 10th July. Danton was tired. He was chided for not having been able to conduct the war abroad, and for not having put down the revolt in the *départements*. In the North his lines of defence were caving in, on the Rhine they had already ceased to exist. Condé, Mainz and Valenciennes had given in, Landau and Cambrai were threatened. In the Vendée the royalist rebels were winning. Lyons, the second town in France, rose at the call of the Girondins, preparing to join forces with Nîmes and Marseilles. Robespierre did not take any part whatsoever in the campaign against Danton, carried on by the Montagnard extremists. People talked ironically of the Committee of Public Loss—a *bon mot* of Marat. On 23rd June, Verdier had denounced to the Convention "the idlers of the Committee".

In the face of these attacks Danton was strangely silent. On 10th July itself, the defeat of his protégé Westermann by the Chouans (rebels in the West led by Jean Chouans) was made known. It was the straw that broke the camel's back.

Nevertheless, Robespierre was not asked there and then to be a member of the newly-elected committee, but only two weeks later, on 26th July, when Gasparin resigned "for health reasons". "He accepted," he said, "against his inclination." It was as always the same repugnance he had for taking public office. He undertook to "spend the nights making useful laws".

The most urgent task in that month of July was to improve the military situation. If the enemy reached Paris, the whole Revolution would collapse. Somewhat curiously Robespierre assumed responsibility for the Girondin war aims: "We will carry freedom and equality to foreign peoples. The true objective of our policy must be to remove the cause of the tyrants in league against us." As far as the immediate future was concerned, he said that the remedy was to dismiss and punish incapable and traitorous generals—to his way of thinking they were all, more or less, traitors. The success of the operations depended on "Republican principles". All the same, Barère suggested calling on a military expert capable of making plans and organizing the armies. It has been said that the great achievement of the Committee was that it saved France by standing up to the European coalition. But it could only accomplish this because of Carnot's membership. Robespierre understood this necessity with regret, and had therefore not opposed the inclusion of his former colleague from the Academy of Arras, despite the fact that there was scarcely any point of agreement between them. They had had no contact since the beginning of the Revolution, and Robespierre regarded him as a moderate.

[[·]]

Military questions were of secondary importance as far as Robespierre was concerned. As he once said: "Victory over enemy armies is not the victory to which one should most aspire." One might even say that he feared them a little, obsessed as he was by the dread of a military *coup d'état*. So although he kept his eye on Carnot and his generals, his chief preoccupation was the home front.

His notebook reveals under this heading three points: supervision of the press, punishment of conspirators and direction of public opinion. The time had long since passed when he demanded from the rostrum of the Constituent Assembly the right of citizens to publish anything and everything in the name of freedom. He now said: "Writers must be proscribed as the most dangerous enemies of the fatherland." He would have liked the government to undertake the publication of an official newspaper, to "spread the principles of Republican conduct and freedom; to stimulate the courage of the French against the enemy without; to put them on their guard against the intrigues of foreign governments, and to unmask conspirators." *La Feuille de salut public*, edited by his friend Garat, and printed by his bodyguard, Nicolas, partially fulfilled this task.

The number of newspapers had multiplied to such an extent—and the interest of readers had at the same time diminished—that most of them had great difficulties in staying in business. Government subsidies helped Jacobin broadsheets: *L'Antifédéraliste*, *Le Moniteur*, *Le Journal universel*, *Le Journal des hommes libres*, and above all Hébert's famous *Père Duchesne*, of which hundreds of thousands of copies were bought by the War Ministry for distribution to the troops.

Robespierre applied to the theatre the same procedure of official intervention. A decree setting out the reorganization contained the disturbing sentence that in a free country the theatre ought to be expurgated and become, under government control, a method of educating the public. Robespierre suspected actors—and above all actresses—of not being civic minded: "The princesses of the theatre are no better than the princesses of Austria. Both are perverse, and both ought to be treated with equal severity." Payan, the National Agent and his friend, demanded that theatre directors substitute the words citizen and citizeness for monsieur and madame "unless the latter is used as an insult or to designate an enemy of the Revolution". He warned Robespierre of the danger of allowing the performance of Marie-Joseph Chénier's play *Timoléon*: "Other authors would imitate it and we would soon see in the theatre only honest kings and moderate republicans." *Paméla*, by François de Neufchâteau was censored and every line that could be interpreted in a counter-revolutionary way was cut. Other plays were simply forbidden. Mercier was quite right to say that these people did not have a true notion of freedom.

The second feature of Robespierre's programme for the home front—the repression of subversive intrigues—involved operations in the Vendée and the destruction of the last Girondins in the provinces. The method he put forward was the dispatching of commissioners "with sound instructions and good principles to restore public opinion to the Republic and unity". Unfortunately, some of these commissioners were keen to get rich, and in so doing made the Republic appear odious. Robespierre saw with consternation that they "directed against the people the terror reserved for its enemies". He declared that these men were hypocritical counter-revolutionaries, who were ruthless and intended to ruin the revolutionary

*Rousseau's dictum that public fêtes benefited the people inspired the Convention to celebrate
the anniversary of the 10th of August 1792 at a newly constructed Fountain of Regeneration*

cause. Hence the necessity of having strict control over the commissioners by
always sending them out in pairs, one to watch over the other. Put "a strong man,
with another whose patriotism is less certain; change them frequently, and keep up
a close correspondence with them".

Such a system, which developed suspicions even concerning the better patriots,
fatally succeeded in setting up a sort of inquisition. Robespierre was not alarmed
about this, as his notes reveal: "So as to purge the revolutionary committees one
must have a list of all their members with all their names, their social positions and
their addresses. In particular, we must have information about the president and
secretary of each committee. Secondly, we must draw up a list of all the counter-
revolutionary agitators in each district and take measures against them. Thirdly, we
must pursue the deputies who are at the head of the conspiracy and get hold of
them; all without exception must be punished. Finally, we must have a detailed list
of all the prisoners, and decree that those who have given refuge to conspirators
should suffer the same punishment as they do."

A revolutionary past was no guarantee. The "constitutional" Bishop of Cantal,
Thibault, a true supporter of Robespierre and one who had voted for the death
of the king, was accused of having been "the agent of a criminal faction which
surrendered itself to religious propaganda".

The problem of food supplies, which was daily becoming more serious, weighed heavily on the Committee of Public Safety. Barely one-tenth of the necessary flour was now reaching the capital, since the peasants absolutely refused to exchange the fruit of their labours for a currency that was continually depreciating. The commissioners out on their missions vainly denounced "the dangerous aristocracy of the farmers". When meat also became hard to find, the population was advised to "observe a civic Lent".

Agitation broke out again, spurred on by the *Enragés*, supported by Hébert. They even had partisans like Chaumette in the Commune. The demonstrations on 4th September, directed against the Committee of Public Safety, infuriated Robespierre. Those who looted shops were not the true people, but "scoundrels under the guise of the people, in the guise of respectable poverty". When a delegation appeared before the Convention on 5th September, Robespierre—who was in the chair—received them with decided frigidity. The people, he said simply, could count on the solicitude of the Committee of Public Safety. He thereupon closed the debate.

That evening at the Jacobins he attacked those delegates with especial vigour: "What is one to make of the propositions of the *Enragés* that equate all tradespeople, even the most humble carrot-sellers, with evil-doers? If a merchant is of necessity a bad citizen it is obvious that no one can sell anything anymore. Hence the natural exchange that gives a livelihood to members of society is destroyed, and consequently society is dissolved. By destroying commerce our enemies mean to starve the people." He went on to say that the *Enragés* were trying to sow dissension among the people. Demonstrations such as those of 4th and 5th September constituted a deviation from the Revolution. A true *sans-culotte* ought to struggle against tyranny, not for such materialistic motives as food-supplies. Such people pretended to love the people more than he. They were in the pay of royalists and foreigners solely to discredit him.

"There are two men whose salaries are paid by the enemies of the people. One of them is a priest known exclusively for two horrible deeds; firstly to have wanted to assassinate merchants and shop-keepers because, he said, they were charging too much, and secondly to have the Constitution rejected by the people. The second person is a young man who proves how corruption may enter a young heart. He has a disarming appearance and an engaging charm. He is Leclerc, a *ci-devant* (aristocrat), and the son of a nobleman—two men denounced by Marat as two plotters: two emissaries from Coblenz and Pitt."

The dealings that the *Enragés* had had with the Friend of the People had stood them in good stead. After they had slandered him, they passed themselves off as his successors and revived his newspaper. Robespierre had the idea of having the "widow" of Marat, Simone Evrard, appear at the bar of the Convention to "read there an address written by him". "In particular I denounce before you two men, Jacques Roux and the man called Leclerc, who pretend to carry on the patriotic paper of Marat and make his ghost speak so as to outrage his memory and deceive the

XXV)   (XXV

SIEGE DE LYON.

Bon pour VINGT-CINQ Sous

A rembourser en Assignats de 25 livres à 400 livres.

XXV

(ABOVE) *The national treasury ran out of funds and the country was flooded with promissory notes called* assignats. *Instead of stemming inflation they only increased it.* (BELOW) *The acute shortage of grain forced the government to issue ration cards to limit the sale of bread*

JOURS.	LIVRAISON DU PAIN.	JOURS.	LIVRAISON DU PAIN.	JOURS.	LIVRAISON DU PAIN.
Primidi		Primidi		Primidi	
Duodi		Duodi		Duodi	
Tridi		Tridi		Tridi	
Quartidi		Quartidi		Quartidi	
Quintidi		Quintidi		Quintidi	
Sextidi		Sextidi		Sextidi	
Septidi		Septidi		Septidi	
Octodi		Octodi		Octodi	
Nonodi		Nonodi		Nonodi	
Decadi		Decadi		Decadi	
Primidi		Primidi		Primidi	
Duodi		Duodi		Duodi	
Tridi		Tridi		Tridi	
Quartidi		Quartidi		Quartidi	
Quintidi		Quintidi		Quintidi	
Sextidi		Sextidi		Sextidi	
Septidi		Septidi		Septidi	
Octodi		Octodi		Octodi	
Nonodi		Nonodi		Nonodi	
Decadi		Decadi		Decadi	
Primidi		Primidi		Primidi	
Duodi		Duodi		Duodi	
Tridi		Tridi		Tridi	
Quartidi		Quartidi		Quartidi	
Quintidi		Quintidi		Quintidi	
Sextidi		Sextidi		Sextidi	
Septidi		Septidi		Septidi	
Octodi		Octodi		Octodi	
Nonodi		Nonodi		Nonodi	
Decadi		Decadi		Decadi	

BUREAU CENTRAL.

Section ,n.°

Carte pour recevoir le pain
chez , boulanger de la section.

Pour personnes composant le
ménage d citoyen
demeurant rue n.°
Présents, ; absents, .

À Bordeaux, le , l'an de
la république Françoise, une et indivisible.

Commissaire du comité des douze.   *Commissaire du comité des douze.*

· 213 ·

people." She called on the Convention to punish these emissaries of England and Austria "who poison public opinion". Then Robespierre spoke: "I demand that the conduct of these usurpers of Marat's name be sent before your Committee of Public Safety, which will take the necessary measures against them." Roux was sent to prison, where he committed suicide on 22nd August, and Leclerc not long afterwards.

The boldness of the *Enragés* in teaching him a lesson annoyed Robespierre enormously. On 17th September he replied to the insinuations of another of their leaders, Varlet, whom he arrested a few days later: "I think that I am as well versed in morality and principles as the spokesman of the petitioners." At the same time, so as to deprive them of their followers, he had part of their economic programme adopted. A law establishing a maximum price for grain and fodder was passed on 11th September 1793, followed on the 29th by one for a general maximum, which taxed both produce and salaries. Since the inflation of *assignats* continued, the effect obtained was the opposite of what had been intended. The result was that goods became even more scarce. Shops remained empty. Application of the tax would have been tantamount to the shopkeeper's selling their goods at a price lower than the one they would have to pay to replace their stock. In order to force them to open up their shops again, recourse had to be made to requisitions, organized watches and house-searches. This dissatisfied many people, some of whom had proved themselves to be good Republicans. Freedom of the individual was disappearing, with no one able to point the way to prosperity as compensation. In the country-side requisitioning of supplies crushed the peasants and cancelled out any effect of low prices charged for the sale of land belonging to the Church and the émigrés. People with private means were ruined through the depreciation of *assignats*; and the underpaid and underfed workers threatened to strike. "The picture of Paris begins to be terrifying," wrote the commentator Latour Lamontagne. "All one sees in the markets and in the streets is a mob of citizens running, rushing at each other, shouting and weeping, and presenting everywhere a picture of despair. One would say, at the sight of all this activity, that Paris was already a prey to the horrors of famine."

[[·]]

In his task of creating a new society, Robespierre had the encouragement and help of Saint-Just, who proposed that the State should regulate the daily lives of the citizens, beginning with their clothing. "Up to the age of sixteen all French people should wear linen in all seasons, and they should be uniformly dressed: from sixteen to twenty a workman's costume; from twenty to twenty-five a soldier's costume, unless they be magistrates. A citizen may dress as an artisan only when he has publicly swum across a river on the day of the festival of youth." Lovers who wanted to break off their relationship should first present themselves to the tribunal. The police would be replaced by "ten worthy old men", responsible for restoring calm and order by their exhortations, and in the event of sedition they would be forced to remove themselves immediately from public positions in the interests of the people.

On 12th October Saint-Just arrived at the Convention to tell them that the plan for the reorganization of the Republic would soon be ready. Woe to anyone who attempted to oppose it, he said, or who did not welcome it with sufficient enthusiasm. "You need no longer treat with caution the enemies of the new order of things, and freedom must win, cost what it will. You must punish whosoever is passive in the affairs of the Republic, and does nothing for it."

On 17th September a law was passed to punish those who were apathetic or in opposition. It was obviously necessary to reorganize the Revolutionary Tribunal to apply the law effectively. Robespierre took care of this. His notes show his preoccupation with the matter. At the beginning of October they read: "The Revolutionary Tribunal is not working well." A month later: "Reorganization of the Revolutionary Tribunal: repeal of the decree setting up Revolutionary Tribunals everywhere." In fact, the Revolutionary Tribunals in the provinces seemed to him irritatingly inclined to slowness and indulgence. By bringing all cases to Paris, the committee itself would be the centre of justice and could keep a better control on sentences.

He saw that this supervision was necessary even in Paris. Judges and juries had showed shameful indulgence towards counter-revolutionaries. In the La Rouerie trial, for example, half the accused had been acquitted. President Montané had shown favour to Charlotte Corday, and was moved by her youth. Girondins would not be condemned by this kind of tribunal.

Consequently the court was reorganized and divided into four sections with new judges and juries appointed by the Committees. Robespierre did not ask for an election. The first matter to be dealt with was the trial of Marie-Antoinette on 14th October. The execution of "the Capet woman" did not interest him, since it did nothing useful for the Republic. Responsibility for it fell above all on Billaud-Varenne. "A woman," he said, "the shame of humanity and of her sex, the widow Capet, must pay her debts on the scaffold." As he did on every occasion when a somewhat extreme proposition was put forward, Robespierre suspected that the people who demanded her trial wanted to detract attention from real problems. Hébert's testimony only confirmed this suspicion. The journalist accused the former queen of having indulged in immoral practices to gain control of her son's mind. It has been suggested that he let himself be bribed in an attempt to save her life. Not being able openly to take her defence, he therefore used a procedure which consisted of making a disgusting and absurd accusation which would in effect throw doubt on others. At all events, the queen then had the chance to make a noble and indignant reply which briefly gained public sympathy for her. From that moment Robespierre suspected Hébert.

AU NOM DE LA RÉPUBLIQUE.

L'ACCUSATEUR PUBLIC, près le Tribunal criminel-révolutionnaire, établi à Paris par la loi du 10 mars 1793, en exécution du jugement du Tribunal *de ce jourd'huy* requiert le citoyen commandant-général de la force armée parisienne, de prêter main-forte et mettre sur pied la force publique, nécessaire à l'exécution dudit jugement rendu contre *Marie antoinette Lorraine autriche Ve de Louis Capet* et qui *la* condamne à la peine de *Mort* laquelle exécution aura lieu *aujourd'huy a Dix* heures *du Matin* sur la place publique de *La Révolution* de cette ville. Le citoyen commandant-général est requis d'envoyer ladite force publique, cour du Palais, ledit jour, à *huit* heures précises du *Matin* —

FAIT à Paris, le *25 du xe mois de* ___ 179 l'an *second* de la République française, une et indivisible. *(reçu fait Mercredy 16e Ving heure du Matin)*

ACCUSATEUR PUBLIC.

A. Q. Fouquier

The Public Accuser orders that this day the widow of Louis Capet be condemned to death and is to be executed this morning at 10 o'clock in the Place de la Révolution. This Wednesday, 16th October 1793, the second year of the Republic, 5 in the morning: Fouquier-Tinville

TRIBUNAL CRIMINEL
RÉVOLUTIONNAIRE.

LE Gardien de la Maison *de Justice de la Conciergerie*

remettra à la Gendarmerie *les nommés Brissot, Vergniaux, Ducos, Boyer Foufrède, Lacaze, Lehardy, Mainville, Duprat, Vigée, Daftier Valaze, gendonne, Duperres, Carra, Gardier, Antiboul, Boilleau, Duchâtel, l'Esterp Beauvais*

pour être conduit au Tribunal criminel-révolutionnaire.

Fait à Paris, ce 9ᵐᵉ jour d2 2ᵐᵉ mois de ~~19~~ , l'an second de la République française, une et indivisible.

Herman
Prot.

The Tribunal issued this order for the arrest of Brissot and twenty of his collaborators. They were to be confined in the Conciergerie before appearing at the Tribunal to answer the charges and defend themselves

[[·]]

The trial of the Girondins, on the other hand, was entirely the work of Robespierre. But it was also his wish that the punishment should affect only the leaders. The arrest of the twenty-two had been followed by a petition of protest from seventy-three members of the party. A report by Amar proposed that they should be arrested provisionally. Subsequently, Danton and Osselin demanded that the trial be closed. The public in the gallery applauded the motion. But Robespierre interrupted to defend them. "Citizens, take care, for beside all those men who were driven by their own ambition whom you have unmasked, there are many more who have strayed." This caused murmurs, but he went on: "I am giving my opinion in the presence of the people. Know this, citizens, that you will only be truly defended by those who have the courage to tell you the truth, even when the circumstances would seem to call for silence. I say that the dignity of the Convention commands that it concern itself only with the leaders. If there are any more, then the people are there, and they will demand justice from you for it. I say that among the men under arrest there is one of very good faith whose handwork has been a surprise."

As for the others [the leaders], Robespierre showed himself to be implacable, despite the numerous appeals he received in their favour. Garat, a moderate whom he held in some regard, was one of the people who approached him. He, first of all, suggested that a special tribunal be set up to judge them. "The Revolutionary Tribunal is good enough for them," replied Robespierre. Garat then asked if there was anything against his being their official counsel for defence.

"They would have a good laugh if they could hear you. They would have had you guillotined quite legally."

"I think that they would use the guillotine very little."

"Little is enough."

To another who also pleaded in their favour he retorted: "Do not talk to me about it anymore. I cannot save them. There are days in the course of a revolution when it is a crime to live, and when you must know how to give your head when it is asked of you."

The trial began on 24th October. From the very first session the proceedings took a favourable turn for the accused. They were brilliant men, many of them barristers, and they knew how to defend themselves. If they were acquitted and made a triumphant return to the Convention, they could well turn the Revolution in a new direction. The Jacobins began to worry. Delegations demanded that the Convention "rid the tribunal of forms that stifle the conscience and obstruct conviction". This circumlocution referred to the calling of witnesses. Only nine of them had been heard in six days. On 29th October Osselin demanded that the debates be stopped. Robespierre opposed his motion which he described as "too vague". The solution that Robespierre proposed, which in his view reconciled the interests of the accused with the safety of the country, consisted in allowing the

No sooner had Brissot and his companions heard the verdict of guilty than they stood up and threw their assignats *to the audience shouting 'These are for you, our friends!'*

President of the court, after three days of debate, to ask the jury if they had enough evidence to satisfy them. In this way any trial might be stopped. At least appearances seemed to have been saved.

When the death sentence was pronounced, a man was seen standing up among the public, overcome and in tears. It was Camille Desmoulins. His neighbours held him back, but he said to them: "Let me go, let me get away from this spectacle. Wretch that I am, it is I who is killing them. My 'Brissot unveiled' is accusing them and judging them. I cannot bear the sight of my work. I feel the drops of their blood falling on the hand that has accused them."

Meanwhile people were astonished to see, one after the other, the men who had led them to Revolution now accused of counter-revolutionary intrigues. Robespierre's correspondent Aigoin wrote to him: "What is to happen if people such as Guadet, Brissot, Gensonné and Vergniaud are not patriots? If they are enemies of the fatherland?" The Terror had begun, and nothing could stop it. It was to devour all those who, whether they were revolutionaries or not, had been involved in events—the Duc d'Orléans, Madame Roland, Bailly, Duport-Dutertre, Barnave, Lebrun-Tondu, d'Eprémesnil and Madame Elisabeth. It seems that

After the sentence the Girondin leaders were escorted out of the chambers by an armed guard. Valozé, who had been stabbed in the preceding mêlée, was borne out on a stretcher

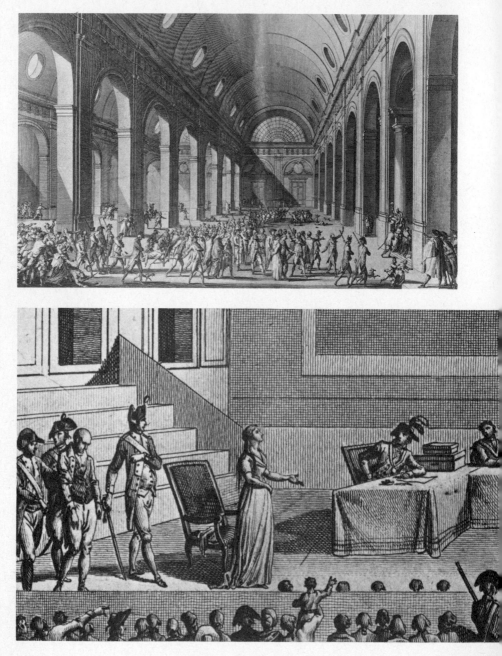

(ABOVE) *A day later the twenty-one men were guillotined in what is now the Place de la Concorde*
(BELOW) *Mme Roland's last words to the Tribunal were: "as you judge me worthy of the fate of those whom you have killed, the least I can do is to go to the scaffold with the courage they showed"*

Robespierre wanted to save the princess. Maret, the librarian of the Egalité palace, reproached him for not having done anything for her, but Robespierre confided that Collot d'Herbois had "torn" her from him.

[[·]]

Robespierre's first speech to the Convention after he had become a member of the Committee of Public Safety was given on 17th November and dealt with foreign policy. Following the spring defeats in Holland and on the Rhine, the victory of Wattignies had restored confidence. The largest part of the speech was devoted to England, contemptuously described by Robespierre as "an island thrown by chance into the ocean". He denounced the "intrigues" of the English government, and more specifically of its leader, William Pitt. He was the instigator of a plot to put the Duke of York on the throne of France. He wanted to capture Dunkirk. According to Robespierre, Pitt had not understood a thing about the Revolution: "He is too immoral to believe in republican virtues and too little of a philosopher to take a step towards the future. George's minister is behind the times. The century was advancing forth towards freedom, but Pitt wanted it to return into barbarianism and despotism." Happily the Jacobins and the Republic had foiled his criminal designs. "Pitt wanted to toy with the French people, and he has been caught out. The French people have disentangled themselves from the tangle of his intrigues like Hercules from a spider's web. Then, in his confusion, he has forced the French people to make war."

To complete his dastardly work, Pitt had had accomplices in France itself, the Girondins. Robespierre particularly accused them "of having saved the Prussian despot and his army [at Valmy]", of having "soaked the soil of Belgium with the purest blood of France [at Neerwinden]", and finally "of having delivered to the enemy [in the retreat from Belgium] our treasures, our provisions, our arms and our defences."

Three countries were still well disposed to France: America, who did not forget that the French people had helped them acquire their freedom; Turkey, France's natural ally against their common enemy, Austria; and Switzerland, who had refused to join the coalition. France would win the friendship of other nations by frankly revealing her policy. "Such is the advantage of a powerful republic; its diplomacy is in its good faith; and as an honest man may open his heart and his house to his fellow citizens without fear, a free people may reveal to other nations the basis of its policy."

After this digression he returned to the hostile nations and their sinister designs. England and Holland were plotting to seize French colonies and trade. Prussia and Austria, "like brigands fighting each other over the remains of a murdered traveller", forgot their differences in Poland to join in the attack on France. Spain was drawn into the coalition by the offer of territory in the Pyrenees, and Sardinia in the hope of annexing the Dauphiné and Provence. Russia, "a country combining the fierceness of savage tribes with the vices of civilization", had only withdrawn from the coalition so as to increase its territory in Poland and Turkey, at the expense of Prussia and Austria.

Robespierre's conclusion, which was rather unexpected, was that the fate of England was in the hands of the French, who could invade it without difficulty. "Whatever anyone says, the only real powers are those which command the land. The moment such a power decides to cross the interval which separates it from a purely maritime power, the latter will cease to exist." The very freedom of the English people, according to Robespierre, depended on France. He explained that, in fact, the English revolutionary movement, deprived of the moral support of the Revolution, could not continue the struggle "against a despotic minister" who attempted to suffocate reason, fetter freedom and oppress the British nation. Finally, not only freedom, but philosophy, humanity and civilization itself, depended on the existence of the Republic. It would survive its ordeals, he was sure, "for the French Republic was invulnerable, like reason, and immortal, like freedom".

One cannot know what the French thought about this speech, in the absence of a free press; the *Feuille de salut public* hailed Robespierre for "the greatness of his ideas, the depth of his principles and the sublimity of his republican eloquence".

[[·]]

Robespierre was entirely taken up with his work on the committee, and during November spoke only once at the Convention and twice at the club. On the 9th he replied to Hébert, who had accused his representative Duquesnoy of having hindered Jourdan's operations. Robespierre said that the generals were now worthy of trust, and that those who criticized the committee for its military policy could only do so with the perfidious intention of embarrassing the government. "I realize that there is a scheme for paralysing the Committee of Public Safety, by seeming to help it in its work, and that people are trying to vilify the executive power so that they can say that there is no longer an authority in France capable of holding the reins of government. The fact is that they want our places. Well, let them take them!" As always, when Robespierre talked about resigning, cries of protest were heard: "No, no, stay where you are!" He went on: "I would like to see *them*, night and day, probing the wounds of the state, and spending their lives in finding a remedy for them. Do they want to extenuate our labours, or do they want to lead us to counter-revolution by betraying patriots in the hearts of the people?" The applause made Hébert realize that he was on the wrong track. Without any shame he withdrew his remarks about Duquesnoy, to whom he gave a brotherly embrace.

Robespierre had, *en passant*, made a brief reference to purging clubs and popular societies. He returned to the matter with further details on the 18th: "We do not want patriots like those of 10th August, and even less like those of 31st May. Even today every royalist poses as a republican and every Brissotin as a Montagnard."

In the forefront of those he was getting ready to exclude as false patriots he put atheists. Not only because their doctrine wounded his deepest convictions and because he regarded them as immoral (he saw no place for them in the republic of virtue that he wanted to found) but also because their anti-religious zeal seemed dangerous to him and more likely to turn people away from the republic than draw them to it. Hébert had had the odd idea of demolishing belfries as being contrary to the concept of equality. Some provincial scenes with their grotesque processions had shocked him. Robespierre had strongly warned the commissioner André Dumont: "It seems to us that, in your latest activities, you have struck out too violently at the objects of Catholic worship. Part of France, above all the South, is still fanatical. One must guard against giving hypocritical counter-revolutionaries, who are trying to start civil war, any pretext which seems to justify their slander. One must not give them the opportunity of saying that we are violating the freedom of worship and that we are making war on religion itself." In addition to the excesses in the provinces, there were those in Paris such as the "depriesting" of Bishop Gobel and the Feast of Reason in Notre-Dame, which had been secularized. Robespierre greeted Anacharsis Cloots, one of the organizers of the ceremony, with marked coldness: "Why are you trying to alienate the Belgians from us, clashing with the doctrines to which you know they are strongly attached?"

"Oh, the damage had already been done. We have been called unbelievers a thousand times over."

"Yes, but there were no facts. Now there are."

Robespierre had been thinking of founding a new faith and wanted Catholicism to disappear, but of its own accord. He did not for one moment think of reviving the constitutional church. As far as priests were concerned, those guilty of counter-revolutionary activities were to be dealt with, but the others left in peace: "Seditious and uncivic priests must be punished, but the title of priest is not in itself to be outlawed."

He was disturbed to see that the Commune, under the influence of Chaumette and Hébert, was following such a strong atheistic policy. The Jacobins also seemed to be letting themselves be carried along. They even thought of electing Anacharsis Cloots as chairman.

Robespierre decided to act without delay. His speech to the Jacobins on 21st November was an energetic denunciation of atheism: "They wanted to make the people believe that the Jacobins had declared war on religion. The acts of atheism, in which some people are indulging, risk making the Republic odious and are compromising it in the eyes of foreigners. To attack fanaticism where it does not exist

All his attempts at being the revolutionary Prince came to nothing, for Philippe l'Egalité was beheaded a bare fourteen months after he had voted for his cousin's death

is to distract the country from its real dangers. The Convention has no intention of outlawing the Catholic religion. Whoever tries to prevent the Mass being said is more fanatical than the priest who is celebrating it."

He explained that atheism was politically dangerous. A philosopher or a private individual might think what he likes on the question of God, but "for the legislator, the public man, to adopt such a system, would be senseless. The National Convention abhorred atheism. Atheism is aristocratic. The concept of a Great Being who watches over oppressed innocence, and who punishes crime is common to all."

[[·]]

One of the most notorious of Jacobin atheists, Hébert, rushed to retract after Robespierre's warning: "I tell the people in the country," he said, "to read the Gospel. This book of morality seems excellent to me, and one must follow its maxims to be a perfect Jacobin. Christ seems to me to be the founder of the people's clubs." This denial saved him for the time being, but three of his followers— Dubuisson, Desfieux and Pereira—were expelled from the club. Another, Guiraud, only just saved himself by telling Robespierre about suspicious meetings at the town hall.

Thus the business of purging the Jacobins began, and it increased in scope during the following weeks. People began to denounce others because they were afraid of being denounced themselves, and to prove their civic virtue. Danton was attacked on 23rd November. He seemed to have changed, and there was little left in him of the fiery revolutionary of 10th August. He had married again, to a very young woman, and he spent more of his time at his house at Arcis-sur-Aube than at the Convention. He worshipped property and had, thanks to bribes, considerably extended the size of his family estate with woods and meadows. He was warned by his friends of the dangers of his retirement, and had returned to Paris to make several speeches denouncing atheism and the policy of de-Christianization practised by certain representatives when they were out on missions. Robespierre could only approve but, at the same time, Danton's speeches show a veiled criticism of the Terror. He said that he was tired of bloodshed and in his turn, feeling threatened, he wanted to see the Revolution brought to an end. His new attitude infuriated Hébert's followers, who wanted the Terror to be intensified. By showing themselves to be ultra-revolutionaries, they hoped that Robespierre's accusations of their being counter-revolutionaries would be forgotten. One of them envisaged reducing the population of France from 20 to 5 million by guillotine. Another, Bichet, proposed guillotining all grocers who were unable to justify themselves in the sale of their provisions. By attacking Danton, who was suspected of being lukewarm, they would have a good springboard. However, Bichet had a weak point—namely, that when he had been at the Ministry, money had passed through his hands, the disappearance of which he somehow or other could not explain. There was also his suspicious behaviour in Belgium. Not without some self-assurance Danton rose to his feet, faced the tribunal and demanded that a committee examine his deeds.

Robespierre came to his aid. He did not want the Hébert faction, whom he wished to defeat, to carry off such a victory. Moreover, Danton was an old companion in arms, and he thought he might still be of use to the Republic. He wanted to save him. Until now they had been in agreement on most things. In semi-retirement, he could hardly appear as a rival. Robespierre said that it was absurd to accuse Danton of having emigrated or having wanted to be Regent to Louis XVII. At the very most he might be reproached for having been too easy on Dumouriez and the Brissotins: "Possibly I am mistaken about Danton but, seen in the context of his family, he only merits praise. In the political context I have watched him. We had a difference of opinion which made me carefully keep my eye on him, sometimes with anger. Although he was not always of the same opinion, should I conclude that he was betraying the fatherland? No. I have always watched him serving it with zeal. Danton wants to be judged. He is right. May I also be judged. Let them come forward, the men who are more patriotic than we."

[[·]]

He was much harder on another Jacobin figure. On 9th December he warned the Jacobins against giving certificates of citizenship too readily.

"The foreigner who insinuates himself among you, disguised in a red cap only to plunge a dagger into your heart, is no less guilty than the Austrian slave who plunges his bayonet into the breast of a defender of freedom."

Everyone recognized Cloots as the "foreigner" belaboured thus. He was a Prussian baron and a millionaire, a picturesque "orator of the human race". What was the crime, then, that this gentle idealist had committed, after having given so many pledges to the Revolution, that brought upon himself the thunder of the Incorruptible? First, there was his atheism, and his part in the anti-religious demonstrations. Then there were the unfortunate words: "King Louis XVI and King Robespierre are more terrifying for France than the Prussian and Austrian armies." Robespierre hated him, then, on three counts: as a foreigner, a rich man and an atheist. On 12th December he attacked him by name, referring first to his 60,000 *livres* income. "Could one look upon as a patriot a foreigner who wanted to be more democratic than the French? Paris bristles with conspirators, English and Austrians. They have been planted in your midst by Frederick's agents. Cloots is a Prussian. I have outlined for you his political life. Judge." His expulsion was voted for immediately, without his being able to defend himself, or a single voice daring to raise itself in his favour.

13

MODERATES AND EXTREMISTS

"Danton will only be discredited after they have proved that they have more energy, more talent and more love of the fatherland. No one has the right to make the slightest reproach against Danton."

ROBESPIERRE, 2nd August 1793

W HEN HE HAD PURGED THE JACOBINS BY EXPELLING THE atheists from their midst, Robespierre realized that there were many thieves among the most prominent of them. The Holy Mountain was corrupt. Men who, from the beginning of the Revolution, had fought alongside Robespierre, were amassing huge fortunes through shameful dealings. These miserable people, "who have taken up the Revolution as a job and the Republic as a prey", had to be unmasked. Some of them were even very close to him. For example the deputy Robert, the husband of Mademoiselle Keralio, in whose house, after a denunciation, several casks of rum were discovered. Robespierre was quite prepared to admit that it was a passing weakness on the part of a good patriot. He intervened. The law on hoarding was not brought into operation against him. But Delacroix, Chabot and Julien de Toulouse were protecting Abbé d'Espagnac, a notorious trafficker in army supplies. Many doubtful foreigners had wormed their way into revolutionary circles, where they took advantage of useful protection. The Englishman Walter Boyd, on the point of being arrested, was able to escape thanks to a false passport supplied by Chabot. The Belgian banker Proli, said to be the natural son of the Austrian Chancellor Kaunitz, was a friend of Camille Desmoulins. Because of his love of good food, Desmoulins frequently dined with rich people, and this alarmed Robespierre. The Spaniard Guzman, who made a living from speculation, entertained Danton. Two Moravian Jews, vaguely bankers, the Frey brothers, were close friends of Chabot, who had married their sister. Hébert himself, the great denouncer of speculators, often visited the Dutch banker Kock.

Thereupon the scandal of the Compagnie des Indes exploded. Baron de Batz, an extraordinary figure, seems to have been the instigator of it. He was a fervent royalist, and had first attempted to save Louis XVI, then Marie-Antoinette, on the way to execution. After that he thought that he could halt the Revolution by corrupting its chief leaders, who would then denounce and destroy each other.

The Compagnie des Indes had been founded by Louis XIV to encourage trade with the East, and was a profitable organization. However, it was decided to wind it up in 1793 as being a vestige of the *ancien régime*. Deputy Delaunay proposed entrusting the liquidation of the company to the company itself which, as Fabre d'Eglantine pointed out, would have allowed the directors to make huge fortunes. A decree then specified that agents of the State would take charge. But when it appeared in the *Bulletin des lois*, the official list of laws passed, the decree appeared to have been altered. Fabre was suspected of having sold himself. To cover himself he denounced to the Committee of Public Safety a "foreign plot", in which he implicated Chabot, Julien and Hérault de Séchelles. Fabre was in turn denounced by Chabot who maintained that he had only taken part in the plot so he could watch the others better. As proof of his good faith he returned the money he had received.

Robespierre suspected both the denouncers and the denounced. He had Chabot and his associates arrested, leaving Fabre for the time being, rightly thinking that they were all guilty. Fabre was a former actor and author, and annoyed Robespierre with his habit of looking at him through a monocle when he spoke to the tribunal, with an ironical smile on his face, as if he were at a play. Chabot was a former Capuchin friar and was repulsive to Robespierre for his dirty appearance, a filthy scarf knotted round his head, and his bare legs emerging from heavy linen trousers. He had none of Marat's redeeming features in Robespierre's eyes.

[[·]]

Fabre was a friend of Danton, whose well-known dishonesty reflected upon him. Something had just happened which might have made Robespierre think that Danton was seeking to get rid of him and take his place. On 25th September there was an attempt to overthrow the Committee of Public Safety. The right wing, the Hébert faction and a variety of malcontents took part in it. A new committee was to have been set up, with Danton at its head. According to Garat, its programme consisted of immediate peace, an end to the Terror, the recall of the émigrés and the freeing of suspects with a general amnesty. If one is to believe the royalist, Mallet du Pan, Danton was even thinking about restoring the monarchy. He no longer believed in the survival of the Republic, nor a French victory over the coalition. He would willingly welcome Robespierre as a member of his committee.

The plotters chose to attack when the Incorruptible was ill and confined to his room for several days. It seems that they did not warn Danton of their intention, so as to force his hand. At least he did not take part in the discussions. One after the other the speakers—Duhem, Goupilleau, Briez and Merlin de Thionville—launched their attacks on the committee, which they accused of incompetence and arbitrariness. The members who were present—Billaud-Varenne, Jean Bon Saint-André and Barère—only offered a feeble defence to their attackers, which presaged their defeat. They were unable to prevent Briez from being elected with a large majority.

Then Robespierre, who had been warned, arrived on the scene. His unexpected appearance changed the atmosphere of the session. He at once launched a counter-attack: "This day has been worth more than three victories to Pitt, I dare say. And if throughout Europe we are taken for imbeciles or traitors, do you think that Europe will have any more respect for the Convention that chose us? We are accused of doing nothing. We have eleven armies to direct; the weight of the whole of Europe to bear; everywhere traitors to unmask; emissaries corrupted by gold; foreign powers to outwit; unfaithful administrators to denounce; all the tyrants to fight; all the conspirators to intimidate, and everywhere obstacles to overcome. These are our functions."

The election of Briez had been a clumsy move. He exposed himself to criticism. When he had been commissioner of the Commune of Valenciennes he had handed the town over to the enemy. This gave Robespierre a weapon: "I tell you that the man who was at Valenciennes when the enemy entered it is not fit to be a member of the Committee of Public Safety. This member would never reply to the question 'Are you dead?' Had I been in Valenciennes in such circumstances, I would never have been in the situation of making a report on the elements of the siege. I would have wanted to share the fate of those who preferred an honourable death to a shameful capitulation."

Briez was terrified at being denounced by Robespierre, and withdrew. He said that he had not wanted to attack the government. If the committee was going to resign as a consequence of his election, then he would renounce it.

When he gave in, the plotters were routed. "The fatherland is lost," shouted Robespierre, "if the government does not have unlimited confidence. I demand that the Committee be renewed." The session ended with a vote of confidence proposed by Barère.

The next day Danton asked to leave Paris for his house in Arcis-sur-Aube.

[[·]]

Danton returned some weeks later to ask Camille Desmoulins to undertake the publication of *Le Vieux Cordelier*. Danton wanted to stop the Terror, partly because he was sick of the bloodshed, but also because he saw himself and his friends threatened. Each of them hoped to enroll Robespierre in their campaign. The Incorruptible had shown undeniable moderation in the application of the Terror, distinguishing the puppets from the leaders. Robespierre thought that it should not strike blindly. Hence his defence of Pache, Bouchotte and Delbarade against extremist attacks. He blamed those who "carried the Terror into all situations, declaring war on peaceable citizens, making it a crime to have unalterable opinions or to be impartial, to find guilty ones everywhere and make the Revolution frightful to the people themselves". He had Carrier recalled. Doctor Souberbielle recounted that when he learned of Fouché's and Collot d'Herbois's mass executions at Lyons, Robespierre cried out: "Blood, endless blood. The wretches. They will end up by drowning the Revolution." He was for the Terror, but a controlled Terror, so as to punish and frighten the guilty. "Woe to whoever dares to abuse the sacred name of freedom, or the fearful arms she has bestowed on it only to bring death or mourning to the hearts of the patriots. Should there be, in the Republic, only one man persecuted by the enemies of freedom, the government must seek him out with vigilance and avenge him with fervour."

Control the Terror, not suppress it—Robespierre's position was as different from the leniency of Danton and Desmoulins as from the ultra-terrorism of Hébert. They were certainly aware of this, but thought that by skill they could lead him on, further than he wanted to go. Desmoulins presented his newspaper which was intended to counter Hébert's policy. Robespierre approved and even agreed to read the proofs, which amounted to giving his guarantee. There was nothing in the first two issues that he could not have written himself. The first, which appeared on 15th Frimaire of the Revolutionary Calendar (5th December 1793), contained a justification of Danton, followed by a vibrant eulogy of the Incorruptible. "Victory has stayed with the Jacobins because in the midst of the ruins of so many colossal civic reputations, that of Robespierre has remained upright. Already strengthened by the ground won during the illness and absence of Danton, the *Enragés*, amidst the most touching and, in his estimation, most convincing of scenes, booed, shook their heads and smiled in pity as if the speech had been condemned by votes. We have won, even so, because, after Robespierre's overwhelming speeches, whose skill seems to grow as the perils of the Revolution increase, and the profound impression that he had left in people's minds, it was impossible to dare to raise their voices against Danton, without giving, as it were, quittance to Pitt's guineas." The remainder of the article revealed the dangers to which the extremists were exposing the fatherland and the Republic.

The second issue bore even clearer evidence of Robespierre's influence, to the point where one might well wonder if the paragraphs dealing with the de-Christianization and the cult of Reason had not been written by his hand. They certainly voiced his opinion exactly. Camille had always been supremely impartial in religious matters. When he dealt with them, it was under Robespierre's guidance. Already in *Les Révolutions* he had, at Robespierre's request, defended priests "who render great service". He took up the argument "that the time had not yet come for the unfortunate ones, old people and women, to give up their old altars and the hope attached to them". One sees here the consoling role that Robespierre

Plots and counter-plots and uprisings were not confined to Paris, nor was the capital alone in wreaking bloody vengeance. In December 1793 there was an uprising in Lyons which was violent and only subdued by the troops commanded by Collot-d'Hérbois

assigned to religion. The rest of the article consisted of an attack against Hébert's faction, "those men who try to destroy principles and patriotism, by exploiting principles and patriotism to extremes. Cloots is a Prussian, Guadet and Vergniaud had him naturalized [a skilful insinuation, intended to pass 'the orator of the human species' off as a Girondin], Hébert has sold himself to the English."

Robespierre demonstrated his satisfaction by defending Camille when it was his turn to be purged on 14th December. He had been accused of uncivic attitudes when the Girondins had been condemned. He was a journalist, and did not speak easily in public. He could only stutter: "I was mistaken about many people. A singular fate has seen to it that of the sixty people who signed my wedding contract, only two friends are still alive—Danton and Robespierre. All the others have either fled or have been guillotined." Murmurs of disapproval were heard on all sides. If Robespierre had not intervened, he would have been expelled from the club there and then. "We must consider Camille Desmoulins," he said, "with his weaknesses and his virtues. Sometimes he is timid and guileless, he is often brave, always Republican. We have seen him in turn the friend of Mirabeau, de Lameth and of Dillon, but we have also seen him smash the idols he worshipped. I beg him to pursue his career, but I also beg him not to be so inconsistent and to stop making mistakes about people who play crucial roles in the political scene."

After such a plea from the Incorruptible, Camille's enemies did not dare insist further.

But at the same time it was a warning not to repeat with Danton the mistake he had made with Mirabeau. Robespierre saw Danton following the path of which he disapproved, namely of forebearance towards the enemies of the Revolution. He could blame the irresponsible and corrupt terrorists, busy himself with sending them to the scaffold, but he had no hesitation about the need to maintain the Terror. "People are glossing the defenders of the Republic with a varnish of injustice and cruelty. The severity used against conspirators is denounced as an attack on humanity. But the people who protect and thus, favour, the aristocrats, by the same token do battle with patriots. The Revolution must be decided by the ruin of one or the other."

Camille, so hesitatingly severe during the time he was "Procurator of the Lanterne", was now entirely won over to the idea of leniency. He persisted, without heeding Robespierre's warning. In fact, he sought to compromise him. After having got him to approve his first two issues of the newspaper, Camille thought his readers could not doubt that the following issues also represented Robespierre's ideas. He took good care not to show Robespierre proofs of the third which paraphrased Tacitus and contained the famous comparison between France under the Terror and the Roman Empire under Nero: "Everything offended the tyrant. If a citizen was popular, he was a rival for the ruler, capable of causing civil war. He was suspect. If, on the contrary, one shunned popularity, and held oneself aloof, this life of retirement gave one pause to think. One was suspect. The courts, protectors of life and property, had become butchers' shops, and what was once called punishment was nothing less than murder. One man was struck down because of his name, or that of his ancestors; another because of his fine house at Alba; Valerius Asiaticus because of his gardens which had pleased the empress; Stabilius because of his face, which did not please; and a multitude of people the reason for whose death it was impossible to guess. Spying was the only way of succeeding. A friend, a son, was found to murder a guest. One had to show joy at the death of a son if one did not want to perish oneself. One was afraid that fear itself made one guilty."

There was a danger that for the word "tyrant" the readers might read Robespierre. To avoid such a mistake, Camille suggested it in the list of victims of the Terror: "It was a crime to have an important position and resign it, but the greatest of all crimes was to be incorruptible."

[[·]]

Such precaution was inadequate to allay Robespierre's displeasure when he read this third issue, which he saw praised by all the counter-revolutionaries. Between the Extremists and the Moderates—both equally guilty in his eyes—he thought that the moment had come to define his position clearly. This was the intent of his *Rapport sur les principes*, which he read to the Convention on 5th Nivôse, year II (25th December 1793).

He began by saying that it had been comparatively easy to conquer external enemies. The danger now came from internal enemies. The government had a duty to defend itself against the factions that endangered it. "Only good citizens are worthy of public protection. The punishment for enemies of the people is death."

The government had to steer its course between two equally dangerous reefs—weakness and rashness—the same individuals being sometimes of one and sometimes of the other faction. In fact, it was difficult to say with certainty to which faction, for example, Hérault de Séchelles belonged. In each could be seen a strange mixture of idealists, adventurers and scoundrels. "If the one proposes a wise measure, but none the less daring, and based on the needs of the fatherland, the other will immediately say that it is inadequate and demand a law that is apparently more popular, but which by their machinations becomes an instrument of destruction. If one puts forward a more solid measure, but still based on the needs of the fatherland, they shout that it is weak, that it is going to ruin the fatherland." It was impossible to make a choice between the two, for "whether one aims too high or not high enough, in both instances one misses". Beneath opposite appearances all the enemies of the fatherland look alike: whether an apostle of federalism or the priest of a universal republic; whether a priest or a prophet of atheism. "There is less difference than one thinks between the red bonnet of patriotism and the red heel of aristocracy."

Dismissing the two enemy factions, Robespierre announced his own programme. It involved a better application of the Terror. He said that the Committee had noticed that the law was not quick enough in punishing the worst criminals. It had chosen badly. The punishment of a hundred petty criminals was of less use to the State than the execution of one major conspirator. A new organization of the Revolutionary Tribunal, he promised, was soon to be set up, which would allow it to act more speedily and more effectively.

[[·]]

Meanwhile Camille Desmoulins had written a fourth and even a fifth issue of *Le Vieux Cordelier*. Taking his plea for indulgence even further, he demanded that a Committee of Clemency be set up, to free suspects. "Release 200,000 suspects from prison, for in the Declaration of the Rights of Man there is no house of suspicion, no suspect people, only prisoners for crimes fixed by law. At the mention of the word clemency, what patriot would not feel deeply moved, for patriotism is the best of all virtues, and in consequence may not exist where there is neither philanthropy, nor humanity, only an arid soul dried up with egoism." An eloquent invocation to Robespierre was intended to get this daring proposition accepted, by placing it in some way under his aegis: "Oh, my old college comrade, whose eloquent speeches posterity will read, do you not recall the lessons of philosophy in which we learnt that love is stronger and more lasting than fear? I am speaking to you at this point, for I foresaw the moment when Pitt had only you to conquer. Without you the ship Argos was in the process of foundering, the Republic turning into chaos and the Jacobins and Montagnards becoming a tower of Babel."

In spite of all the flattery it contained, Robespierre certainly had reasons for being displeased with this piece, realizing that his former fellow disciple was trying to force his hand. He was himself thinking about setting up a Committee of Justice to free the innocent and patriotic who had been unfairly arrested, but not the suspect. Camille's project compromised his plan because of the similarity between the two, and forced him to abandon it so as not to appear temperate himself.

All the same, he still loved Camille sufficiently to save him once again from being expelled. At the Jacobins, Collot d'Herbois, who had just returned from Lyons, read a very brutal report of his activities. This former actor-author, who liked strong drink and gambling, was his colleague on the Committee of Public Safety and was the sort of terrorist whom Robespierre disliked. Even so, he did not come down in favour of expulsion, but reprimand. At the next session the names of Fabre, Bourdon and Camille were called out for purging. None of them was present. It seems that Robespierre wanted to take advantage of their absence to have the matter sorted out. "The champions who ought to be fighting are not present in the arena. Since those who have flung down the challenge are at present avoiding the fight, let the club call them to the tribunal of public opinion. It will judge."

But Camille arrived shortly afterwards. He was asked several questions to which he stammered his replies, alluding to his good faith: "Look, citizens, I do not know where I am any more. My head is in a whirl. People accuse me and slander me on all sides. Do you consider it a crime to have been mistaken?"

"Explain yourself in *Le Vieux Cordelier*," someone shouted.

Robespierre got up. Much has been said about his speech which was a defence tinged with blame. In fact, it expressed exactly the feelings he then had for Camille. He disapproved of his present attitude but was indulgent out of respect for his past history, and to be assured by him of better behaviour in the future. "Some time ago, citizens, I defended Camille Desmoulins when he was accused by the Jacobins. Friendship allowed me some mitigating thoughts on his character. But today I am obliged to speak in a different way. He had promised to give up those political heresies that covered the pages of *Le Vieux Cordelier*. Swollen by the prodigious success of his pamphlet and by the perfidious praise that the aristocrats lavished on him, he has not abandoned the path that terror has traced for him. He is a child led astray by bad company. We must be severe against his writing, which Brissot himself would not have disowned, and preserve his person. I demand that his papers be burnt."

Unhappily Camille did not understand Robespierre's intention. He only saw the blame, which mortified him. *Le Vieux Cordelier* would be burnt by the Jacobins as once before his *France libre* had been by a decree of the Parliament of Toulouse. Then what was the point of having had the Revolution? He retorted: "I will answer you as Rousseau did, to burn is not to answer." However accurate the saying might have been, Robespierre in turn was wounded by it. In order to save the headstrong Camille, at the risk of compromising himself, and with him the fate of the Republic, he had gone to the limit of what his conscience allowed him, and the other rejected the branch he held out to him. "How dare you," he exclaimed, "justify pages that delight the aristocracy. You must realize, Camille, that if you were not Camille, one could not be so forebearing with you. The way you want to justify yourself proves to me that you have evil intentions. 'To burn is not to answer.' Does this quotation have any application here?"

It was one of those days when everything Camille did was wrong. "You condemn me here and now, but did I not come to your house? Did I not read my articles to you, beseeching you in the name of friendship to enlighten me with your advice and point out the way for me?" It was an inopportune reminder. There was nothing in the world that Robespierre wanted less than that it should be thought that he shared Camille's ideas. His voice became drier: "You showed me only some of your articles. Since there was nothing particular to quarrel over, I did not want to read the other issues. They would have said that I had dictated them."

Danton interrupted here. Camille's case had been confused with his own. "Citizens, Camille Desmoulins ought not to be worried by the chastisement that

Robespierre is giving him. Let justice and calm always preside over your decisions. In judging Camille, take care that you do not strike a fatal blow at the freedom of the Press." But the days had gone when the Jacobins listened to him. Danton should have remained silent. His intervention only upset Robespierre, who held him responsible for Camille's errors. He adopted a totally different tone of voice: "So be it. Let us not burn, but reply. A man who sticks so strongly to his dangerous writings is perhaps more than a lost soul. His courage is only a borrowed front, and reveals the hidden men, at whose dictation he writes his newspaper." A secretary then read issue No. 4 in its entirety. Since it was late, it was decided to postpone the reading of numbers three and five until the next day.

When Momoro had finished No. 3 and was preparing to begin No. 5, Robespierre stopped him. There is no doubt that it was a last effort to save his friend. "There is no point in going on with this reading. Camille is a mixture of truth and lies, of polity and absurdity, of healthy views and illusionary designs. It is of little consequence whether the Jacobins expel him or keep him. He is only one individual. What is more important is that freedom should triumph and that the truth be recognized." In similar terms of disdain he had tried to save Madame Elisabeth. What was necessary, he went on—and here his intention of distracting attention became apparent—was to protect oneself from the two factions which threatened the interests of the fatherland, the counter-revolutionaries and the ultra-revolutionaries. "I take up the cause of no one. Camille and Hébert are equally wrong in my eyes."

As he spoke, he noticed Fabre d'Eglantine who was getting ready to leave without making any noise. He had thought for a long time that the man who had devised the republican calendar was an honest patriot. The affair of the Compagnie des Indes had showed that he was nothing more than a speculator and a forger. Robespierre challenged him violently, accusing him of having inspired Camille's writings. Doubtless he also hoped that he could still deflect the club's anger. The poet's expulsion from the Jacobins was voted there and then unanimously. That of Camille came twelve days later.

On 28th January 1794—9th Pluviôse, year II—Robespierre delivered a speech at the Jacobins on foreign policy in which he recalled and expanded the ideas in his speech to the Convention on 5th Nivôse. The club was in the grip of a war fever, and had begun to discuss the "crimes" of the English government. The time was gone when Robespierre would warn the Jacobins against such behaviour. War seemed to him the means of uniting the French around the Committee of Public Safety. Peace would have signified success for the Danton faction—in other words, the end of the Revolution. "There is no point in talking about the English people. All that we want is that they witness our debates. You are fools to believe that the English people are as moral and as enlightened as you." These people, he explained, were still two centuries behind in the matter of enlightenment and morality, because their government's policy had always been to hide the truth.

Oppressed and ruined, they would also one day have their revolution. Pitt, the mad minister of a mad king, would be overthrown. He must be out of his mind to think that with ships he could starve France and dictate terms to her.

Two days later, 11th Pluviôse (30th January), he spoke again on the same subject, since he felt that some of the other speakers lacked conviction. With her liberal traditions, England had long been a model for revolutionaries, Robespierre well knew. Now war divided them. This time he no longer made a distinction between those who governed and the governed, who were "accomplices in the crimes of this perfidious government. I do not like the English because the very name recalls the idea of an arrogant people daring to make war on a generous people who have regained freedom. I do not like the English because their government, perfidiously machiavellian towards the very people who support it, has dared to proclaim that it has no code of honour, no faith to keep with the French in this war, and because some of the people, the sailors and the soldiers, maintain this hateful declaration by force of arms. As a Frenchman, as a representative of the people, I declare that I hate the English people."

[[·]]

In Robespierre's eyes it was not only a political reform that the Revolution was to bring to the French, but a total transformation of their morals. This was the aim of the *exposé* he made to the Convention on 27th Pluviôse, year II (15th February 1794), published under the title "Report on the principles of moral policy that ought to guide the National Convention in the administration of the Republic."

What, he asked, was the aim in view? "The peaceful enjoyment of freedom and equality; the reign of this eternal justice whose laws have been engraved not on marble and stone, but in the hearts of all men, even in that of the slave who forgets them, and the tyrant who denies them."

The object of the laws, therefore, was to create a new order in which all base and cruel passions would be suppressed, and all beneficial and generous passions aroused. Morality would replace egoism; honesty, honour; principles, customs; duty, decency; the rule of wisdom would replace the tyranny of whim; the scorn of vice would replace the scorn of misery; pride, insolence; greatness of soul, vanity; love of glory would replace love of money; good character, good times; merit, intrigue; genius, cleverness; truth, brilliance; the charm of happiness would replace the boredom of lasciviousness; the humanity of man, the manners of great people; a magnanimous, powerful, happy, likeable people, would replace frivolous and miserable people—in other words, all the virtues and all the achievements of the Republic would replace all the vices and inanities of the monarchy.

To bring about a new order of things Robespierre thought that in time of peace, virtue alone would suffice. But in time of war terror had to be added. For then, without terror, virtue was powerless, since without virtue the terror was deadly.

This terror, the support of virtue, he defined as prompt justice, severe and inflexible, without emotion—even that of virtue—the momentary despotism of freedom against tyranny. "Whoever does not hate crime is incapable of loving virtue. Even so, one or the other must yield. Some people cry for leniency for the royalists, and pity for the scoundrels. No. Pity for innocence, pity for the weak, pity for the unfortunate, pity for humanity."

[[·]]

Once again a fresh bout of illness forced Robespierre to absent himself from the club for some time. While he was secluded in his apartment a loyal delegation went along to Duplay's house to learn the news. When, finally recovered, Robespierre returned, his reappearance was greeted by the members in a display of wild enthusiasm. "Would to God," he said, "that my physical strength were equal to my moral courage. I could then—today even—confound these traitors and bring down national vengeance on their guilty heads."

For if the reality of the Revolution did not correspond to his dreams, the fault was theirs. They were responsible for the desolate spectacle that the nation presented. Instead of bringing happiness, the Revolution had only brought war and misery. The new laws were being disregarded, people were refusing to accept the depreciated *assignats*, and recruitment was being ignored. In the provinces the discontented shouted: "Long live the king!" They also wore the white cockade. As for freedom, it had been necessary to replace local elected authorities by appointing agents. Never, even in its most difficult moments, had France been subjected to such supervision. The reports of the national agents showed that everywhere reaction was gaining, at least in people's minds. Jérôme Gillet, of Lyons, wrote to Robespierre: "Wherever I go in the countryside, it is no longer recognisable. Stupefaction, wanness, sadness and consternation are painted on all faces. All the peaceful inhabitants—or almost all—once blessed the Revolution, and now they curse it and long for the *ancien régime*." The reports were the same, whether they came from Lorient, Strasbourg or Calais. Letters from Monsieur and Madame Buissart in Arras expressed the same complaints. The *département* was under the control of Lebon, the former priest, whom Robespierre was protecting. This person, thinking that "'head strong men' were causing all the trouble for France", had consequently sent a large number of them to the guillotine. "Permit an old friend," wrote Madame Buissart, "to address to you a feeble and slight picture of the ills with which the fatherland is overwhelmed. You advocate virtue, but for six months we have been persecuted by all the vices; scorn for all good men; outrages on nature, on justice, on reason' greed for riches; thirst for the blood of brothers. Our ills are indeed great, but our fate is in your hands."

[[·]]

In the eyes of Robespierre the people responsible for this situation were the aristocrats, the "Moderates", and the followers of Hébert and the factions. He would crush them all, beginning with those he thought most dangerous, either because of their number, or at least because they were the most enterprising: the Extremists. The Moderates might be strays, but they were simply perfidious, false revolutionaries, whose manoeuvres he denounced: "The false revolutionaries oppose strong measures and exaggerate them when they have been unable to prevent their being passed. They are severe towards innocence but lenient towards crime. They even accuse the guilty who are not rich enough to buy their silence, or important enough to warrant their zeal, but they are careful enough not to compromise themselves to the point of defending slandered virtue. Sometimes they reveal plots, or unmask the exposed and even decapitated traitors, but praise living and still accredited traitors, set great store by the appearance of patriotism and are devoted to sedition. They would prefer to wear a hundred red bonnets than do one good deed."

Their headquarters was the Cordeliers Club, Danton's old domain which he no longer visited. Predominant there were Hébert, Momoro, Vincent and Carrier, the disgraced terrorist. Hébert was not an adversary to be treated lightly. He had previously been a dealer in tickets for people who wanted to leave and then return at the Théâtre des Variétés. He had a newspaper with a circulation of 600,000, a proportion of which was distributed to the armies through Bouchotte, the Minister of War. He had filled the ministry with his men. All these people pretended to think of Robespierre as a man unaware. On 24th Pluviôse (12th February), they launched a general attack against him, without ever naming him. Vincent talked about unmasking plotters, the names "of whom people would be amazed". Momoro stigmatized "all the worn out men of the Republic, the broken legs of the Revolution, who look on us as extremists because we are patriots, and they no longer want to be patriotic". Hébert said: "These men, greedy for the power they are accumulating, but ever insatiable, have concocted, and in great speeches, pompously spread the word of ultra-revolution to destroy the friends of the people who watch over their plots—as if one person were allowed to set limits to the national will."

The factionists nurtured the hope of getting their hands on power through a new revolution. They organized an uprising against the Convention which they expected to be another 31st May. In the way that the Jacobins had beaten the Girondins, they in their turn would beat the Jacobins. In the very heart of the Committee of Public Safety they hoped for the support of Billaud-Varenne and above all that of Collot d'Herbois, who opposed Robespierre with jealous rivalry. Thinking himself to be the second person in the Republic, the ex-actor-dramatist was ambitious to become the first.

Led by Hébert, the Cordeliers gambled on the help of the Sections to bring down Robespierre. They failed in their attempts to unite Robespierre's enemies, and on 12th March the club was invaded and the conspirators arrested

At the beginning of March posters appeared, calling for the dissolution of the Convention and the establishment of a dictatorship. In the hall where the Cordeliers met, the panel of the Rights of Man was symbolically covered with a black veil. On 14th Ventôse (4th March), Hébert openly called for revolt. The protection that Robespierre had given Desmoulins, his personal enemy, was a stab in his heart. "Remember that Camille was driven out, struck off by the patriots, and that one man, led astray no doubt, otherwise I would not know how to describe it, found it only right to have him reinstated." Hébert had chosen his moment well. The committee found itself weakened by the absence of several of its members. Prieur de la Marne was on a mission, Robert Lindet and Couthon were ill. But after four years of revolution, Paris had enough of riots. Out of forty-eight Sections, only one answered Hébert's call. The mayor of Paris, Pache and Hanriot, commander of the National Guard, declared themselves against an insurrection.

When a rising fails, its organizers are lost. They vainly tried to retract. Carrier said that it had never been a question of an actual insurrection, and Hébert explained that by insurrection he had meant "a more intimate union of the Montagnards with the Jacobins and the patriots, so as to obtain justice for all unpunished traitors". Nor did it gain them any advantage by tearing the black veil as a sign of reconciliation. On 22nd Ventôse (12th March), the Committee of Public

Safety decided on the arrest of Hébert, Ronsin, Vincent and Momoro. The next day Saint-Just read a report to the Convention denouncing Moderates and Extremists. It was the sort of thing he excelled in. Following the more and more commonly used process of amalgamation and before the trial took place, there were added to the followers of Hébert "atheists" such as Cloots, and the anti-clerical bishop, Gobel, and a group of people described as "foreign agents", namely Kock, Proli and Pereira. In this way no one knew any more who was accused on political grounds, who was a swindler or who was a traitor. On 24th Ventôse (14th March), they were all guillotined in front of the baffled populace. So the people who had denounced treason so much were only traitors themselves.

Between their arrest and their execution, Robespierre made several speeches. Amar, a member of the Committee of General Security, had made a report on the liquidation of the Compagnie des Indes which displeased him. Amar presented it as a pure swindle, which of course it was. Robespierre insisted on seeing it as "a foreign plot". Fabre, Chabot and their accomplices cared nothing for foreigners. Not only did Robespierre demand that the report be re-written, but he also decided that he would have to denounce publicly the international nature of the affair. After Pitt he blamed the English parliament, "this parliament associated with crimes against freedom that I have just pointed out to you, which at this moment, together with all our enemies, has its eyes on France to see what the results will be of the dreadful schemes they are directing against us. Do you know what the difference is between them and the representatives of the French people? This illustrious parliament is essentially corrupt, and we have in the National Convention a few individuals affected by corruption. Before the eyes of the British people, the members of parliament boast of the traffic of their views and sell them to the highest bidder, whereas we, when we discover a traitor or a corrupt man, we send him to the scaffold."

[[·]]

Before his execution, one of the Hébertists, Ronsin, exclaimed: "The party that is sending us to death will go there in its turn, and it will not be long in doing so." Meanwhile the Moderates were rejoicing in the fall of their enemies as if it were a personal triumph. Camille Desmoulins pushed lack of feeling to the point of proposing that the journey to the scaffold be transformed into a sort of cavalcade preceded by "Père Duchesne's Furnaces". They should have realized that Robespierre, so as not to appear to be a moderate, would be forced to strike at them in turn. On 30th Ventôse (20th March), he announced that the proscription of the Hébert faction would soon be followed by that of the Moderates.

In fact, measures against them had already been taken on 27th Ventôse (17th March), with the arrest of Hérault de Séchelles. Robespierre suspected him of being a spy and some months previously had dismissed him from the Committee of

Ten days after their trial and conviction Hébert and his colleagues were put into the tumbrils. The route to the guillotine took them along the rue Saint-Jacques passing the entrance to the Jacobin club whose members had brought them to this fate

Public Safety. He was a former noble, a rake, and had once been an assiduous member of the queen's circle and that of Madame de Polignac. He had gone into the Revolution without conviction. He retained the spirit of the *ancien régime* and had allowed himself "some jokes at the expense of the committees, which offended Saint-Just. The man who makes fun of the head of a government is inclined towards tyranny."

In common with Fabre, Hérault de Séchelles was a friend of Danton. By striking at them first, it is possible that Robespierre wanted to warn Danton, to bring him back on to the straight and narrow; and if it were necessary to strike him down, he would thereby be deprived of support. Billaud-Varenne and Saint-Just were putting a great deal of pressure on Robespierre for the proscription of Danton. All the same, he hesitated to give his consent. Danton aroused conflicting feelings in him. His sensuality, his venality and his atheism displeased Robespierre. He could not delude himself that such a man would ever be virtuous. On the other hand, he had considered his enthusiasm, his strength and his energy useful to the fatherland. They could, if need be, still be so. His death would divide the Mountain and risk disastrous consequences for the Revolution. When Billaud-Varenne first proposed to the committee that Danton be arrested, Robespierre protested indignantly and charged him with wanting to destroy their finest citizens.

Danton's enemies reported despicable things about him, which were more or less authentic, and Robespierre kept a record of them. Moreover, Danton was one of those people who say things without thinking: of Robespierre, "That bugger couldn't even cook an egg"; or again, "Can't one scratch his skin without making patriotism bleed?" Robespierre also recalled the occasions on which he had "with anger" noted Danton's behaviour and his dealings with suspects such as the Belgian financier Proli and the Spaniard Maria de Guzman. "If only Danton were honest," he said, regretting the fact that such a man had been lost to the Republic. One of Danton's remarks about Robespierre's religious projects, which he referred to as "Latin American Jesuitry", had deeply wounded Maximilien.

On the other hand, friends they had in common tried to reconcile them and arranged several meetings between the two. The first seems to have taken place at the house of Deforgues, either in the Marais or at Charenton. There are two contradictory versions of the meeting, but one thing is certain—that it only succeeded in making the chasm between them wider. Danton was not circumspect and talked with abandon, while Robespierre thought that he could see a wilfully wounding allusion in everything he said. Danton is supposed to have said: "Let us come to an understanding and save freedom. It is under attack from very wicked people. They slander and deceive the people, who look upon them as their friends." Robespierre replied: "What do you mean? What are you alluding to? You may put whatever interpretation you wish on my speeches. Your mission to Belgium is possibly not without reproach—you have been badly seconded and badly advised. Delacroix covered this mission with disgrace." Danton then replied: "You are talking like the aristocrats, who want to dishonour the Convention and the patriots who compose it; I will never permit such an attack. The Republic must not be defamed by slandering the people who founded it." Robespierre registered silent disapproval while Danton went on to evoke the dangers to freedom if the Terror continued, "in which the innocent was confused with the guilty". Robespierre replied sharply: "Who has told you that an innocent person has perished?"

In his speech of 8th Ventôse (26th February) to the Convention, Saint-Just gave an apology for the Terror, of which every word was aimed at Danton: "Those who want to tear down the scaffold because they are afraid of going to it themselves. . . . One is guilty against the Republic because one had pity for the detainees. . . . One is guilty because one does not want virtue . . . One is guilty because one does not want the Terror . . . what constitutes the Republic is the destruction of everything that is opposed to it."

With his usual optimism, Danton made the mistake of underestimating the danger. If, over the course of those decisive weeks, he had showed as much energy before the tribunal, the outcome might have been different. He was now only intermittently energetic. As if he were dreaming, he said that he was weary of events, sickened with politics, "drunk with men", and too proud to believe that they could send such a revolutionary as himself to the guillotine. When people tried to warn him he replied: "I will put Robespierre on the end of my thumb and make him spin like a top." Or again: "If I imagined that he had only even thought about it I would eat his guts."

The fall of Hébert and his friends had increased Danton's illusion of security. He had been unwise enough to make a triumphant speech announcing the end of the Terror: "The time has come when only deeds will be judged. The masks are falling, and the masks will no longer deceive people. Those who want to slaughter patriots will no longer be confused with the real magistrates of the people. Were there amongst all the magistrates only one who had done his duty, then we must put away, rather than make him drink, this chalice of bitterness." The deputies who had for several months trembled for their lives, enthusiastically voted that his speech be printed.

As Robespierre listened to Danton, he must have thought that Danton was throwing his cap into the ring for the leadership of the next government. Danton, who had seemed withdrawn, at one blow re-established his position, and became the rallying point for the discontented. More so since Tallien, who was considered his partisan, had been elected president of the Convention and his friend, the butcher Legendre, president of the Jacobins. If Robespierre did not counter-attack quickly, the Moderates would possibly carry the day. . . . That would mean the end of the Republic of virtue.

Nevertheless, the two men were to have one last meeting on 2nd Germinal (22nd March), at the home of their mutual friend Humbert. Also present at this dinner were Legendre, Panis, Deforgues and Courtois, who left an account of the evening. According to him, Danton behaved warmly and exhorted Robespierre: "Let us forget our resentment and only consider the fatherland; its needs and its dangers. You will see that the Republic, triumphant and respected outside, will soon be loved inside by those very men who, up till now, are its self-evident enemies." Robespierre said nothing for quite some time and then replied: "With your principles and your morals, would any guilty people be found and punished? Would you be angry if there were no guilty people to punish?" Courtois says that Danton was so moved that he began to weep. Another witness, Daubigny, said that he embraced Robespierre.

But the Incorruptible remained cold. In fact, their conversation had wrecked his final hopes for an understanding with Danton. At that very moment he decided to send him to the scaffold. The next day he began to prepare material for denunciation, with the intention of entrusting the writing of it to Saint-Just: Danton had been the friend of Mirabeau and the de Lameths in 1790 and 1791. It did not occur to Robespierre that some of his accusations could easily be applied to himself. As a minister Danton had let his friends—in particular Fabre—enrich themselves out of the treasury. In that he was free from any reproach. When he had proposed crushing the Brissotins, Danton had refused "under the pretext that he could only concern himself with the war". He had "ensured the safety of the King of Prussia and his army". Once Danton had said: "Public opinion is a whore and it is stupid to talk of posterity." The word "virtue" made Danton laugh. "There was no virtue more solid," he said jokingly, "than that which he practised every night with his wife." How could a man to whom any idea of morality was so alien be a defender of freedom?

During the incident of the Champ-de-Mars Danton had fled to Arcis-sur-Aube, allowing 2,000 patriots to be slaughtered. He had played no part in the rising on 10th August. During the night of 9/10th August he took it upon himself to go into hiding. He had renounced Marat, Robespierre and the Mountain, and attacked the Convention. He had only spoken against the Right because they had demanded an account of him. He had not wanted the death of the Tyrant, he had only voted for it because of the strength of public opinion. He had "seen with horror the revolution of 31st May and tried to make it fail". He had tried to save the Girondins. He wanted to "dissolve the Convention and establish the Constitution (of 1793)". On 18th Ventôse, year I (8th March 1793), he had organized a false insurrection to give Dumouriez "the pretext to march on Paris". Finally, ultimately, he had asked for "an amnesty for all the guilty".

Saint-Just did not have to alter anything in Robespiere's notes to build up his indictment. There followed a few notes on Danton's "accomplices"—Fabre, Delacroix, and Hérault de Séchelles. And Desmoulins? Was it too painful for Robespierre to send his old college friend to death, or did he think that he could still be saved? He granted him the excuse of having been mistaken about Mirabeau and Lafayette. The tribunal, knowing that the remarks were Robespierre's, might bring acquittal. But Saint-Just suppressed it. His hatred would not pardon the young journalist for having one day mocked his arrogant manner. Robespierre, who possibly already reproached himself for this weakness, did not protest.

Danton, meanwhile, did nothing. His bout of liveliness had not lasted. His friend Legendre was amazed at his inactivity, but Danton told him that he would rather be guillotined than guillotine.

[[·]]

Saint-Just presented his report to the committees of Public Safety and General Security on 11th Germinal (31st March). As usual where important decisions were involved, they met together. "He was so convincing," said Lavicomterie. "Saint-Just told it all with so much soul that when he had finished and asked if anyone wanted to speak, everyone replied: 'No, no!' " Even so, two members refused to sign the decree (for the arrest of the Dantonists). One was Lindet, purveyor of supplies, who stated his principle: "I am here to feed the citizens, and not to kill patriots." The other was the Alsatian, Rühl, who out of friendship for Danton simply warned him. Carnot warned his colleagues: "Think carefully about it. A head such as his will drag many others after it."

Vadier said that Saint-Just's intention was then to read his indictment to the Convention, in front of the accused, before the warrant for the arrest would be issued. Did he believe that the accused would let him speak without interruption? Danton's impetuous defence before the tribunal allows one to imagine what would have happened. The Tribune would have drawn himself up and with his powerful voice would have crushed the presumptuous young man. As later events were to prove, it was not so difficult to reduce Saint-Just to silence. This is doubtless what the members of the committees feared when they exclaimed that by postponing the arrest they risked their own dissolution. Saint-Just became angry, and said that they wanted to deprive him of his effect: "Seeing our formal opposition he completely lost his head in rage and left us in the lurch." Robespierre was also of the opinion that to arrest the Dantonists before the report had been read to the Convention was reprehensible. He was overruled by Vadier who said: "Since fear was an irresistible argument with him, I used this weapon to fight him. You may run the risk of being guillotined if that is your pleasure, as far as I myself am concerned I want to avoid this danger by having them arrested at once, for we must not fool ourselves about the decision we ought to take. It is all summed up in these words: 'If we do not guillotine them, we shall be guillotined ourselves.' "

Finally a warrant was executed, and the arrests made during the night (30th March). That of Desmoulins certainly troubled Robespierre's conscience. However, he must be absolved of the act of hypocrisy which, according to Riouffe's *Mémoires* was that he never treated his old college friend with more affection than on the eve of his arrest, in order to reassure and deceive him. He had stopped seeing

Camille, who for that very reason was expecting arrest. When Desmoulins met Joseph Planche a few days earlier, he had said: "I am lost. I went to call on Robespierre and he refused to see me." Charlotte claims that even then he "went to the prison to ask Camille to return to the true principles of the Revolution. Camille did not want to see him, and my brother—who would probably have guaranteed his defence and perhaps have saved him if he had been able to persuade him to foreswear his political heresies—abandoned him to the terrible justice of the revolutionary tribunal."

The Convention met the next day at eleven o'clock in an atmosphere of tension. If Danton could find no guarantee in his revolutionary past, no one could feel safe. Legendre, the butcher, took the floor: "Citizens, four members of this assembly were arrested last night. I know that Danton is one of them, but I do not know the names of the others. I demand that the arrested members be brought to the bar of the house to be accused or set free by us. I affirm that I believe Danton to be as pure as myself." If the motion had then been put to the vote for the accused to appear, it would have had every chance of being accepted—as the members of the committee had rightly feared (the day before). If Danton had been allowed to confront his accusers, the situation might easily be reversed.

Assemblies, however, are prone to waste their time at important moments. Robespierre was warned of what was happening and hastened to the Convention. When he appeared there was total silence, then shouts of: "Down with the dictatorship", began to be heard. Slowly he went up the steps of the rostrum and then began: "There has been secret unrest for some time in this assembly, and it is easy to see that it is of great importance. In fact, it is a question of knowing whether some men today should prevail over the fatherland; if the interest of a few ambitious hypocrites should prevail over the interest of the French people." The deputies applauded this declaration, as they had applauded that of Legendre a few moments earlier. Robespierre went on: "We want no privileges, we want no idols. We will see whether, today, the Convention will be able to break a supposed idol that has been rotten for a long time, or if in its fall the idol will crush the Convention and the French people." With his eyes fixed on Legendre he added, spacing out his words: "The man who trembles is guilty." The butcher was not a timid man, but he was afraid and retracted. Robespierre had been expecting more resistance. Apparently that evening when he returned to the rue Saint-Honoré he made this disillusioned comment to Duplay: "Danton has some very cowardly friends."

There remained nothing more for Saint-Just to do than to read out the report of accusations which he did, according to Barras, "one hand motionless, and making only one gesture with the other, lifting his right arm and letting it fall in an inexorable way, without recourse, like the very blade of the guillotine."

"Danton, you have served tyranny [having prepared his indictment with the vision of Danton in front of him, head lowered, ashamed and humiliated, he had not changed a word of the original text]. . . . Would you dare deny having sold your-self to the three most violent conspirators against freedom. . . . Evil citizen, you have conspired . . . wicked man, you have compared public opinion to a woman of loose morals; you have said that honour was ridiculous, that glory and the past were foolishness. These maxims should endear you to the aristocracy." After which he turned to Desmoulins "who was first duped, and ended up being an accom-plice", to Fabre, who at the idea of a Committee of Clemency "began to cry. But the crocodile also cries." Finally Hérault de Séchelles, who made the mistake of "being facetious in intimate conversation".

He finished amidst a terrorized silence on the part of the deputies. No one came forward to reply, and the Convention voted unanimously for the decree against "Danton and his accomplices . . . guilty of having dabbled in conspiracy towards re-establishing the monarchy and destroying the national representation and the republican government."

Every precaution was taken to assure that the tribunal would bring in the desired verdict. One could count on the president, Herman, as well as the public prosecu-tor, Fouquier-Tinville. The jury was reduced to seven, eliminating all those suspected of being lenient. As usual three groups were lumped together—the politicians, Danton and his friends Delacroix, Desmoulins, Philippeaux, Wester-mann; the monopolists of the Compagnie des Indes, Chabot, Delaunay and Basire; and finally those who it was agreed to call "qualified foreign agents", Diedrichsen, Guzman and the Frey brothers, who were in reality only swindlers, with no interest in politics, come to enrich themselves in the troubled waters of the Revolution.

At the approach of danger, Danton found all his energy once more and wanted to fight. The president was unable to stifle his stentorian voice. The public went on applauding his tirades. There is one interesting point: he did not believe that Robespierre was to blame. At one point he shouted: "I must talk about the three rascals who dished Robespierre."

The president and the public prosecutor did not know what to do. The trial was in danger of ending in an acquittal. The accused then demanded that witnesses for the defence be heard. The prosecutor could not refuse on legal grounds, so he wrote to the committees. There are no traces of Robespierre's intervention, but Saint-Just acted. He imagined a plot hatched in prison by General Dillon and several other people, with the complicity of Lucile Desmoulins, to save Danton and his friends, "to stir up a movement, to murder the patriots and the tribunal". In support of this terrible lie, the Convention passed a decree depriving "any prisoner who resists or insults national justice" of the right to defend himself.

After this decree was read, several of the condemned wrote to Robespierre to try to placate him. Since his arrest, Chabot had never stopped sending him totally servile letters: "I prostrate myself, my face to the ground, to worship Providence, who has established you as the protector of the patriots." Delacroix maintained that he was an "austere republican, an enemy of conspirators and traitors", and denouncing to him the members of the committee—Vadier, Voulland and Barère. Others, such as Lulier and Deforgues, invoked their long careers in the service of the Revolution. The most touching of these letters was on behalf of Camille Desmoulins. Madame Duplessis, his mother-in law, reminded Robespierre of the evenings spent at her house and that of her friend, where he had held little Horace on his knees, and of his hope at one point of becoming her son-in-law. But Robespierre would have thought himself lacking in his duties if he had let himself be moved by such appeals.

The Dantonists mounted the scaffold on 16th Germinal (5th April). The tumbril passed through a silent crowd of onlookers who were stunned to see these pioneers of the Revolution taken to their deaths. Camille Desmoulins, his hands tied behind his back and his shirt undone, shouted in an attempt to incite the crowd to riot, to remember the 14th July. "Leave this vile rabble," Danton said to him. As the cortège passed along the rue Saint-Honoré and in front of Duplay's house, he shouted the prophetic words: "You will follow us, Robespierre."

· 14 ·

THE 120 DAYS

*"The revolution is frozen, its fundamental concepts are under-
mined. All that remains is the red bonnet worn by intrigue.
The workings of the Terror have made crime pall, as strong
drink dulls the palate."*

ROBESPIERRE

NOW THAT THE EXTREMISTS AND THE MODERATES HAD BEEN
beaten, Robespierre felt that the moment had come to set up the republic
of virtue. Even so, there were still a large number of factions. They had to
be fought "relentlessly". This was the aim of the laws of Prairial. "We will rescue
freedom by plunging the dagger of justice into the hearts of all the criminals who
are determined to destroy it."

Meanwhile, the people needed a religion to replace Catholicism, which was now
outlawed. That of the jurist priests, lacking a foundation, no longer existed, and the
cult of Reason was no more than a scandalous orgy. Rousseau had taught Robespierre
the moral value of ceremonies, and recent events had only reinforced his deism.
Victories on the frontiers had brought proof of the intervention of Providence in
favour of the Republic.

With these ideas in mind, Robespierre addressed the Convention on 18th Floréal,
year III (7th May 1794) with his speech "on the relation between religious and moral
ideas and republican principles". He had devoted three weeks to its preparation.

He began by taking a general view of the world. How, he asked, had Europe
been able to make such astonishing progress in the arts and sciences when she had
still been ignorant of the first notions of public morality? He provided the answer
himself. It was because hitherto the kings who had controlled the destinies of the
earth, feared neither the great geometricians, nor the great painters or poets, whereas they feared the strict philosophers and the defenders of humanity.

Nevertheless a hope was born. Reason was on the march against thrones. New concepts were to be employed in the government of peoples. The art of governing had hitherto been the art of deceiving and corrupting men and it must now become the art of enlightening them and making them better. Since the sole foundation of society was morality, the legislator must enact laws and the administration put into practice the moral truths handed on in the books of philosophers.

The leaders of the two rival factions, Girondins and Moderates—Condorcet "the academician despised by all the parties", and Danton "the most dangerous of the conspirators if he had not been the most cowardly"—for a moment put the Republic in danger. The people had struck them down. Now the threat came from the atheists, who were making war on religion:

> They have elevated immorality not only into a system, but into a cult. They have tried to smother all the noble sentiments of nature by their examples as much as by their precepts. What did these people want when, surrounded as we were by conspiracies, burdened as we were with such a war, and at a time when the torches of civil discord were still smouldering, they suddenly and violently attacked religion? What was the motive that drove these propogandists, foreigners, and conspirators to plan this great operation in the shadows of the night and kept secret from the National Convention? Was it patriotism? The fatherland had already inflicted punishment on traitors. Was it hatred of priests? The priests were their friends. Was it horror of fanaticism? It was the only way of supplying fanatics with arms. Was it the desire to hasten the triumph of reason? But they never stopped outraging reason; by their extravagant scheming they made it hateful.

Was it not the policy of the most relentless enemies of the Republic, the policies of Pitt, of the émigrés, and of the kings allied against France?

In a lyrical flight he took these atheists to task, who denied the existence of Providence:

> Who then has given you a mission to announce to the people that the Divinity does not exist, you who are so passionate about this arid doctrine, but are never passionate about the fatherland? What advantage do you find in persuading man that a blind force presides over his destinies and strikes indiscriminately at crime and virtue, that his soul is nothing more than a gentle breath that is extinguished at the gates of the tomb? Does the idea of his annihilation inspire in him the purest sentiments, more uplifted than that of his immortality? Will it inspire in him more respect for himself and for those like him; more devotion to the fatherland; more daring in facing the tyrant; more scorn for death and for sensuality? Innocence on the scaffold makes the tyrant turn pale in his chariot; would it have this effect if the tomb was the same for the oppressor and the oppressed?

Deism, with its role of consolation, was socially useful, whereas the negation of God and the immortality of the soul only offered despair:

> You regret a virtuous friend, you like to think that the finest part of him escapes death. You weep over the coffin of a son or a wife, but are you consoled by the man who tells you there is nothing left of them but vile dust? You unfortunate people who die at the hands of a murderer, your last sigh is a call to eternal justice. Unfortunate sophist. By what right do you come to snatch the spectre of reason from innocence, to put it in the hands of crime, to throw a funeral veil over nature, to make the unfortunate desperate, to rejoice in vice, to sadden truth and degrade humanity? The more a man is gifted with sensitivity and genius, the more he embraces the ideas that enlarge his being and lift up his heart. The doctrine of men of this stamp becomes that of the universe. How could these ideas not be truths? I cannot in any way conceive how nature could have suggested to man fictions that are more useful than all the realities; and if the existence of a Supreme Being, if the immortality of the soul, were nothing more than dreams, they would still be the finest of all the conceptions of the human spirit.

Robespierre then delivered his proposed decree, the first article of which declared: "The French people recognize the existence of the Supreme Being and of the immortality of the soul." The second and third enumerated the duties of citizens: hatred of tyrants; punishment of traitors; brotherhood and the practice of justice. Articles four to seven enumerated various festivals to be named after the glorious events of the Revolution, the virtues which are most dear to men, and the chief blessings of nature: the 14th July 1789, 10th August 1792, 21st January 1793 and 31st May 1793; justice, modesty, frugality, conjugal faith, Stoicism, etc., etc.

The speech was greeted by the applause of the whole assembly and was passed unanimously without discussion. Even so, the atheist majority hated the ideas put forward by Robespierre. It seemed too dangerous, however, to express any doubt. Several deputies, ready to permit anything in the realm of politics, did not spare their vote for Robespierre. Meanwhile, at the request of Couthon, the Convention decided that the decree should be translated into all languages, so that the whole world knew what France thought. It was also decided to print 200,000 copies, to be sent to the armies and popular clubs and to be displayed on placards in camps and public squares. The Committee of Public Safety ordered that the first article of the decree be carved on the façades of "churches". The national agents, priests of the new religion, were told to read aloud the decree in the Temple of Reason for thirty days in succession.

The majority, under a mask of approval, remained silently reticent, but Robespierre's friends and admirers demonstrated their enthusiasm. Payan, one of the national agents, proclaimed that the report contained "great, new and sublime" ideas, proving that the government would never deprive the people of the consoling dogmas of religion. The Commune voted its congratulation and the poet Sylvain Maréchal composed a hymn in honour of the Supreme Being, although personally he scarcely believed in it. But there are limits even in flattery, and a man called Julien de la Drôme was to learn this lesson to his cost. Thinking that he would pay court to Robespierre, he proposed at a meeting of the Jacobins that any citizen who did not believe in the Divinity should be banished from the Republic. Despite the fact that this motion had Rousseau's authority behind it, Robespierre opposed it, suspecting de la Drôme of seeking, through his "extremism", to make his project ridiculous.

[[·]]

At this time there was a man called Henri l'Admiral living in Paris. He had once been a valet, but the Revolution, by destroying the nobility, had deprived him of his job. It was natural that he did not like the Revolution at all. He lived by a variety of expedients, and finally was reduced to selling his furniture. In his eyes, one man symbolized the Revolution that had brought him to a state of misery— Robespierre. He decided to avenge himself by killing him.

He got hold of two pistols and went to Robespierre's house. He asked to see him and was told that Robespierre was not there. Admiral went away, without further ado, in the hopes of finding him at the Convention. On the way, doubtless to give himself courage, he treated himself to a good lunch. Then to be able to watch his man, to follow him and strike him down when he had left the Convention, Admiral took his place in the public gallery. There, during the recitation of a boring report by Barère, he fell asleep. When he woke up the session was over and Robespierre had left. Admiral rushed off in search of him; hours went by when about midnight, worn out with fatigue and furious at his failure, he decided to go home. It was then that he realized that another great figure of the Revolution, Collot d'Herbois lived in the same house as himself. Instead of Robespierre, he would kill that man. He lay in ambush on the doorstep and waited for Collot's return. He fired twice without hitting him, merely wounding a neighbour who tried to intervene.

By chance the next day there was another attempt on Robespierre's life—or at least something that looked very much like it. Cécile Renaud, a pretty and naïve girl of twenty, lived quietly at home with her modest family who fondly remembered the guillotined king. She heard people around her saying that the fault was all Robespierre's. Doubtless the news about Charlotte Corday's deed had reached her. (On 22nd May) she left her house, taking with her two little knives and a packet of laundry. She did not know where Robespierre lived, and had to ask people she met in the street. Since she had never left her district, it took her quite some time to find the rue Saint-Honoré. On the way she stopped in a café, where she put down her parcel, saying as she left "that she was going to see a man who was much today, but who would no longer be anything to-morrow". At the Duplay's Eléonore

Cécile Renaud, inspired by Charlotte Corday, decided to kill Robespierre. With knives hidden in her basket, after losing her way she finally reached the house, only to be arrested

stopped her at the door and told her that she could not see Robespierre. She insisted on entering, but some men who were there took her to the Committee of General Security, where she made no bones about telling her story.

Robespierre had often talked about the daggers of murderers directed at him, and so took these two failed attempts very seriously, since he saw in them "a foreign plot". He persuaded his colleagues on the committee to write an urgent letter to Saint-Just, who was then on a mission to the armies, requesting him to come back to Paris without delay "where freedom was exposed to new dangers. The committee needs to assemble the brilliance and energies of all its members," said the letter which, in his agitation, he signed twice. Barère, possibly in order to flatter Robespierre, formally accused England before the Convention of having been the instigator of the two attempts. He drew up an imposing list of England's crimes, which filled nine columns of *Le Moniteur*, and proposed that by way of reprisal no quarter should henceforth be granted to English and Hanoverian soldiers taken prisoner.

The meeting at the Jacobins that evening bordered on hysteria. The account runs as follows: "At this interesting session [according to the official record] the club and all the citizens in the galleries welcomed with tenderness and applauded with

Robespierre, faithful to the teachings of Rousseau, solemnly inaugurated the Feast of the Supreme Being in the Champs de Mars. It was not successful and reflected poorly on him

delight two of the most ardent defenders of the people's rights [Robespierre and Collot], whom the wickedness of the British government had marked down as companions to Marat and Lepelletier." Legendre was anxious to have his defence of Danton forgotten, and excelled himself in flattery: "The god of nature has not allowed the crime to be committed."

The feelings of his friends were doubtless a balm for Robespierre, but, all the same, one thing disappointed him, as when Marat had been assassinated. The attack might really have been meant for Collot d'Herbois, deflecting some of the attention from him. Even more so since his colleague talked a lot. At the Jacobins a man called Rousselin proposed that "civic honours" be granted to the locksmith who had been wounded as he went to help Collot, but Robespierre saw this proposal as a malevolent thrust at himself, and had Rousselin expelled from the club. "I am not," he said, "one of those people whom recent events should concern in the least. All the same, I cannot prevent myself from making several reflections. It was only to be expected that the defenders of freedom should be prey to the daggers of tyranny. I have always said as much. What I warned about has happened. I no longer believe in the necessity of living, but only in virtue and Providence. I find myself more disassociated than ever from the wickedness of men. The crimes of tyrants and the fire of assassins have made me freer, and more formidable to all the enemies of the people. My mind is more disposed than ever to unmask traitors."

A few days later, at the Convention, he declared: "I have lived enough. I no longer hold to a transient life, except through love of my country and a thirst for justice."

The 20th Prairial (8th June) was the Feast of the Supreme Being. Robespierre was chosen unanimously by his colleagues in the Convention to preside over the ceremonies. As far as his friends were concerned, it was an honour he deserved. This enabled others to shake off on to him the responsibility for a demonstration of which they did not approve.

That day the sun rose in a cloudless sky. Robespierre, permeated with the grandeur of the act that he was going to perform, dressed with particular care. He wore a blue coat and buff cotton trousers. He did not have any breakfast, doubtless because of nerves. He left with a bouquet of red, white and blue flowers given him by Eléonore.

As he was crossing the Tuileries garden he met one of his friends, young Vilate, a juryman on the Revolutionary Tribunal, who invited him to his apartment in the Pavillon de Flore for a few moments. From the window Robespierre enjoyed looking at the assembled crowd. He exclaimed with emotion: "There is the most interesting part of humanity. Oh Nature, how sublime and delightful is your power! How tyrants must turn pale at the idea of this celebration." The two men stopped to gossip, so that Robespierre arrived late at the place where the deputies were to meet. His colleagues were impatient. Some did not disguise their displeasure at being forced to take part in this religious ceremony which seemed to them a masquerade: "Is he making us wait so he can play at being king?" they murmured.

When the Convention had taken its place in a large amphitheatre built against the wall of the palace, Robespierre read his first speech, which was in praise of the Divinity. "Frenchmen, republicans, the day has at last arrived that will be forever blessed, which the French people have devoted to the Supreme Being. Never has the world that he created offered him a spectacle so worthy of his sight. He has seen reigning over the earth tyranny, crime and imposture. He sees at this moment an entire nation, at grips with all the oppressors of the human race, suspend its heroic work to lift its thought and its vows towards the Great Being who has given these people the mission to undertake those vows and carry them out."

While he was talking, ironic comments were heard from among the deputies: "Listen to the pontif." The former Abbé Barthélemy murmured in a bantering tone in Courtois's ear: "Without Monsieur de Robespierre we would not know that there is a God and that the soul is immortal." As for the people of Paris, they cared little about the Supreme Being, a divinity of philosophy. Even so, they welcomed the ceremony with pleasure. Since the Feast of the Federation they had been deprived of this sort of spectacle. It is always pleasant, when the sun shines, to watch processions with music and singing. Some remembering the Corpus Christi processions of old, thought that the old faith was being revived, and arrived with missals or rosaries.

Meanwhile Robespierre went on with his homily: "God did not create kings to devour the human race. He did not create priests to harness us, like vile animals, to kings' chariots, and to give the world an example of baseness, pride, perfidy, debauchery and lies; but he created men to help each other and to love each other and to arrive at happiness by the path of virtue."

After this the Convention went in procession to the Champ-de-Mars, Robespierre walking twenty paces ahead of his colleagues. Barère said: "This proud affectation of being the first among the deputies, who were all equal, was offensive." Baudot remarked that the deputies deliberately allowed Robespierre to be some way ahead of them. Even so, the distance was not great enough to prevent Robespierre hearing their murmurs: "There are still some Brutuses." He recognized one voice, that of Bourdon de l'Oise, who was saying that: "The Tarpeian Rock was not far from the Capitol." Moreover, the deputies were not the only ones to protest. Vilate said that he had heard the *sans-culotte* standing beside him make this observation: "That bastard isn't satisfied with being master, he's got to be God as well."

The climax of the ceremony was to be the symbolic destruction by fire of the statue of Atheism, the victorious emergence of the image of Wisdom. She rose before the eyes of spectators so smeared in soot that they broke into laughter. Robespierre delivered his second speech: "The monster that the genie of kings vomited out on France has returned to the void. With him may all crimes and all the ills of the world disappear. Armed alternatively with the daggers of fanaticism and the poisons of atheism, kings always plot the assassination of humanity. If they can no longer disfigure the divinity by superstition and compound it with their crimes, they labour to banish it from the earth in order to reign alone with their crime."

The official account goes on: "A barrage of artillery signifying national vengeance, rang through the air, and all the male and female citizens embraced each other, ending the festival by lifting to the heavens the shouts of humanity and civicism, 'Vive la Republique'." The festival was over.

All the same, the murmurs of Robespierre's colleagues had tarnished the day

The immediate reaction to the decree of the Feast of the Supreme Being was elation. People thought that the days of deprivation and terror had ended and that the promises of the Revolution were about to be realized. Their joy was short-lived with news of further restrictions

that had begun so well for him. Returning home that evening to his friends the Duplays, he was a prey to a grim foreboding. He said to them: "You will not see me much longer."

[[·]]

In one of his speeches (during the Festival of the Supreme Being) he had proclaimed: "People, let us give ourselves up today to the transports of pure levity. Tomorrow we will be fighting vice and crime again." This was his way of suggesting that more severe laws were to come. Many people at the celebration had nevertheless applauded, imagining that it was to herald a new era of clemency. Also the proclamation brought Robespierre several flattering letters from the deputies of the Plain, who did not like the Terror. Boissy d'Anglas wrote to him that he had seemed "to hear Orpheus teaching men the first principles of civilization and morality". Abroad, the impression was the same. The royalist pamphleteer Mallet du Pan, then an émigré, wrote: "The Feast of the Supreme Being produced an extraordinary effect outside. People really thought that Robespierre was going to close the abyss of the Revolution."

They were all mistaken. It was, on the contrary, the start of a period of even greater repression. The ceremony had shown Robespierre that there were still atheists, intriguers and scoundrels in influential positions in the Republic. These counter-revolutionaries had to be struck down to establish the happiness of the people through virtue. The two attempts at assassination had convinced him of the need for swiftness. "The more they [his enemies] hasten to end my career on earth, the more I want to hasten to replenish my career with deeds that are useful to the welfare of my kind. At least I will leave them a testament that will make tyrants and their accomplices tremble." Already the decrees of 27th Germinal (16th April) and 14th Floréal (3rd May) had suppressed provincial courts in order to bring political trials to Paris. However, this concentration, which Robespierre hoped would bring about a speedier repression of the counter-revolution, had contrary results. The prisons were choked with prisoners transferred to the capital; and at the tribunal, in spite of the batches of accused, the trials dragged on.

The procedure then had to be speeded up. The law of 22nd Prairial suspended all formalities that slowed things down. When he presented the plan worked out by Robespierre and himself, Couthon said: "The tribunals are only intended to punish the enemies of the Republic. Lenience towards them is atrocious, and clemency parricide." To begin with, there were to be no more lawyers, since to allow them was tantamount to giving royalists a platform and an advantage to the rich at the expense of the poor. "The natural form of defence and the necessary friends of the accused citizens are patriotic jurymen. Conspirators should find none."

Interrogation of the accused was also abolished, since it only served to "confuse the conscience of the judges". There were to be no more witnesses. In the absence of written proof or testimonials, the juries would be satisfied with "moral proof". Above all, speed was of the essence. "The time to punish the enemies of the fatherland should only be the time needed to recognize them. It is less a question of punishing them than annihilating them." There were only two possible verdicts: acquittal or death.

The reasons for bringing a citizen before the dreaded tribunal were many and vague. "The fatherland has as enemies not only those who conspire with foreigners and rebels. The most criminal are those who seek to deprave and corrupt political conscience. For a citizen to become suspect," Couthon ended, "it is sufficient that rumour accuses him."

The Convention was dismayed at these propositions. Although the Committee of Public Safety knew the object of the law (of the 22nd Prairial) in general terms, the text had not been submitted to them. In particular, they did not know of the clause that suspended parliamentary immunity. As for the Committee of General Security, Robespierre had not deigned to inform them about the law. Since Amar's report on the Compagnie des Indes, he had suspected his devotion to the Revolution. Several deputies (to the Convention) demanded an adjournment to allow them to examine the clauses. But adjournment implied the possibility of amendments. Robespierre did not want any. He demanded an immediate discussion. When there were factions, he said, the Mountain was the patriots' party. Now that factions had ceased to exist, the Convention, the Mountain, and the committees, "were all one". This was a debatable point, but no one dared not applaud. The law was passed.

All the same, the following day, when Robespierre was absent, opposition appeared. The arrest of members of the Convention and their appearance before the tribunal simply by dictate of the Public Prosecutor, or the committees, seemed a terrible thing. Bourdon de l'Oise, whom Robespierre called "a despicable intriguer", and Merlin de Douai put forward an amendment proclaiming the inalienable right of the Convention to impeach and try its own members. The motion was passed.

This amendment destroyed the very purpose of the law, which was to strike at suspect deputies without their having a chance to defend themselves. Robespierre and Couthon demanded its suppression, accusing the men responsible of being intriguers who were trying to persuade a part of the Mountain and make it the head of a new faction. Bourdon protested that he had no such intention: "I demand that proof be given for what is put forward. It has just been said quite clearly that I was a scoundrel." Robespierre replied: "I did not name Bourdon. Woe to the person who names himself." He went on, giving a description of the "intriguers" that was very disturbing for the deputies who could not help but think how perfectly it applied to themselves. One such was Tallien. Staring as if to single him out, Robespierre said that two nights previously one of the deputies, as he left the Convention, insulted the clerks of the Committee of Public Safety, treating them like spies. "If the assaulted patriots were to be defended, you can be assured that they would not fail to empoison this business; they would only come before you the next day complaining." In this incident Robespierre saw the proof of an intrigue hatched against the committee. "Who has said to those I have named that the Committee of Public Safety intended attacking them? Who told them that there was proof against them? Has the committee even threatened them? If you know anything, citizens, you know that there is more cause for accusing us of weakness." Tallien wanted to protest. He was called a liar and silenced. The amendment was rejected.

With the law of 22nd Prairial, Robespierre's dictatorship became a reality. It was no longer only virtually, but actually so, not so much so on the committees, but ruled by means of the Jacobins, who, through their provincial branches, made his wishes known throughout the whole of France. He filled the ministries with his own men. Hanriot, one of his henchmen, was military governor of Paris. Since Chaumette had been guillotined and Pache put in prison, the Commune was in the hands of his followers: Payan the National Agent and Lescot-Fleuriot the mayor. There was no longer any question of elections. Revolutionary government is not compatible with control by the people. The president of the Revolutionary Tribunal was Dumas, the vice-president Coffinhal, both his vassals. Among the jurymen was Duplay, his landlord, and Souberbielle, his doctor. His usual body-guards, Nicolas and Garnier, were judges. At the head of administration he put his fellow townsman Herman, whom he had brought from Arras for that very purpose.

Letters from admirers reached him from all corners of France. They have sur-vived because he preserved them preciously. One said: "Mere pawns of warring factions, yet patriots forget their ills on hearing of Robespierre's virtues." Another: "The irreproachable reputation that you have made for yourself, through your deeds and your writing, of a true French citizen who combines in himself the energy of an ancient Spartan or of a Roman of the earliest days of the Republic, and the eloquence of an Athenian." Speeches made at provincial clubs spoke of him as "founder of the Republic, father of patriotism, torch, pillar and corner stone of the Revolution." Others even went as far as calling him: "Messiah", or "tri-umphant genius". Mirabeau's sister wrote: "You are an eagle soaring in the heavens; your mind, your heart are irresistible, love of good is your cry, mine is that you long for the happiness of a Convention that I love." A young widow from Nantes offered him her hand in marriage and her fortune.

Meanwhile the executions increased in number. Between 20th June and 27th July 1,258 death sentences were passed, very often condemning simple people. Eighty-five per cent of the victims of the Terror belonged to the Third Estate, as against 8·5 per cent from the nobility and 6·5 per cent from the clergy. Danton had been right—as he entered the prison and said to the inmates who looked at him with curiosity—that up to that point they had seen nothing but roses. Obviously Robespierre saw no contradiction between his opposition to the death penalty and the Terror, having admitted once and for all that in time of war and revolution one practised a different policy and a different morality from that of normal times. Moreover he never, unlike so many others, attended an execution, aware no doubt that he would lose courage to carry on with the severity that he thought necessary. It is surprising only that he never tried to stop executions being carried out in public. He had once written that such a sight "brutalizes and coarsens the spirit of the people".

[[·]]

The disappearance of Catholicism had fostered the appearance of all sorts of little sects. One of them was quite successful in its own district, at least. It was founded

A false rumour linking his name with Cathérine Théot, a madwoman and reputed faith-healer, was barely suppressed by Robespierre. It was a step on the path to his inevitable ruin

by an illiterate old woman known as Mother Théot, who had been put away as a madwoman until 1782. There was a constant stream of people to her house in the rue de la Contrescarpe: invalids asking for miraculous cures, soldiers wanting magic potions to make them invulnerable in battle. Mother Théot preached the early advent of a Messiah, one who would regenerate the world. She had joined up with an ex-Carthusian, Dom Gerle, who was almost as mad as she, and had been a deputy of the Clergy. Together they carried out rites, the chief of which consisted of "sucking" her chin.

At this time any meeting apart from those of the popular clubs appeared more or less suspect. Following a denunciation, the police made a raid on the rue de la Contrescarpe and arrested everyone. Dom Gerle presented a certificate of *civisme* to the interrogating commissioner which was signed by Robespierre. "I certify that Dom Gerle, my colleague in the Constituent Assembly, has walked in the true principles of the Revolution, and always seemed to me—despite being a priest—a good patriot."

The dossier on the case passed into the hands of Vadier, a member of the Committee of General Security. The discovery of Robespierre's name gave him the wildest ideas. The old Gascon, who was an atheist, had not forgiven the Incorruptible for what he called his masquerade of the Feast of the Supreme Being. Vadier was going to get his revenge by playing one of his own tricks on Robespierre.

In the report that he read to the Convention, he presented the affair as an Orléanist plot. Among those involved he had in fact discovered a former doctor of the Duc d'Orléans—Quésuremant Lamothe—and, luck being with him, a sister-in-law of the cabinet-maker Duplay, who lived at Choisy. To flavour it all he altered the name of the old woman from Théot to Theos which, as he pointed out, means God in Greek. She thus became the mother of God. The Convention, which did not often have a chance to laugh, thoroughly enjoyed the reading of the report, which was delivered with many gestures and in a screamingly funny southern accent.

Vadier was very careful not to mention Robespierre's name, for that would have been too dangerous. However, he put about a rumour that a letter to Robespierre had been found in the priestess's straw palliasse, in which she called him "her dear son", and talked about his "mission" foretold by Ezekiel, and thanked him for having contributed to the re-establishment of religion by ridding it of priests. That the mother of god should call Robespierre "her son" led to a humorous conclusion. The letter obviously did not exist and, in any case, Robespierre could not be held responsible for what a madwoman had written to him. But Vadier well knew that when rumours fly around, the public is not much bothered with logic. Moreover, it was easy for gossip to turn a letter *to* Robespierre into a letter *from* Robespierre.

Robespierre was fully aware of the purpose behind this comedy. "The first attempt that evil-doers made was to find ways to belittle the noble principles you had proclaimed, and to erase the touching memory of the national festival." Others understood it also, as Fouquier-Tinville's commentary shows: "This affair is a genuine counter-revolution." A public trial would have the whole of France laughing at the expense of the Incorruptible. It would be difficult to defend oneself from such an imputation. If he were to prevent the trial, his enemies would not hesitate to say that he was protecting suspects. If he were to intervene, then that would be proof of his relationship with the sect. Even so, that is precisely what he did. He summoned Dumas, President of the Tribunal, and Fouquier-Tinville, the Public Prosecutor. The former, totally devoted to Robespierre, let himself be convinced easily. But the latter was a prosecuting maniac and made difficulties. He finally submitted and left the dossier, but immediately went and complained to the Committee of General Security that Robespierre was against the trial. "He . . . he . . . he will not have it."

This unlikely affair caused dissension among the Committee of Public Safety. Truth to tell, since the Law of the 22nd Prairial there had been a certain amount of tension between Robespierre, Saint-Just, Couthon and their colleagues. "Saint-Just's unbearable pride," said Barère, "was particularly distasteful to them." Carnot, a good and sincere man who knew his job inside out, became impatient when Robespierre and Saint-Just interfered in military matters. "I shall be waiting for you at the first defeat," he had threatened Robespierre after a stormy discussion. With Collot d'Herbois, who protected the ultra-terrorist proconsuls—particularly Fouché, his accomplice in the Lyons massacres—relations were no less strained. No doubt Robespierre had him in mind one day when he said: "Sometimes I have feared, I confess, that I will be sullied in the eyes of posterity by the unhealthy association with these perverse men."

His quarrel with Billaud-Varenne is even more astonishing. This sober man was no less virtuous than Robespierre. They both supported the Terror, not in order to have bloodshed, but to gain victory at all costs. A stupid incident seems to have made them fall out. Robespierre had decided on the arrest of the members of the revolutionary committee of the Indivisibilité Section who were accused of fraud. Billaud saw in this an intent to hound the last Cordelier, and lost his temper with Robespierre when the matter came up for discussion at the committee. He did not dare contradict him to his face, but he was heard mumbling an aside: "You are beginning to bore me with your Supreme Being." One day he put this hidden warning into one of his speeches: "The rascal Pericles used base lies to conceal the chains he was forging for the Athenians."

Barère's memoirs give us an idea of the atmosphere prevalent between Robespierre and his colleagues. Both of the committees, according to him, wanted Robespierre to give up the laws of Prairial. "It was a very stormy session. Vadier and Moïse Bayle were among those on the Committee of General Security who attacked the laws, and the people who devised them, with the utmost force and indignation. The Committee of Public Safety declared that it had had no part in their conception and fully disowned them. The members were in agreement to have the laws repealed the next day; and it was after this decision that Robespierre and Saint-Just declared that they would refer the matter to public opinion, and that they saw that a party had been formed to assure immunity for the enemies of the people, for the sole purpose of confusing the most ardent defenders of freedom. But they would surely warn the worthy citizens against the combined manoeuvres of the two committees of the government. They withdrew, threatening the members of the committee.

For his part, Billaud-Varenne told how on 23rd Prairial (11th June) such a stormy scene occurred that Robespierre wept with anger and "so that the people would no longer witness the storms that disturbed us, it was agreed that the committee would hold its meeting on the floor above".

It seems that the cause of this quarrel was Robespierre's demand that the Théot trial be suppressed. His colleagues were only too happy to refuse. Billaud-Varenne soberly said that it would be a direct violation of a formal decree of the Convention.

On the following days there was lively opposition between Saint-Just and Carnot. Couthon said to the latter: "I knew that you were the wickedest of men."

"And you the most traitorous," was the reply. Billaud-Varenne shouted at the Triumvirate: "As dictators you are grotesque." Robespierre left, banging the door: "Save the country without me." From 15th Messidor (3rd July) he stopped attending the committee meetings.

[[·]]

This was not, however, a political retirement, but a strategic withdrawal before engaging in the final battle, which he hoped would be decisive—a purge of the Convention and the committees. Then every obstacle to his plans would have disappeared. In order to win, he thought he had at his disposal the forces—namely, the Commune and the Jacobins—that had succeeded in the great revolutionary days of the last years. On 13th Messidor (1st July), at the club, he referred for the first time to his differences with the committees: "Previously the thoughtless faction consisting of the remnants of Danton, and Camille Desmoulins attacked the committees as a body. Now they prefer to attack a few members in particular so as to break up the unity. Previously they did not dare attack national justice, today they think themselves strong enough to slander the revolutionary tribunal. And people believe their slander, which they sow abroad with tender care. They have talked of a dictator and they have named him. It is I they have named, and you would tremble with fear if I tell you for what reason. Truth is my only refuge against crime. Never fear, slander does not discourage me, but it leaves me undecided as to what course to pursue."

His henchmen had no such hesitation. Payan, Coffinhal, Lescot-Fleuriot and Hanriot were pressing him to act without delay. Another 31st May would rapidly put the situation right. "You cannot choose a more favourable moment," Payan, the National Agent, wrote to him. "Teach every French citizen that an infamous death awaits all who oppose the revolutionary government. Prepare a great statement, which includes conspirators, revealing all the conspiracies gathered today into one, and involving the Lafayette faction, the royalists, the federalists, the Hébert faction, and those of Danton and Bourdon. Work on a grand scale."

THERMIDOR

"They call me tyrant. If I were, they would grovel at my feet, I would gorge them with gold, I would give them the right to commit any crime."

ROBESPIERRE

T HE OPPOSITION AGAINST ROBESPIERRE—EVERYONE WHO FELT threatened by him—was disparate and disunited. There were his colleagues on the committees, with whom he had quarrelled; the terrorist representatives, Fouché and Carrier, who knew that he was getting ready to send them before the tribunal; old friends of Danton, such as Courtois, Legendre and Thuriot, who wanted to avenge his death; and by no means least, the "corrupt" of the Assembly, such as Barras, Bourdon, Lecointre, Fréron and Tallien. Especially Tallien, who trembled for the life of his beautiful mistress, Thérèsa Cabarrus, who had been imprisoned by order of the Incorruptible.

Aware of the struggle that was to begin, the Committee of Public Safety took an initial measure to deprive Robespierre of his means of action. A decree signed by Collot d'Herbois and Billaud-Varenne sent some of the Revolutionary sections to the front. Nevertheless, a solution that had the merit of being less risky was one of reconciliation with Robespierre, rather than bringing him down. Barras and Fréron, returning from their mission to Provence, where they had shamelessly abused their power, wanted to attempt a reconciliation. They were distinctly ill at ease when Robespierre, meeting them, said not one word to them. Fréron, as an old friend, decided to visit him and take his colleague with him. Barère relates the interview in his memoirs:

Robespierre was standing up and wearing a kind of dressing gown. He had just left the hands of his hairdresser, and his hair was dressed and powdered. The spectacles that he usually wore on his forehead were not there, and through the powder covering his face, already so white by being naturally pallid, we saw two anxious eyes which we had never noticed before, hidden by the mask of glass. His eyes turned on us with a fixed look, quite amazed at our appearance. We greeted him in our way, without embarrassment, with the customary simplicity of the time. He did not reply to our greeting, but turned first towards a mirror which hung on the window overlooking the courtyard, then alternatively to a small mirror that was doubtless intended to hang on a chimney piece. . . . He took his toilet knife and scraped the powder that hid his face, carefully inspecting the arrangement of his hair. He then took off his dressing gown, putting it carefully on a chair near us in such a way as to dust our coats with powder, but without asking any pardon, and without any semblance of noticing our presence. He washed himself in a bowl that he held in his hand, cleaned his teeth, spat several times on the floor at our feet, without giving us any sign of attention. Fréron thought that he could get to him by introducing me in this way: "This is my colleague Barras, who was more decisive at the capture of Toulon than either I or any other soldier was. We have done our duty at the risk of our lives on the battle field, as we will do so in the Convention. It is very distressing, when one is as honest as we are, to see not only injustice done to us, but to see ourselves the object of the most iniquitous accusations and the most monstrous slander. We are quite sure that at least the people who know us as you do, Robespierre, will do us justice and we will do it in return."

Confronted by Robespierre's continued silence, Fréron thought that he could detect a frown on Robespierre's face, perhaps denoting displeasure at the use of the Revolutionary *tu*; and in the remainder of his speech, he substituted *vous*, in the hopes of reconciling himself with this touchy and haughty man. Robespierre did not show any satisfaction at this mark of deference. He remained standing without asking us to sit down. I told him politely that our initiative was inspired by the esteem felt for his political principles. He still said nothing, and his face was expressionless. I have seen no expression as impassible on the icy marble faces of statues or on the faces of the dead.

The man who was to unite all the various elements opposed to Robespierre was Fouché. This strange man had a genius for plots. In Arras, Robespierre had taken him for a good patriot, but he was enraged by massacres at Lyons and had Fouché recalled. He was bold enough to go to Robespierre, with a show of cordiality. On this occasion Robespierre did not remain silent, as he had done with Fréron and Barras, but burst into violent reproaches and showed him to the door.

Fearing arrest, Fouché then went underground. Throughout the first two weeks of Messidor he wandered from hiding-place to hiding-place. But at the same time he was doing things. His method was very simple and consisted of seeking out colleagues in the Convention whom he knew had good reason to fear Robespierre's harshness: "You are on the list," he said to them, "as well as me." In this way he instilled them with fear; fear that was to give them courage to risk everything.

Robespierre, warned of these activities, summoned Fouché to the Jacobins. He was careful not to attend and was expelled. Fouché's hiding-place had to be found before he could be arrested. There is no doubt that one must attribute to Fouché the bizarre rumours circulating at the time about Robespierre, which were intended to discredit him in the eyes of the public. One rumour said that he was preparing to marry Madame Royale and found a new dynasty. He was supposed to have attended meetings held at Madame de Sainte-Amaranthe's gambling den in the Palais-Royal as well as her amorous salon in the rue Grange-Batelière, the meeting-place of "monopolists and gamblers". Although Robespierre had never set foot in these places, Augustin and a nephew of the Duplays' had been taken to the salon by a friend who wanted to "amuse himself".

Twenty or so terrorists and plotters were not enough to bring Robespierre down. The majority of votes in the Convention were held by the Marais. They certainly did not like the Incorruptible, but they thought that he was the lesser evil and preferred him to other terrorists who might succeed him. There was a kind of tacit agreement between Robespierre and the Marais deputies—they would support him in exchange for the lives of the seventy-three imprisoned Girondin deputies.

At first the leaders of the Plain hesitantly welcomed the advances made to them by men who, a few weeks earlier, talked only about sending Moderates to the guillotine. In order to get them to promise to withdraw their support from Robespierre, they would have had to give a formal undertaking that the Terror would stop. "It is not possible," Durand-Maillane said later, "to see sixty to eighty heads fall each day, without being horrified."

In fact, the executions redoubled, disturbing public opinion even more. People no longer understood. Up to a certain point the Terror had been justified by reverses in the war, but France was now victorious. How could one believe that all the people whom one saw mount the scaffold were a danger to the Republic? Among those condemned for the fictitious "Luxembourg Plot" was the worthy Abbé Fénelon, an octogenarian and founder of a charitable organization called Les Petits Savoyards. Then there was the "Foreign Plot" in which fifty-four people were sent to the guillotine, among them Admiral; Cécile (Renaud), together with her father, her brother and her aunt; the entire Sainte-Amaranthe family—an incredible conglomeration of victims.

Nevertheless, on Barère's advice, the Committee of Public Safety attempted to bring about a reconciliation. In trying to bring down a man as powerful as Robespierre its members risked death. If they succeeded, Robespierre's fall could mean a blow fatal to the regime. A bargain was therefore proposed to the two other members of the Triumvirate, Couthon and Saint-Just, who had continued their work and obviously deplored the quarrel (between Robespierre and the Committee).

On 4th Thermidor (22nd July), at the request of his friends, Robespierre agreed to attend a meeting of the two committees. Saint-Just spoke a few conciliatory words showing that the overthrow of the revolutionary government would only profit the enemies of the Revolution, and denying that Robespierre had ever aspired to being a dictator. David, for the Committee of General Security, supported these conciliations.

Robespierre, however, showed himself in a less accommodating mood. "He spoke," said Barère, "as a man who had orders to give and victims to pick out." He walked up and down, glaring disdainfully through his spectacles, and took the offensive.

He reproached the committees for not having put into operation the laws of Ventôse, passed more than four months ago by the Convention; he attacked Vadier for his report on the Théot affair, and criticized Amar for his handling of the Compagnie des Indes affair. He had bitter words for Collot d'Herbois and Billaud-Varenne. The latter, nevertheless, sincerely wanted a reconciliation and tried to appease Robespierre. "We are your friends, we have always agreed with each other."

A compromise was reached. Saint-Just was appointed to make a report to the Convention to give greater speed to the application of the laws of Ventôse. At the request of Collot d'Herbois and Billaud-Varenne, he promised to make no reference in his report to the cult of the Supreme Being. A decree was also signed, ordering new detachments of artillery to be moved from Paris (to the front).

It seemed as if agreement had been reached. Barère assured the Convention that harmony reigned in the government. At the Jacobins, Couthon said reassuring things: "If there are any differences of personality, there are none of principle." Voulland, a member of the Committee of General Security, wrote to his electors to gainsay all rumours of discord.

But his colleagues were deceived. Robespierre no more wanted a reconciliation with them than he had in the past with Brissot or Danton. When he left the meeting he made a resolution to make his last stand, by attacking all his opponents at once. He would ask the Convention for the heads of corrupt deputies and a purge of the committees.

Robespierre knew about the lists of suspects that Fouché was circulating. He had warned about them in his speech of 21st Messidor (9th July) at the Jacobins: "Someone is trying to persuade each member that he has been proscribed by the Committee of Public Safety. He wants to terrorize the Convention. I urge all members to be wary of the insidious remarks of certain people who, fearing for their lives, want others to share their fear." Fouché could not have been more clearly indicated. It would, moreover, have been easy for Robespierre to call his bluff by revealing the names of those Fouché wanted arrested. He could also have made contact with the leader of the Marais. He disdained to do so, convinced that, on the day, his decisive eloquence would be enough to rally them. Their alliance was tacit, and he had no intention of making any promises respecting the Moderates. The only precaution he took in attempting to strike down his enemies was to prepare a speech.

Even so, during these decisive days he was overwhelmed by weariness, and went for long walks on his own at Issy, Choisy, in the woods at Ville d'Avray; he also made a pilgrimage to Rousseau's tomb as if to ask his master to inspire him. He wrote to a friend: "Count on my tender devotion, but have some forebearance for the state of exhaustion that my painful work sometimes puts me in."

Dissatisfied with Saint-Just, who had accepted the compromise, he did not inform him of the content of his speech; nor did he tell Couthon. On 8th Thermidor (26th July), towards noon, he appeared at the Convention, dressed in the blue coat he had worn for the Festival of the Supreme Being. He at once went to the rostrum where he was to speak for two hours. As a start he denounced the "perfidious deputies", the "scoundrels responsible for our ills", "the league of thieves who have accomplices in the Committee of General Security, and to whom are joined members of the Committee of Public Safety". In these few sentences he combined all his opponents. One, he went on, charges me with being a dictator and then conciliates me, saying that he has always been my friend. Billaud-Varenne must have recognized himself at this point. Another enemy used agents whose civic qualities were dubious; another deprived Paris of its guns and surrounded himself with the aristocrats he had protected. Here he was getting at Carnot. The Committee of Public Safety had to be "purified", and the agents of the Committee of General Security dismissed in view of their dishonourable" conduct.

Then he dealt with the deputies who had mocked the Festival of the Supreme Being. One of them, "just to swell the number of malcontents", had thought up a plot with "some stupid devotees, and had made out of it a despicable matter of indecent and puerile sarcasm". Then "military administration was enveloped in a suspect authority", and he maintained that it had had dealings with the enemy. "England, so abused in our speeches, is comforted by our arms." As for victory, "it has only armed ambition, put patriotism to sleep, awakened pride, and with its gleaming hands hollowed out the tomb of the Republic".

The Terror, "the dreadful system of the Terror", was the fault of the rogues who wanted to dishonour the Revolution. "Let us purge the national supervision, instead of using vice. The arms of freedom ought to be touched only by pure hands." He disclaimed any responsibility for himself:

Who am I, the person they accuse? A slave of freedom; a living martyr to the Republic, the victim as much as the enemy of crime. All rogues insult me. Let them prepare hemlock for me; I will wait for it on these sacred seats. I have promised to leave a redoubtable testament to the oppressors of the people. I leave to them truth . . . and death. Did we plunge the patriots into cells and bring terror to all manner of men? Did we, forgetting the crimes of the aristocrats, and protecting traitors, declare war on peaceful citizens, make it a crime to favour prejudice or to be indifferent to matters, and find guilty people everywhere, rendering the revolution fearsome to the people themselves?

When the victims of their perversity complain, they excuse themselves by saying: "Robespierre wants it, we can't avoid it." They said to the nobles: "He is the only person who has outlawed you." At the same time they said to the patriots: "He wants to save the nobles." They said to the priests: "He is the only person who pursues you. Without him you would be in peace and triumphant." They said to the fanatics: "He is the only person who is destroying religion." They said to the persecuted patriots: "He is the one who ordered it, or who wants to stop it." I was sent all the complaints, the cause of which I was not able to prevent. They said: "Your fate depends on him." There are some unfortunate people condemned. Who is responsible? Robespierre. They are particularly determined to prove that the Revolutionary Tribunal is a tribunal of blood, created by me alone, and that I was absolute master who had all the worthy people slaughtered, as well as the rogues, because they wanted to make all sorts of enemies for me. There is possibly not one condemned citizen to whom it was not said: "There is the person responsible for your distress. You would be happy and free if he did not exist." This charge has echoed through all the prisons. This plan of proscription was carried out in every department simultaneously. I had done everything, demanded everything, commanded everything, for you must not forget my title of dictator.

I will say only that for the last six weeks, nature and the pressure of slander, the impetus to do good and stop evil, have forced me to abandon absolutely my functions as a member of the Committee of Public Safety. My dictatorship has been ended for six weeks. Has the country been happier as a result? I hope so.

He then went on to justify the very Terror he had just denounced:

Without the revolutionary government the Republic cannot be made stronger. If it is destroyed now, freedom will be no more tomorrow. At the point at which we are now, if we stop prematurely, we die. We have not been too severe. They talk about our rigorousness, and the fatherland reproaches us for our weakness.

Citizens, remember that unless justice alone rules in the Republic, freedom is a mere name . . . Remember that there exists in your midst a swarm of rascals who are fighting against public virtue. Remember that your enemies want to sacrifice you to this fistful of rogues. Any man who rises to defend the cause of public morality will be overwhelmed with insults and outlawed by the unprincipled.

The speech was greeted with the usual applause. The plotters, thinking that they had been abandoned, lost courage. Lecointre, who had intended to launch an attack against the government after Robespierre had finished speaking, thought that the game was up, and wanted only to attract the dictator's goodwill. He proposed that Robespierre's speech be printed, and the Assembly immediately agreed.

Victory for the Incorruptible appeared absolute. Vadier, in abject fear, exonerated himself. Bourdon de l'Oise had more courage. It was true that he no longer had anything to hope for, so he might as well risk all. "I oppose the printing of this speech. It contains matters that are serious enough for discussion."

Then Barère went to the rostrum. Desmoulins had said spiritedly that the great man was two-tongued. Two days previously he had dined with Robespierre, who had not taken him into his confidence. His colleagues were murmuring that Robespierre had prepared two speeches, according to how the session turned out. The one he delivered certainly lacked clarity; it seemed, moreover, that he accepted the tag.

Of all his opponents, Robespierre named only one, Cambon, the President of the Finance Committee, whom he had accused of "fomenting monopolism, disturbing public credit, ruining the poor and reducing them to despair, increasing the number of malcontents, depriving the people of national assets, and gradually bringing about the ruin of the national wealth". This assigned him to the revolutionary tribunal. Cambon's opposition to Robespierre was of long standing. He was an honest man, and did not belong to Fouché's band, but was a resolute character. The day before Cambon had sent a copy of *Le Moniteur* to his family in the country, and on a corner of it had written: "Tomorrow, of Robespierre and myself, one of the two will be dead." Seeing that he was going to carry the day, he leapt to the rostrum: "Before I am dishonoured, I will speak to France. It is time to tell the whole truth. One man alone is paralysing the will of the National Convention. This man is Robespierre. Judge, therefore."

Almost unanimous applause greeted these words. Robespierre was visibly unsettled. Instead of making an indignant reply to crush his opponent, Robespierre excused himself, citing his incompetence in financial matters. "I have never had anything to do with that side of things." He explained that he had simply spoken his mind, declaring that Cambon's decree of 23rd Floréal (12th May) had dismayed the impoverished citizens. "I do not think that this is a crime." Then some delegates shouted that profiteers were attacking the decree. Was it Robespierre's intention to protect them? He stammered: "That may be true, I do not know what profit they may draw from this action. I do not concern myself with such things."

It was now Billaud-Varenne's turn to enter the lists. Robespierre's public attack on him, when he had thought they were reconciled, had made him furious. He demanded that before the speech was printed it be submitted for examination by the committees. Robespierre protested: "It is not the committee as a whole that I have attacked. I demand that I be able to explain myself." His voice was at once lost amid shouts of: "We all demand it."

When they saw that Robespierre was shaken, the plotters took heart. Panis, who had long been his friend, reproached him for tyrannizing the Jacobins. He demanded that he explain the latest proscription lists. Was he to be proscribed? It would surely be easy for Robespierre to reassure the Convention by giving names. But he simply replied: "In throwing down my shield, I have exposed myself to my enemies. I have flattered no one; I fear no one; I have slandered no one." "And Fouché?" shouted someone. "I do not want to talk about him at this moment, that is not the question."

Those who had feared that their names were on the list felt consoled—they well knew that if he had named them, the Convention would certainly hand them over. Since it seemed that the danger was over, they no longer hesitated to reveal themselves. Bentabole, Charlier, Amar and Thirion spoke in turn to demand, along with Bréard and Bourdon de l'Oise, that the assembly should go back on the two previous votes. "What," shouted Robespierre, "I have the faith to entrust to the Convention the truths I believe essential for the good of the country and they return my speech to be examined by the committee I accuse!" They paid no attention to him, and the two decrees were annulled.

[[·]]

That evening Robespierre is reported to have said to his friend Duplay: "I expect no more from the Mountain . . . but the mass of the Convention will listen to me." The adverse vote of the assembly seemed no more than an accident which would be put right the next day. This could have happened had he met the leaders of the Plain, instead of letting his opponents strengthen their bargain with them. It never occurred to him. That evening, after dinner, he went for a walk in the Champs-Elysées with Eléonore and his dog, Brount. The sun was setting in a red sky. "That means a fine tomorrow," Robespierre said.

For his victory he was counting on the Jacobins. He was received with wild enthusiasm by most of the audience when he appeared (at the club on the evening of the 26th). But Billaud-Varenne and Collot d'Herbois had arrived before him and questioned Robespierre's right to speak first. After a stormy debate, the protests of Collot and Billaud were silenced by their expulsion from the club. They left the hall to boos and shouts of: "To the guillotine." Dumas shouted at them: "I will be waiting for you tomorrow at the Revolutionary Tribunal."

Robespierre went to the rostrum. "From the agitation here, I see that you all know what happened this morning at the Convention." He then proceeded to repeat all of his speech delivered to the Convention, which was at times interrupted with bursts of applause. According to tradition, he added at the end: "This is my last will and testament. My enemies, or rather, those of the Republic, are so numerous and so powerful that I cannot hope to escape their blows much longer." The Jacobins could not listen to their idol speak of his imminent death without expressing their emotions. In a spontaneous movement they surrounded him, shouting to him to save the fatherland. Hanriot shouted that he was ready to mobilize the artillery. But Robespierre went on: "If you support me, the new traitors will share the fate of the old. If you forsake me, you will see how calmly I shall drink the hemlock." The painter, David, with his usual emotionalism, rushed towards Robespierre: "If you drink it, I will drink it with you." The whole place was galvanized and shouted: "Yes, we will all drink it; we swear."

However, his friends in the Commune, Payan, Lescot-Fleuriot and Coffinhal were more practical, and begged him to dislodge his enemies from a position in which they could harm him. A few soldiers would suffice to purge the Convention and the committees, as on 31st May. He refused to carry out a *coup d'état*: he was sure that his eloquence would carry the day. Meanwhile, the plotters continued their dealings with the still wavering leaders of the Marais, who were hesitating. They renewed their undertaking to repeal the law of 22nd Prairial.

After their expulsion from the Jacobins, Billaud-Varenne and Collot d'Herbois returned to the Pavillon de Flore. Saint-Just was in the committee room, a little apart from his colleagues (Carnot, Barère, Lindet, Lacoste and Prieur de la Côte d'Or), busy writing a report that he was to present to the Convention the next day. Collot d'Herbois went in first. "We plied him with questions," said Carnot. Saint-Just did not look up, but asked coldly: "What is new at the Jacobins?" Collot strode up and down the room two or three times without replying, then suddenly stopped in front of Saint-Just, and roughly seized his arm. "Are you writing out our bill of indictment?" Saint-Just stammered and tried to hide his papers. "These evasions are useless," said Collot. "You are writing out our accusation." Saint-Just boldly then got up. "Well, you are right, Collot, my report will incriminate you." He then turned to Carnot. "You have not been left out of the report, either, and you will see yourself described there with a master's hand."

Carnot merely shrugged his shoulders. At this moment Billaud-Varenne arrived. More angry words and threats were exchanged. Saint-Just's colleagues reproached him for wanting to repeat Couthon's *coup* of 22nd Prairial (10th June) by bringing a report to the Convention that had not been debated (by the Committee). Saint-Just finally undertook to read his work before the session, and even to suppress it if they wanted. At about five o'clock (the morning of the 27th) he left the committee room, promising to return about ten.

His colleagues waited all morning in vain. Noon had already struck when an usher delivered a curious note: "Injustice has withered my heart. I intend to open it to the Convention." This "runny-nose", as Carnot called him, had tricked them. They all hurried to the debating chamber.

Saint-Just had just gone to the rostrum: "I belong to no faction," he began. "I have fought them all." He thought that Robespierre had made a mistake the day before by not naming the people he was attacking. He intended to mention them by name—Billaud-Varenne, Collot d'Herbois and Carnot—ending none the less with a call for reconciliation. His speech was full of such aphorisms as: "Pride alone engenders factions"; and "governments perish by factions". "If virtue did not show itself sometimes, thunder in hand, reason would succumb to force."

But the Convention was not prepared to listen to these aphorisms. Hardly had Saint-Just delivered his opening sentences when Tallien rushed to the rostrum and interrupted him. "I demand the right to speak on a point of order." Collot d'Herbois, who was in the chair, quickly gave him it. "Citizens, Saint-Just has just told us that he belongs to no faction. I say the same. That is why I am going to speak the truth. Yesterday a member isolated himself from the government and delivered a speech in his own name. Today another is doing the same. They have done nothing but aggravate the ills of the fatherland, tearing it apart, throwing it into the abyss. I demand that all pretences be torn assunder."

At these words there was a volley of applause from the Convention. Then the unimaginable happened. Saint-Just the handsome, proud Saint-Just, who until this very moment had made everyone tremble, was silent, not attempting to continue his speech. He had let himself be interrupted by vulgar Tallien, the man who had thought himself capable of standing up to Danton. He stood motionless at the foot of the rostrum, as if he were finished, emptied out. He was not heard again for the rest of the session.

Billaud-Varenne then went towards the rostrum, as if replying to Tallien's invitation. As he passed by, the hypocritical Barère gave him this wise advice: "Attack only Robespierre. Leave Couthon and Saint-Just alone." Billaud was very angry at the memory of the boos of the previous evening at the Jacobins. "Yesterday," he began, "the Jacobin Club was full of apostates, with not one honest member there. Yesterday in that club plans for slaughtering the National Convention were elaborated. Yesterday I saw men openly spew out the vilest infamies against those who have never deviated from the Revolution. I can see," he went on with his arm extended, "on the Mountain, one of those men who threatened the representatives of the people. There he is." The person pointed out was immediately expelled from the hall.

He reproached Saint-Just for not having submitted his report to the Committee as promised. He then turned to Robespierre and delivered his indictment. Robespierre had protected the Hébert faction in the person of Hanriot; given special treatment to nobles such as Lavalette; persecuted the patriots of the Indivisibilité Section; plotted with Dumas over new proscriptions; and aspired to personal power. "You will tremble when you learn that during the period when representatives of the people were to be sent to the departments, this man could not find, on the list that was presented to him, twenty-five members of the Convention who seemed worthy of the mission." This revelation—that he had despised them—could only unite the Convention against the Incorruptible; but Billaud, carried away by his bitterness and without thinking of the effect he might have on the Plain, then accused Robespierre of moderation: "When I first denounced Danton to the committee, Robespierre got up in a fury, saying that I wanted to destroy the best patriots."

Billaud-Varenne, breathless from his diatribe, concluded his speech, and Robespierre hurried to the tribune. Before he could get there, he was greeted by shouts: "Down with the tyrant!" The conspirators' plan was to prevent him from speaking. Tallien, who had armed himself with a dagger, brandished it with a theatrical gesture and said he would strike down the tyrant if the Convention did not decree his accusation. He then demanded the immediate arrest of Hanriot, so as to prevent another 31st May. Billaud-Varenne supported him and added Dumas to the list of names on the decree.

Once more Robespierre tried to mount the rostrum. But there were shouts for Barère to speak. Robespierre was refused leave to speak, and Barère began another neutral speech. Without even mentioning Robespierre, he apologized for the revolutionary government and demanded a reorganization of the National Guard. Then Vadier spoke. He had been tortured by the excuses he had hesitatingly made the day before. Today he would take revenge: "There was," he said, "under the mattress of the mother of God, a letter addressed to Robespierre. This letter told him that his mission had been foretold by Ezekiel." Because of the assembly's amusement at these remarks, Tallien feared that its anger might evaporate, and he interrupted Vadier, demanding that the discussion be brought back to the point. "I can do that," shouted Robespierre, but his voice was drowned out by his opponents, and Vadier exclaimed: "This man, whose patriotism and virtue were so vaunted, this man hid himself on 10th August, and only reappeared three days after the victory. . . . At a time when our armies were in a critical situation, this man deserted the Committee of Public Safety, which alone saved the fatherland."

Then Robespierre, as if he were lost, ran to left and right, up and down the steps, repeating: "Death, death." Someone shouted: "You have deserved it a thousand times." The tumult increased. Robespierre turned to the main body of the assembly: "It is to you, honest men, that I speak." When he was preparing to sit down among what was left of the Girondin deputies, they protested: "Wretch, that was Vergniaud's seat." As if pursued by a ghost, he turned towards the rostrum. "President of murderers . . ." he shouted at Thuriot, another of his enemies, who had replaced Collot d'Herbois in the chair. Robespierre's voice failed him. A deputy—possibly Garnier de l'Aube—was heard to say: "Danton's blood chokes you." He remained still, as if turned to stone, then said: "Ah! So he is the one you wish to avenge."

It was all over. An obscure deputy from the Mountain, Louchet, proposed the arrest of Robespierre and another, Lozeau, seconded the motion. Augustin stood up: "I am as guilty as my brother, I share his virtues, I want to share his fate." The president put the arrest of the two Robespierres to the vote. All hands, from the Mountain to the Plain, were raised. As with the vote against Danton, it was unanimous. His comrades tried to restrain young Philippe Le Bas, who also demanded his own arrest: "I will not share the disgrace of that decree." Along with Saint-Just and Couthon, his arrest was decreed by the Assembly. Fréron's voice was heard: "Freedom and the Republic are finally going to rise from the ruins," and Robespierre tried once again to make himself heard: "Yes, because brigands have won."

Collot d'Herbois, who had taken the chair again, ordered Saint-Just to give his speech to one of the secretaries. With the motion of an automaton he handed over the roll of paper. "Citizens," said Collot, "you have just saved the fatherland. The fatherland with its torn breast has not spoken to you in vain. It was rumoured that the Robespierrists had planned another 31st May against you." Robespierre shouted: "That's not true, you lied, I . . ." Once again he was silenced by his opponents. These were Robespierre's last words to the Convention. An usher, doubtless too frightened to hand Robespierre the decree of arrest, placed it on the seat next to him. Robespierre was motionless and seemed not to see the decree. Thuriot shouted: "He refuses to obey a decree of the Convention." Again the assembly was in an uproar and demanded that the prisoners come to the bar. The *gendarmes* were called to lead the prisoners away. One of them hoisted the paralysed Couthon on to his shoulders, and the others followed.

The session was over. It was 3.40 p.m.

[[·]]

As soon as the news of Robespierre's arrest was made known, Lescot-Fleuriot and Payan called a meeting of the Commune at the Hôtel de Ville. The Commune immediately pronounced itself to be in a state of revolt (against the Committees and the Convention), while the Jacobin Club declared itself to be in permanent session. An executive committee of nine members was immediately set up and installed in the Egalité hall. Orders were sent to all the Sections calling on National Guardsmen to meet on the Place de Grève.

Of the 50,000 men the Sections could produce, only about 20,000 assembled themselves. In addition, Hanriot attempted to organize a revolt in the Faubourg Saint-Antoine. He rode his horse at a gallop up and down the street shouting: "To arms!" But after five years of revolution the zeal of the *sans-culottes* was well nigh exhausted. No one moved. The tumbrils proceeded through the rue Saint-Antoine to the guillotine (moved to the eastern part of the city). Some of the spectators who knew what had happened and thought that as a result there would be changes, urged the arrest of Hanriot. But he ordered the *gendarmes* to speed up the convoy.

The second attempt to free the prisoners from the headquarters of the Committee of General Security (where they were given dinner) was no more successful than Hanriot's earlier call to arms. The general broke into the room where the Robespierrist leaders were and let himself be overpowered by the *gendarmes* and arrested.

To avoid any more rescue attempts the Committee decided to assign the prisoners to different prisons. Robespierre was taken in a carriage to the Luxembourg; Augustin and Le Bas to La Force; Couthon to Port-Libre (formerly Port-Royal), and Saint-Just to the Écossais.

Meanwhile, the Commune despatched an order to all prisons not to accept any new prisoners. Only the gate keeper at the Luxembourg paid any attention, and refused to open up for Robespierre. The other prisoners were put under lock and key.

Robespierre had hesitated to break prison—it was said because of legal scrupulousness. That explanation fits quite well with his character; but no doubt he had other motives too. He must have remembered Marat who had been acquitted by the Revolutionary Tribunal and returned in triumph to the Convention. Why should it not be the same for him? Because he had been refused imprisonment at the Luxembourg, he asked to be escorted to the town hall. To be detained in the administration's offices probably seemed to him a sort of semi-arrest, and evidence of his wish to obey the law.

When the carriage stopped at the entrance to the Mairie, a *gendarme* went to present himself to the chief of police. His words must have caused a sensation. The staff members came out at once (to greet Robespierre), wearing their sashes round their waists. One of them opened the door of the carriage to embrace Robespierre, who was holding a white handkerchief over his mouth. He was pushed out of the carriage and fell into the arms of one of the patriots. "Take courage," he said. "You are among friends."

Robespierre was then escorted into the offices, where it was proposed that he be taken to the Hôtel de Ville. He refused. To have agreed would have been the same as declaring himself in revolt against the government, which he wanted to avoid.

By nine o'clock in the evening, Coffinhal (the judge of the Tribunal), not knowing the latest events of the day, set off for the Tuileries to free the prisoners. On the way he was arrested by one patrol of *gendarmes* and set free by another. Poor men. At that time the police had to obey without really understanding the contradictory orders given by their superiors, on a day when everyone seemed to be a rebel and a conspirator. It was impossible to know who represented legal authority. When Coffinhal reached the Tuileries he learnt that Robespierre and the other leaders had been taken away and that Hanriot had been arrested. Hanriot and his officers were immediately set free.

Coffinhal had been accompanied to the Tuileries by quite a large armed force (*gendarmes*, gunners and volunteers). Hanriot took command of the army, and if he had there and then given the order for the Convention and the Committees to be occupied, as on 2nd June, history would have taken a different course. As, unbelievable as it may seem, since the adjournment of the session at 3.40 p.m., neither the Convention nor the Committees had taken the slightest precaution to ensure their security. The Tuileries were unguarded. The members of the Convention were thrown into panic when they heard that Hanriot was at the door with soldiers. Lecointre, finding a cache of arms, distributed some of them, but what could the deputies have done against the riflemen of Paris! "Citizens," exclaimed Collot, who was presiding over the evening session, "this is the time to die at our posts." Thibaudeau tells how: "This moment was impressive and sublime, for I had no doubt that our last moment had come." But Hanriot was the sort of soldier who could only obey commands and returned to the Hôtel de Ville with his men.

Meanwhile the Commune was attempting to secure the release of the other four detainees. Augustin (released from La Force) went to the Hôtel de Ville, where he made a speech saying that "he had not been arrested by the National Convention, but by cowards who had been plotting for the past five years". It was immediately decided to bring Maximilien from the Mairie to the town hall. "The citizen-mayor demanded that a deputation be ordered to go and fetch the older Robespierre, and to point out to him that he did not belong to himself but to the country and to the people."

Much to the messenger's dismay, Robespierre refused to leave the Mairie and busied himself with sending snippets of advice to the Commune: "Close the gates, if they are not yet closed (which they were), shut down all the newspapers, and order the police commissioners to arrest all journalists and traitor deputies."

A second note, signed by Payan and Lescot-Fleuriot, was then despatched to persuade him to come. "The executive committee appointed by the council needs your advice. Come here at once!"

It must have been about 10.30 or 11 p.m.

Robespierre arrived almost unnoticed at the Hôtel de Ville, where he was taken at once to the Egalité hall. Augustin, Saint-Just and Le Bas were already there. They in turn sent a message to Couthon to join them; but he too was making difficulties about leaving prison: "All the patriots are outlawed. The entire nation is aroused. Not to come to the Commune—where we are now—would betray them."

While they were waiting for his arrival, a letter to the Piques Section was prepared: "Courage, patriots of the Piques Section, freedom is winning. Already those whose steadfastness made them fearsome to traitors have been released. Everywhere people are showing themselves worthy of their reputation. The Commune is the meeting place, and brave Hanriot will carry out the orders of the Executive Committee which has been set up to save the country."

The victorious tone was a little premature. Beside the other signatures, that of Robespierre is incomplete—"Ro". Did he hesitate, was he suddenly interrupted and the paper taken away? At the bottom of the page there is a rusty stain that seems like blood. For a long time it was thought that Robespierre was shot as he was signing the letter. But chemical analysis of the stains has shown them to be ink.

Couthon arrived at the town hall. Robespierre, taking the hand of the *gendarme* who was carrying the paralytic, said to him: "Good *gendarme*, I have always loved and admired your men; always be faithful to us. Go to the doorstep and do something to turn the people against the rebels."

As soon as he had taken his place among his friends Couthon urged them to

COMMUNE DE PARIS.

DÉPARTEMENT DE POLICE.

Le

L.R.N? 37. Couus. 12.

L'an deuxième de la   République Française,

N° 4.

une et indivisible.

*coulhoy, tous les patriotes sont
proscrits, le peuple tout entier est
levé, ce seroit le trahir que
de ne pas te rendre avec nous à
la Commune. où nous sommes actuelle-
ment.   Robespierre je*

Robespierre   Le Just

*Arrested and ordered to be detained on 9th of Thermidor, Robespierre was bundled here and
there across Paris. This did not deter him from sending notes and instructions to his admirers.
He firmly believed, like Marat in his time of deep travail, that the verdict against him would
be reversed and that he would be returned to power triumphant*

write to the armies. "In whose name?" "In the name of the Convention. Has not that always been our place?" Robespierre said a few words to his brother in a low voice. "No, we must write in the name of the French people."

Rather than concerning themselves with those at the front, they would have done better to be worried about the troops of the Commune assembled in the square outside the town hall since six o'clock, tired and disheartened by inaction, who were beginning to disperse. It was late, the men were weary and going home to bed, thinking they were no longer needed. In any event they were prepared to return the next day. At first they left in little groups, then in crowds, as the precedent became contagious. Hanriot did nothing to keep them. By two o'clock in the morning (of the 28th) there were no more troops in the square.

The corridors of the Hôtel de Ville were also empty, as a result of an unfortunate undertaking of Payan. Hoping to arouse the people's indignation against the Convention he read out a decree outlawing the Commune "as well as any citizen present at its meeting". There was an immediate stampede.

[[·]]

At the Convention, when the alert was over, they finally made an effort to decide what measures to make. Fréron proposed giving the "command" to Barras, who was believed to have some military knowledge. He accepted. He had about 10,000 men at his command from the loyalist Sections. With this force he thought that he could hold the Tuileries if they were attacked. But Billaud-Varenne had a better idea. Messages had just revealed that there were no longer any Communal troops at the Hôtel de Ville. They had to seize the opportunity and march on the Hôtel de Ville without delay. "It must be surrounded now. Would you give the Commune and Robespierre the chance to murder us?"

Barras gave the order to move off and divided his men into two columns—one under his command went along the rue Saint-Honoré, and the other, under Léonard Bourdon, advanced along the banks of the river Seine to arrive first at the Hôtel de Ville.

The Place de Grève was deserted—not even a sentry at the door. Bourdon entered the building with a young *gendarme* called Merda, who was the first to enter the Egalité hall. A shot was fired, and Robespierre fell. What had happened? Did Merda fire, as he later boasted, or did Robespierre attempt to commit suicide? This is one of the mysteries of history. When Bourdon later returned to the Convention he presented Merda as the hero of the night, but Barère's report, a few days later, talked of Robespierre's attempted suicide. How could he, since the bullet had shattered his left jaw?

Seeing his master fall, Le Bas put a pistol to his own head. Augustin climbed out of a window to escape. In order to run more easily along a cornice, he took off his shoes, but slipped, fell and broke his thigh. Coffinhal confronted Hanriot, who had

Accounts vary as to how Robespierre's jaw came to be shattered by a bullet. Some thought it an attempt at assassination; others that he had tried to kill himself

botched the job of the defence. He shouted abuse at him, threw him out of a window on to an inner courtyard, where he died. Saint-Just did not flee but let himself be taken prisoner. Coffinhal managed to escape, but Payan and Lescot-Fleuriot were arrested. Couthon was dragged by someone on to a staircase, but in his flight he fell down stairs and wounded his forehead.

[[·]]

It was five o'clock in the morning. Robespierre and his friends were taken to the
Tuileries. Barras had just given the Convention an account of the night's events.
"The villain Robespierre is there. Do you want him to come in?" The deputies
refused, and Thuriot declared that: "To expose before the Convention the body of

a man covered with every sort of crime would be to deny this splendid day all the glory it deserves."

He was carried on a plank to the audience chamber of the Committee of Public Safety and laid on a table, and under his head was placed a white wooden box containing some pieces of army bread. He had no cravat and his shirt and jabot were covered with blood. His stockings had fallen round his ankles.

Drawn by curiosity, many deputies and other people came to see him. Some sneered sarcastically: "Sire, your Majesty is in pain." "It seems you have lost your power of speech." "Well, are you going to put your head in the little window?" Motionless, he seemed to hear nothing. Legendre was chief amongst the offenders: "Well, tyrant, the Republic wasn't big enough for you, but you've wound up with only the two foot width of this little table."

Then he made a movement with his hand, trying to unbuckle his garters, which a secretary did for him. "Thank you, sir," he murmured. He wiped the blood that was dripping from his wound with a leather pistol cover, then someone handed him some sheets of white paper. As morning approached a surgeon came and examined the wound. He removed some broken teeth and fragments of bone from Robespierre's mouth and made a temporary dressing. Shortly afterwards Robespierre slid himself off the table and sat in a chair.

Saint-Just, Payan and Dumas were brought to the committee room. The *gendarmes* pushed away the curious who surrounded Robespierre. "Let them see that their king is just like any other man." Saint-Just did not break his silence, except when he saw the Rights of Man hanging on the wall he was heard to murmur: "There, whatever you say, is our work."

Towards ten o'clock Couthon and Robespierre were carried on stretchers to the Conciergerie. Robespierre was put in a cell near that once occupied by Marie-Antoinette. It is said that he signalled to the jailer to bring him pen and ink. But the man refused and mocked him: "What do you want to do with it? Write to your Supreme Being?"

Twenty-two prisoners appeared before the Revolutionary Tribunal. The interrogation was swift, following the procedure created by Robespierre. "The time taken to punish the enemies of the fatherland should only be the time taken to recognize them. It is less a question of punishing them than of annihilating them." Fouquier-Tinville raised a judicial problem. According to the law, the municipal officers had to identify the accused men. They were themselves on the bench of the accused, or had fled. Commissioners were appointed to replace the officers. Fouquier was able to read his indictment and the jury the condemnation.

Towards 5 o'clock in the afternoon three tumbrils left the prison yard. In the first were Robespierre and his brother; in the second Saint-Just; in the third Couthon and Hanriot. The procession covered the journey from the Conciergerie to the Place de la Revolution in an hour, to the slow hoofbeats of the horses, along the rue Saint-Honoré. Everywhere the crowd demonstrated its joy, shouting abuse

The wounded man was carried to the ante-chamber of the Committee for Public Safety and stretched out on a table, a box for his pillow. He was not to be left in peace. The curious came to see for themselves and the vengeful to mock and gloat over the fallen Incorruptible

and sarcasm, while the *gendarmes* pointed sabres at the condemned. "To the guillotine." When Danton had been led to his death, as Dyanière wrote, there was mourning all over Paris. In front of the Duplays' house the tumbrils made a brief halt. A child with a brush smeared the door with blood. "Down with the tyrant," yelled the crowd.

Couthon was guillotined first, then Augustin, Saint-Just, Hanriot and the twelve municipal officers. Robespierre was the last but one to mount the scaffold.

In his *Souvenirs thermidoriens*, Duval wrote: "The executioner, when he had tied him to the plank, and before bringing down the blade, roughly pulled the dressing off the wound. He gave a groan like that of a dying tiger, which was heard in the far corners of the square."

[[·]]

By way of an epilogue, here are the minutes of the meeting of the Jacobin Club on 11th Thermidor, year II (29th July 1794).

. . . How did it come to pass that this rogue who, consorting with his vile accomplices, placed the Republic within inches of its death was not unmasked sooner? Why wasn't the spirit of free men aroused sooner against the tyranny of thought, against the fiend who displayed the most oriental kind of despotism? It was because the mask with which he hid himself was almost impenetrable. It was because whilst favouring crime, he always spoke using words of virtue and probity. It was because by skilfully suppressing, under insidious pretexts, simple innocence, he loudly proclaimed himself the protector of the oppressed. By favouring the conspirators, he was able to give skill to their defence, and he coloured it with the specious pretext of love of the public good. It was because coveting both the sceptre and the censer, he was consumed with the ambition of the fiend Mohammed—without having his genius or, above all, his courage. Pontif and despot at the same time, he gathered a great number of followers for himself, pretending to believe, so that all would believe, that the French people had forgotten the existence of a superior intelligence. It was because he appeared to be restoring the cult of the Supreme Being, as if the French nation had ever renounced it. It was because the protection he had given to priests had increased tenfold the number of his worshippers, and because he had in his pay an infinite number of slanderers, and even more women to slander. And who would have dared suspect this monster? We did not know that he no longer attended the committee sessions, who every day worked unceasingly for the safety of the fatherland. Every day new victories were immortalising the armies of the Republic. Freedom seemed to be walking to its goal with a firm and rapid step. Who was able to arouse suspicion? One

(OPPOSITE)
Behold a Samson of supreme intelligence!
Having killed everything with that fatal knife
He finds himself in a quandary, what is left for him to do?
Well, he could guillotine himself.

thought that this monster was untouchable by the thirst for gold, and his despotism was looked upon as the fierce authority of a sincere republican.

The mask has fallen. Catiline is no more. He and his infamous accomplices have paid with their heads for their horrible parricide, and the pen of the patriotic writer will no longer be restrained by fear.

[[INDEX]]
Numbers in italic are for illustrations.